# HANDBOOK TO PRAYER

Praying Scripture Back to God

**KENNETH BOA**

**Trinity House Publishers Inc.**
One Piedmont Center, Suite 130
Atlanta, Georgia 30305
(800) DRAW NEAR (372–9632)
trinityhousepublishers.org

Scripture translation and adaptation
by Kenneth Boa

**Handbook to Prayer**
Paperback edition © 2020
Original copyright © 1993 by Kenneth Boa

All rights reserved.
Library of Congress Catalog Card Number 93–61512
ISBN 1–884330–21-5

# CONTENTS

Introduction .................................................................... 7

**PART ONE**
Morning Affirmations ................................................ 17

**PART TWO**
Daily Prayer Guide ..................................................... 25

    The First Month ................................................... 26

    The Second Month ............................................. 164

    The Third Month ................................................ 294

**PART THREE**
One-Week Prayer Guide ......................................... 421

**PART FOUR**
Personal Prayer Pages ............................................. 493

About the Author ..................................................... 501

Other Trinity House Publications ......................... 503

# DEDICATION

*To my bride Karen*

My beloved companion, colaborer,
and fellow sojourner
in our spiritual journey
to the celestial city of God.

# INTRODUCTION

## THE PURPOSE OF THIS HANDBOOK

Spiritual growth is impossible apart from the practice of prayer. Just as the key to quality relationships with other people is time spent in communication, so the key to a growing relationship with the personal God of heaven and earth is time invested in speaking to Him in prayer and listening to His voice in Scripture.

As central as these twin disciplines of prayer and Scripture are to our spiritual life, most believers in Christ are frustrated by hit-or-miss approaches to both. As a result, their time in prayer and God's Word can become unsatisfying, routine, and even boring. It is no surprise, then, that most people spend a minimal amount of time in either of these disciplines and fail to develop intimacy with the One for whom they were created.

The problem with prayer is heightened by the fact that people often succumb either to the extreme of all form and no freedom, or to the opposite extreme of all freedom and no form. The first extreme leads to a rote or impersonal approach to prayer, while the second produces an unbalanced and undisciplined prayer life that can degenerate into a litany of one "gimme" after another. *Handbook to Prayer* was designed to make prayer a more enriching and satisfying experience by providing both form and freedom in the practice of prayer.

Introduction

# THE STRUCTURE OF THIS HANDBOOK

Think of this handbook as a tool that combines the Word of God with prayer and guides you through the process of praying Scripture back to God. It will enable you to think God's thoughts after Him and to personalize them in your own thinking and practice. It will also provide you with a balanced diet of prayer by guiding your mind each day through eight kinds of prayer. Because it is based on Scripture, you can be assured that the content of these prayers will be pleasing to God. This book will encourage you in your walk with God by enriching and enhancing the quality of your experience of prayer.

Years ago, Max Anders and I were profoundly influenced by the *Private Devotions* of Lancelot Andrewes, a seventeenth-century Anglican bishop and prominent translator of the King James Bible. Andrewes adapted Scripture into various forms of prayer, and this idea prompted Max and me to create a guide to prayer called *Drawing Near*. In the years since that book appeared, I have become increasingly impressed with the need to create a more powerful tool for personal and group prayer. *Handbook to Prayer* contains approximately three times as many biblical passages and utilizes a three-month Daily Prayer Guide rather than a one-month cycle. In addition, it contains a One-Week Prayer Guide, which you can use occasionally when you want a more in-depth time of prayer.

To create this collection of biblical prayers, I consulted several translations of the Bible as well as the original language of every passage. The result is essentially my own translation, though it shares much in common with existing translations. My intention in doing this was to remain as close to the biblical text as possible while still retaining clarity and readability. I then adapted the passages into a personalized format so that they could be used readily in the context of individual and group prayer.

This handbook is structured around eight forms of prayer that are based on the model of the Lord's Prayer. Our Lord told His disciples to pray in this way:

> Father in heaven,
> Hallowed be Your name.
> Your kingdom come;
> Your will be done
> On earth as it is in heaven.
> Give us today our daily bread,
> And forgive us our debts as we also have forgiven our debtors.
> And lead us not into temptation,
> But deliver us from the evil one.
> For Yours is the kingdom and the power and the glory forever.
> (Matthew 6:9–13)

The eight forms of prayer—adoration, confession, renewal, petition, intercession, affirmation, thanksgiving, and closing prayer—are all illustrated in this model prayer:

"Father in heaven, hallowed be Your name"—The prayer principles of ***adoration*** (praise for who God is) and ***thanksgiving*** (praise for what He has done).

"Your kingdom come; Your will be done on earth as it is in heaven"—The principle of *affirmation*, that is, agreeing with God's will and submitting to it.

"Give us today our daily bread"—The principle of *supplication*, in which we make requests both for ourselves (petition) and for others (intercession).

"And forgive us our debts as we also have forgiven our debtors"—The principle of *confession* in view of our need for forgiveness of sins.

"And lead us not into temptation, but deliver us from the evil one"—The necessity of *renewal* as we face the temptations of the world, the flesh, and the devil.

"For Yours is the kingdom and the power and the glory forever"—A *closing prayer* that honors the Lord and completes our thoughts.

The prayers of petition and intercession are formatted around a seven-day cycle:

### Petition

- Growth in Christ
- Growth in wisdom
- Spiritual insight
- Relationships with others
- Faithfulness as a steward
- Family and ministry
- Personal concerns

### Intercession

- Churches and ministries
- Family
- Believers
- Evangelism
- Government
- Missions
- World affairs

Introduction

# HOW TO USE THIS HANDBOOK

*Handbook to Prayer* consists of four parts:

- Morning Affirmations
- Daily Prayer Guide
- One-Week Prayer Guide
- Personal Prayer Pages

## Part One: Morning Affirmations

This set of affirmations is a tool designed to help you renew your mind at the beginning of each day. It guides you through a biblical perspective on the fundamental issues of life: *Who am I? Where did I come from? Why am I here? Where am I going?* In this way, you review God's perspective on your faith, your identity, your purpose, and your hope.

Don't feel compelled to go through all the passages in Morning Affirmations every time. As the content becomes more familiar, avoid the trap of reducing these affirmations to a set of words you repeat by rote. Use them as a preliminary to prayer and Bible reading, not as a substitute.

## Part Two: Daily Prayer Guide

This is the heart of the handbook. Because these prayers are on a three-month cycle, you will encounter each passage only four times a year. Thus, this guide can be used indefinitely without resulting in excessive repetition.

Introduction

Be sure to use the prayer prompts so that you do not merely read the prayers. It is essential that you personalize them so they can be incorporated into your own thoughts and experience.

You can adapt the prayers for each day to differing time formats. The prayers can be used with profit in a short period of time, or you can move through them more slowly, as you see fit.

Although you can tie these daily prayers to the day of the month, there is no need to do so, particularly if you find yourself falling behind. You may decide to mark your place and continue wherever you left off.

## Part Three: One-Week Prayer Guide

This seven-day prayer guide is particularly appropriate for longer times of meditation and devotional prayer. You may wish to move through this cycle on an occasional basis.

## Part Four: Personal Prayer Pages

I encourage you to use these pages to add your own thoughts and prayers as they come to mind when using this handbook. You can also use this section to record your petitionary and intercessory prayer lists as well as specific answers to prayer.

# THE PHILOSOPHY UNDERLYING THIS HANDBOOK

The God of the Bible is infinite, personal, and triune. As a communion of three Persons, one of God's purposes in creating us is to display the glory of His being and attributes to intelligent moral creatures who are capable of responding to His relational initiatives. In spite of human rebellion and sin against the Person and character of the Lord, Christ bore the awesome price of our guilt and inaugurated "a new and living way" (Hebrews 10:20) by which the barrier to personal relationship with God has been overcome. "By this the love of God was manifested in us, that God has sent His only begotten Son into the world so that we might live through Him. In this is love, not that we loved God, but that He loved us and sent His Son to be the propitiation for our sins" (1 John 4:9–10).

Since God is the initiator of a loving relationship with us, our high and holy calling is to respond to His offer. Our Lord, in encapsulating the Law and the Prophets, gave us the essence of this response: "'You shall love the Lord your God with all your heart, and with all your soul, and with all your mind.' This is the great and foremost commandment. The second is like it, 'You shall love your neighbor as yourself'" (Matthew 22:37–39). The quality of our vertical relationship with God has a direct bearing on the quality of our horizontal relationships with others. As we grow in His grace, we will have an enhanced capacity, through the power of the indwelling Holy Spirit, to respond to others with the Christlike qualities of humility, gentleness, patience, and forbearance (Ephesians 4:2).

Introduction

This *agapē*, which we receive from the Lord and which flows through us toward others, is rooted in volition (our willingness to receive and display it) and is expressed through thinking and feeling in the deeds of others-centered love.

Another way of summarizing our calling and purpose as followers of Christ is to love God completely, to love ourselves correctly, and to love others compassionately.

*Loving God completely* is a growth process that involves the personal elements of communication and response. By listening to the Holy Spirit in the words of Scripture and speaking to the Lord in our thoughts and prayers, we move in the direction of knowing Him better. The better we know Him, the more we will love Him, and the more we love Him, the greater our willingness to respond to Him in trust and obedience.

To *love ourselves correctly* is to see ourselves as God sees us and to allow the Word, not the world, to define us by telling us who and whose we really are. The clearer we capture the vision of our new identity in Christ, the more we will realize that our deepest needs for security, significance, and satisfaction are met in Him and not in people, possessions, or positions.

A biblical view of our identity and resources in Christ moves us in the direction of *loving others compassionately*. Grasping our true and unlimited resources in Christ frees us from bondage to the opinions of others and gives us the liberty to love and serve others regardless of their response.

Since we cannot serve two masters, the focus of our heart will be either the temporal or the eternal. If it is the temporal, we cannot love God completely because of a divided heart. When Christ is a component instead of the center of life, our lives become complicated; the worries of the world, the deceitfulness of wealth, and the desires for other things choke the word of truth in our lives and we do not bear lasting fruit (Mark 4:19). On the other hand, if the focus of our heart is the eternal, we will love Christ above His created goods and pleasures and begin to fulfill the enduring purpose for which we were created.

# PART ONE

# MORNING AFFIRMATIONS

## 1. Submitting to God

Because of all You have done for me, I present my body to You as a living sacrifice for this day. I want to be transformed by the renewing of my mind, affirming that Your will for me is good and acceptable and perfect. (Romans 12:1–2)

## 2. Adoration and Thanksgiving

Offer a brief word of praise to God for one or more of His *attributes* (e.g., love and compassion, grace, mercy, holiness, goodness, omnipotence, omnipresence, omniscience, truthfulness, unchanging character, eternality) and/or *works* (e.g., creation, care, redemption, loving purposes, second coming).

Thank Him for the good things in your life.

## 3. Examination

Ask the Spirit to search your heart and reveal any areas of unconfessed sin. Acknowledge these to the Lord and thank Him for His forgiveness. (Psalm 139:23–24)

## 4. My Identity in Christ

"I have been crucified with Christ; and it is no longer I who live, but Christ lives in me; and the life which I now live in the flesh I live by faith in the Son of God, who loved me, and delivered Himself up for me." (Galatians 2:20)

> I have *forgiveness* from the penalty of sin because Christ died for me. (Romans 5:8; 1 Corinthians 15:3)

Morning Affirmations

I have *freedom* from the power of sin because I died with Christ. (Colossians 2:11; 1 Peter 2:24)

I have *fulfillment* for this day because Christ lives in me. (Philippians 1:20–21)

By *faith*, I will allow Christ to manifest His life through me. (2 Corinthians 2:14)

## 5. Filling of the Spirit

Ask the Spirit to control and fill you for this day:

I want to be filled with the Spirit. (Ephesians 5:18)

When I walk by the Spirit, I will not carry out the desire of the flesh. (Galatians 5:16)

If I live by the Spirit, I will also walk by the Spirit. (Galatians 5:25)

## 6. Fruit of the Spirit

Pray on the fruit of the Spirit: love, joy, peace, patience, kindness, goodness, faithfulness, gentleness, self-control. (Galatians 5:22–23)

"Love is patient, love is kind, and is not jealous; love does not brag and is not arrogant, does not act unbecomingly; it does not seek its own, is not provoked, does not take into account a wrong suffered, does not rejoice in unrighteousness, but rejoices with the truth; bears all things, believes all things, hopes all things, endures all things." (1 Corinthians 13:4–7)

## 7. Purpose of My Life

I want to love the Lord my God with all my heart, and with all my soul, and with all my mind, and I want to love my neighbor as myself (Matthew 22:37, 39). My purpose is to love God completely, love self correctly, and love others compassionately.

I will seek first Your kingdom and Your righteousness. (Matthew 6:33)

I have been called to follow Christ and to be a fisher of men. (Matthew 4:19)

I will be a witness to those who do not know Him and participate in the Great Commission to go and make disciples. (Matthew 28:19–20; Acts 1:8)

I want to glorify the Father by bearing much fruit, and so prove to be Christ's disciple. (John 15:8)

## 8. Circumstances of the Day

I will trust in the Lord with all my heart, and not lean on my own understanding. In all my ways I will acknowledge Him, and He will make my paths straight. (Proverbs 3:5–6)

God causes all things to work together for good to those who love God, to those who are called according to His purpose. (Romans 8:28; also see 8:29)

I acknowledge that You are in control of all things in my life, and that You have my best interests at heart. Because of this I will trust and obey You today.

Review the events of this day and commit them into the hands of God.

## 9. Protection in Spiritual Warfare

### Against the World: Renew

I will set my mind on the things of the Spirit. (Romans 8:5)

Since I have been raised up with Christ, I will keep seeking the things above, where Christ is, seated at the right hand of God. I will set my mind on the things above, not on the things that are on earth. (Colossians 3:1–2; also see Colossians 3:3–4 and Hebrews 12:1–2)

I will be anxious for nothing, but in everything by prayer and supplication with thanksgiving I will let my requests be made known to God. And the peace of God, which surpasses all comprehension, shall guard my heart and my mind in Christ Jesus. Whatever is true, whatever is honorable, whatever is right, whatever is pure, whatever is lovely, whatever is of good repute, if there is any excellence and if anything worthy of praise, I will let my mind dwell on these things. (Philippians 4:6–8; also see 4:9)

**Against the Flesh: Reckon**

I know that my old self was crucified with Christ, so that I am no longer a slave to sin, for He who has died is freed from sin. I will reckon myself as dead to sin, but alive to God in Christ Jesus. I will not present the members of my body to sin as instruments of unrighteousness, but I will present myself to God as one alive from the dead, and my members as instruments of righteousness to God. (Romans 6:6–7, 11, 13)

**Against the Devil: Resist**

As I submit myself to God and resist the devil, he will flee from me. (James 4:7)

I will be of sober spirit and on the alert. My adversary, the devil, prowls about like a roaring lion, seeking someone to devour. But I will resist him, firm in my faith. (1 Peter 5:8–9)

I will take up the full armor of God, that I may be able to resist and stand firm. I put on the belt of *truth* and the breastplate of *righteousness*; I put on my feet the preparation of the gospel of *peace*; and I take up the shield of *faith* with which I will be able to extinguish all the flaming missiles of the evil one. I take the helmet of *salvation* and the sword of the Spirit, which is the *Word* of God. With all *prayer* and petition I will pray at all times in the Spirit and be on the alert with all perseverance and petition for all the saints. (Ephesians 6:13–18)

## 10. The Coming of Christ and My Future with Him

Your kingdom come, Your will be done. (Matthew 6:10)

You have said, "I am coming quickly." Amen. Come, Lord Jesus. (Revelation 22:20)

I consider that the sufferings of this present time are not worthy to be compared with the glory that is to be revealed to me. (Romans 8:18)

I will not lose heart, but though my outer man is decaying, yet my inner man is being renewed day by day. For momentary, light affliction is producing for me an eternal weight of glory far beyond all comparison, while I look not at the things which are seen, but at the things which are not seen; for the things which are seen are temporal, but the things which are not seen are eternal. (2 Corinthians 4:16–18)

My citizenship is in heaven, from which also I eagerly wait for a Savior, the Lord Jesus Christ. (Philippians 3:20)

Also consider 2 Timothy 4:8; Hebrews 11:1, 6; 2 Peter 3:11–12; and 1 John 2:28; 3:2–3.

# PART TWO

# DAILY PRAYER GUIDE

Daily Prayer Guide

# The First Month

# THE FIRST MONTH
# **DAY 1**

### Adoration

O Lord, our Lord,
How majestic is Your name in all the earth!
You have set Your glory above the heavens! (Psalm 8:1)

Great and marvelous are Your works,
Lord God Almighty!
Righteous and true are Your ways,
King of the nations!
Who will not fear You, O Lord, and glorify Your name?
For You alone are holy.
All nations will come and worship before You,
For Your righteous acts have been revealed. (Revelation 15:3–4)

*Pause to express your thoughts of praise and worship.*

### Confession

The Lord is in His holy temple;
The Lord is on His heavenly throne.
He observes the sons of men;
His eyes examine them. (Psalm 11:4)

*Ask the Spirit to search your heart and reveal any areas of unconfessed sin. Acknowledge these to the Lord and thank Him for His forgiveness.*

## Renewal

O Lord my God, may I fear You, walk in all Your ways, love You, and serve You with all my heart and with all my soul. (Deuteronomy 10:12)

I have not been made perfect, but I press on to lay hold of that for which Christ Jesus also laid hold of me. I do not consider myself yet to have attained it, but one thing I do: forgetting what is behind and stretching forward to what is ahead, I press on toward the goal to win the prize of the upward call of God in Christ Jesus. (Philippians 3:12–14)

*Pause to add your own prayers for personal renewal.*

## Petition

My body is a temple of the Holy Spirit, who is in me, whom I have from God, and I am not my own. For I was bought at a price; therefore may I glorify God in my body. (1 Corinthians 6:19–20)

- **Growth in Christ**
  - Greater desire to know and please Him
  - Greater love and commitment to Him
  - Grace to practice His presence
  - Grace to glorify Him in my life
- My activities for this day
- Special concerns

## Intercession

We must take heed to ourselves and to all the flock of which the Holy Spirit has made us overseers to shepherd the church of God, which He purchased with His own blood. (Acts 20:28)

### Churches and Ministries

- My local church
- Other churches
- Evangelism and discipleship ministries
- Educational ministries
- Special concerns

## Affirmation

The love of Christ compels me, because I am convinced that One died for all, and therefore all died. And He died for all, that those who live should no longer live for themselves but for Him who died for them and was raised again. (2 Corinthians 5:14–15)

Christ redeemed us from the curse of the law by becoming a curse for us, for it is written: "Cursed is everyone who hangs on a tree." (Galatians 3:13)

*Pause to reflect upon these biblical affirmations.*

## Thanksgiving

In Your unfailing love You have led the people You have redeemed.
In Your strength You have guided them to Your holy dwelling.
You brought them in and planted them in the mountain of Your inheritance—
The place, O Lord, You made for Your dwelling;
The sanctuary, O Lord, Your hands have established.
(Exodus 15:13, 17)

You are the Lord our God, who brought Your people out of Egypt so that they would no longer be their slaves; You broke the bars of their yoke and enabled them to walk with heads held high. (Leviticus 26:13)

*Pause to offer your own expressions of thanksgiving.*

## Closing Prayer

Whom have I in heaven but You?
And there is nothing on earth I desire besides You.
My flesh and my heart may fail,
But God is the strength of my heart and my portion forever.
Those who are far from You will perish;
You have cut off all who are unfaithful to You.
But as for me, the nearness of God is my good.
I have made the Lord God my refuge,
That I may tell of all Your works. (Psalm 73:25–28)

# THE FIRST MONTH
# **DAY 2**

## Adoration

How great are Your works, O Lord!
Your thoughts are very deep.
The senseless man does not know;
Fools do not understand
That when the wicked spring up like grass
And all the evildoers flourish,
They will be destroyed forever.
But You, O Lord, are exalted forever. (Psalm 92:5–8)

You are the Lord, that is Your name.
You will not give Your glory to another,
Or Your praise to idols. (Isaiah 42:8)

*Pause to express your thoughts of praise and worship.*

## Confession

I will endure discipline, for God is treating me as a son. For what son is not disciplined by his father? If I am without discipline, of which all have become partakers, then I am an illegitimate child and not a true son. Moreover, we have all had human fathers who disciplined us, and we respected them; how much more should I be subjected to the Father of spirits and live? (Hebrews 12:7–9)

*Ask the Spirit to search your heart and reveal any areas of unconfessed sin. Acknowledge these to the Lord and thank Him for His forgiveness.*

## Renewal

Christ must increase; I must decrease. (John 3:30)

You are the true vine, and Your Father is the vinedresser. He cuts off every branch in You that bears no fruit, while every branch that does bear fruit He prunes, that it may bear more fruit. May I abide in You, and You in me. As the branch cannot bear fruit of itself, unless it abides in the vine, neither can I, unless I abide in You. (John 15:1–2, 4)

*Pause to add your own prayers for personal renewal.*

## Petition

May I follow Abraham's example of willingness to offer all that I have to You, holding nothing back and trusting in Your character and in Your promises. (Genesis 22:2–12, 16)

- **Growth in Wisdom**
    - Developing an eternal perspective
    - Renewing my mind with truth
    - Greater skill in each area of life
- My activities for this day
- Special concerns

## Intercession

May we rejoice, become complete, be of good comfort, be of one mind, and live in peace; and the God of love and peace will be with us. (2 Corinthians 13:11)

### Family

- My immediate family
- My relatives
- Spiritual concerns
- Emotional and physical concerns
- Other concerns

## Affirmation

When I give, it will be given to me; good measure, pressed down, shaken together, running over, will be poured into my lap. For with the measure I use, it will be measured back to me. (Luke 6:38)

He who sows sparingly will also reap sparingly, and he who sows bountifully will also reap bountifully. Each one should give as he has decided in his heart, not reluctantly or under compulsion; for God loves a cheerful giver. And God is able to make all grace abound to us, so that always having all sufficiency in everything, we may abound in every good work. As it is written: "He has scattered abroad His gifts to the poor; His righteousness endures forever." Now He who supplies seed to the sower and bread for food will also supply and increase our seed and will increase the fruits of our righteousness. (2 Corinthians 9:6–10)

*Pause to reflect upon these biblical affirmations.*

## Thanksgiving

We give thanks to You, Lord God Almighty, the One who is and who was, because You have taken Your great power and have begun to reign. (Revelation 11:17)

There will no longer be any curse. The throne of God and of the Lamb will be in the new Jerusalem, and His servants will serve Him. They will see His face, and His name will be on their foreheads. And there will be no night there; they will not need the light of a lamp or the light of the sun, for the Lord God will give them light. And they shall reign for ever and ever. (Revelation 22:3–5)

*Pause to offer your own expressions of thanksgiving.*

## Closing Prayer

Blessed be the name of God for ever and ever,
For wisdom and power belong to Him.
He changes the times and the seasons;
He raises up kings and deposes them.
He gives wisdom to the wise
And knowledge to those who have understanding.
He reveals deep and hidden things;
He knows what is in the darkness,
And light dwells with Him. (Daniel 2:20–22)

# THE FIRST MONTH
# DAY 3

## Adoration

The Lord Most High is awesome,
The great King over all the earth!
God is the King of all the earth,
And I will sing His praise.
God reigns over the nations;
God is seated on His holy throne. (Psalm 47:2, 7–8)

You must be treated as holy by those who come near You, and before all people, You will be honored. (Leviticus 10:3)

*Pause to express your thoughts of praise and worship.*

## Confession

Lord, I have heard of Your fame, and I stand in awe of
  Your deeds.
O Lord, revive Your work in the midst of the years,
In our time make them known;
In wrath remember mercy. (Habakkuk 3:2)

*Ask the Spirit to search your heart and reveal any areas of unconfessed sin. Acknowledge these to the Lord and thank Him for His forgiveness.*

## Renewal

May I not turn aside from following the Lord, but serve the Lord with all my heart. May I not turn aside to go after worthless things which do not profit or deliver, because they are useless. (1 Samuel 12:20–21)

The works of the flesh are evident, which are: immorality, impurity, sensuality, idolatry, sorcery, hatred, discord, jealousy, fits of rage, selfish ambition, dissensions, factions, envyings, drunkenness, revelries, and the like. Those who practice such things will not inherit the kingdom of God. But the fruit of the Spirit is love, joy, peace, patience, kindness, goodness, faithfulness, gentleness, self-control; against such things there is no law. (Galatians 5:19–23)

*Pause to add your own prayers for personal renewal.*

## Petition

When I ask, it will be given to me; when I seek, I will find; when I knock, the door will be opened to me. For everyone who asks receives; he who seeks finds; and to him who knocks, the door will be opened. (Matthew 7:7–8; Luke 11:9–10)

- **Spiritual Insight**
  - Understanding and insight into the Word
  - Understanding my identity in Christ
    - Who I am
    - Where I came from
    - Where I'm going
  - Understanding God's purpose for my life

- My activities for this day
- Special concerns

## Intercession

For God is my witness, whom I serve in my spirit in the gospel of His Son, how unceasingly I make mention of you in my prayers. (Romans 1:9)

### Believers

- Personal friends
- Those in ministry
- Those who are oppressed and in need
- Special concerns

## Affirmation

The Lord is a jealous God, punishing the children for the sin of the fathers to the third and fourth generation of those who hate Him, but showing lovingkindness to a thousand generations of those who love Him and keep His commandments. (Exodus 20:5–6; Deuteronomy 5:9–10)

God is not a man, that He should lie, nor a son of man, that He should change his mind. Has He spoken and not done it? Has He promised and not fulfilled it? (Numbers 23:19)

*Pause to reflect upon these biblical affirmations.*

## Thanksgiving

I will remember the works of the Lord;
Surely, I will remember Your wonders of long ago.
I will meditate on all Your works
And consider all Your mighty deeds.
Your way, O God, is holy.
What god is so great as our God?
You are the God who works wonders;
You have revealed Your strength among the peoples.
You redeemed Your people with Your power,
The descendants of Jacob and Joseph. (Psalm 77:11–15)

*Pause to offer your own expressions of thanksgiving.*

## Closing Prayer

O come, let us sing to the Lord;
Let us shout joyfully to the Rock of our salvation.
Let us come before His presence with thanksgiving;
Let us shout for joy to Him with psalms. (Psalm 95:1–2)

O sing to the Lord a new song;
Sing to the Lord, all the earth.
Sing to the Lord, bless His name;
Proclaim the good news of His salvation day after day.
Declare His glory among the nations,
His marvelous works among all people. (Psalm 96:1–3)

# THE FIRST MONTH
# DAY 4

## Adoration

The Lord is great and greatly to be praised;
He is to be feared above all gods.
For all the gods of the nations are idols,
But the Lord made the heavens.
Splendor and majesty are before Him;
Strength and joy are in His place.
I will ascribe to the Lord glory and strength.
I will ascribe to the Lord the glory due His name
And worship the Lord in the beauty of holiness.
Tremble before him, all the earth.
The world is firmly established, it will not be moved.
(1 Chronicles 16:25–30)

You are the God of Abraham and the Fear of Isaac.
(Genesis 31:42)

*Pause to express your thoughts of praise and worship.*

## Confession

Save me from bloodguilt, O God,
The God of my salvation,
And my tongue will sing aloud of Your righteousness.
O Lord, open my lips,
And my mouth will declare Your praise.

For You do not desire sacrifice, or I would bring it;
You do not delight in burnt offering.
The sacrifices of God are a broken spirit;
A broken and contrite heart,
O God, You will not despise. (Psalm 51:14–17)

*Ask the Spirit to search your heart and reveal any areas of unconfessed sin. Acknowledge these to the Lord and thank Him for His forgiveness.*

## Renewal

May I remove the places of idolatry from my life, and like Asa, let my heart be fully committed to God all my days. (2 Chronicles 15:17)

May I trust in the Lord and do good; may I dwell in the land and feed on Your faithfulness. When I delight myself in the Lord, You will give me the desires of my heart. I will commit my way to the Lord and trust in You, and You will bring it to pass. You will bring forth my righteousness like the light, and my justice like the noonday. May I rest in the Lord and wait patiently for You; I will not fret because of him who prospers in his way, with the man who practices evil schemes. (Psalm 37:3–7)

*Pause to add your own prayers for personal renewal.*

## Petition

May I not pervert justice, show partiality, or accept a bribe, for a bribe blinds the eyes of the wise and perverts the words of the righteous. (Deuteronomy 16:19)

- **Relationships with Others**
  - Greater love and compassion for others
  - Loved ones
  - Those who do not know Christ
  - Those in need
- My activities for this day
- Special concerns

## Intercession

We are the fragrance of Christ to God among those who are being saved and among those who are perishing; to the one an aroma from death to death; to the other, an aroma from life to life. And who is sufficient for these things? (2 Corinthians 2:15–16)

### Evangelism

- Friends
- Relatives
- Neighbors
- Coworkers
- Special opportunities

## Affirmation

There is no one who has left house or brothers or sisters or mother or father or children or fields for Your sake and the gospel's, who will not receive a hundred times as much in this present age—houses, brothers, sisters, mothers, children, and fields, along with persecutions—and in the age to come, eternal life. (Matthew 19:29; Mark 10:29–30)

If anyone comes to You and does not hate his father and mother, his wife and children, his brothers and sisters—yes, even his own life—he cannot be Your disciple. And whoever does not carry his cross and follow You cannot be Your disciple. (Luke 14:26–27)

*Pause to reflect upon these biblical affirmations.*

## Thanksgiving

You have loved me with an everlasting love;
You have drawn me with lovingkindness. (Jeremiah 31:3)

You led Your people with cords of human kindness,
With bands of love;
You lifted the yoke from their neck
And bent down to feed them. (Hosea 11:4)

*Pause to offer your own expressions of thanksgiving.*

## Closing Prayer

You are the Lord, the God of our fathers—the God of Abraham, the God of Isaac, and the God of Jacob. This is Your name forever, the name by which You are to be remembered from generation to generation. (Exodus 3:15)

I will sing to the Lord, for He is highly exalted.
The Lord is my strength and my song;
He has become my salvation.
He is my God, and I will praise Him,
My father's God, and I will exalt Him. (Exodus 15:1–2)

Daily Prayer Guide

# THE FIRST MONTH
# DAY 5

## Adoration

The Lord my God is God of gods and Lord of lords, the great God, mighty and awesome, who shows no partiality and accepts no bribes. He executes justice for the fatherless and the widow and loves the alien, giving him food and clothing. (Deuteronomy 10:17–18)

My soul magnifies the Lord
And my spirit rejoices in God my Savior,
For the Mighty One has done great things for me,
And holy is His name.
His mercy is on those who fear Him,
From generation to generation. (Luke 1:46–47, 49–50)

*Pause to express your thoughts of praise and worship.*

## Confession

God's eyes are on the ways of a man,
And He sees all his steps.
There is no darkness or deep shadow
Where the workers of iniquity can hide.
He does not need to examine a man further,
That he should go before God in judgment. (Job 34:21–23)

*Ask the Spirit to search your heart and reveal any areas of unconfessed sin. Acknowledge these to the Lord and thank Him for His forgiveness.*

## Renewal

May I flee from sexual immorality. All other sins a man commits are outside his body, but the immoral person sins against his own body. (1 Corinthians 6:18)

May I not set my heart on evil things, or be an idolater, or commit sexual immorality. (1 Corinthians 10:6–8)

*Pause to add your own prayers for personal renewal.*

## Petition

Let me hear Your unfailing love in the morning,
For I have put my trust in You.
Show me the way I should walk,
For to You I lift up my soul. (Psalm 143:8)

- **Faithfulness as a Steward**
    - Of time
    - Of talents
    - Of treasure
    - Of truth
    - Of relationships
- My activities for this day
- Special concerns

## Intercession

May I honor all people, love the brotherhood of believers, fear God, and honor the king. (1 Peter 2:17)

### Government

- Spiritual revival
- Local government
- State government
- National government
- Current events and concerns

## Affirmation

All Scripture is God-breathed and is useful for teaching, for reproof, for correction, for training in righteousness, that the man of God may be thoroughly equipped for every good work. (2 Timothy 3:16–17)

We have the prophetic word made more certain, to which I will do well to pay attention, as to a light shining in a dark place, until the day dawns and the morning star rises in my heart. (2 Peter 1:19)

*Pause to reflect upon these biblical affirmations.*

## Thanksgiving

The Lord my God is the faithful God, who keeps His covenant and His lovingkindness to a thousand generations of those who love Him and keep His commands. (Deuteronomy 7:9)

I will tell of the lovingkindnesses of the Lord,
The praises of the Lord,
According to all the Lord has done for us,
And the great goodness toward the house of Israel,
Which He has bestowed on them according to His mercies,
And according to the multitude of His lovingkindnesses.
(Isaiah 63:7)

*Pause to offer your own expressions of thanksgiving.*

## Closing Prayer

I know that my Redeemer lives
And that in the end He will stand upon the earth.
And after my skin has been destroyed,
Yet in my flesh I will see God;
Whom I myself will see
And behold with my own eyes and not another.
How my heart yearns within me! (Job 19:25–27)

God is exalted beyond our understanding;
The number of His years is unsearchable. (Job 36:26)

Daily Prayer Guide

# THE FIRST MONTH
# DAY 6

## Adoration

Oh, the depth of the riches both of the wisdom and knowledge of God! How unsearchable are Your judgments, and Your ways past finding out! For who has known the mind of the Lord? Or who has been Your counselor? Or who has first given to You, that You should repay him? For from You and through You and to You are all things. To You be the glory forever! Amen. (Romans 11:33–36)

Hallelujah! Salvation and glory and power belong to our God, because His judgments are true and righteous. (Revelation 19:1–2)

*Pause to express your thoughts of praise and worship.*

## Confession

The Lord your God is gracious and compassionate, and He will not turn His face from you if you return to Him. (2 Chronicles 30:9)

*Ask the Spirit to search your heart and reveal any areas of unconfessed sin. Acknowledge these to the Lord and thank Him for His forgiveness.*

## Renewal

Like Josiah, may I do what is right in the sight of the Lord, walking in the ways of David and not turning aside to the right or to the left. (2 Chronicles 34:1–2)

Like Josiah, give me a tender and responsive heart, so that I will humble myself before You when I hear Your word. (2 Chronicles 34:27)

May I walk in the steps of Jesus, who often withdrew to lonely places and prayed. (Mark 1:35; Luke 5:16)

*Pause to add your own prayers for personal renewal.*

## Petition

May my conscience testify that I have conducted myself in the world in the holiness and sincerity that are from God, not in fleshly wisdom but in the grace of God, especially in my relations with others. (2 Corinthians 1:12)

- **Family and Ministry**
    - Family
    - Ministry
        - Sharing Christ with others
        - Helping others grow in Him
    - Career
- My activities for this day
- Special concerns

## Intercession

Remember us, O my God, and do not blot out what we have done in Your name. Remember us, O my God, for good. (Nehemiah 13:14, 31)

### Missions

- Local missions
- National missions
- World missions
- The fulfillment of the Great Commission
- Special concerns

## Affirmation

The hour is coming and now is, when true worshipers will worship the Father in spirit and truth, for the Father is seeking such to worship Him. God is spirit, and those who worship Him must worship in spirit and truth. (John 4:23–24)

Those who obey Christ's commandments abide in Him, and He in them. And this is how I know that He abides in me: by the Spirit whom He has given me. (1 John 3:24)

*Pause to reflect upon these biblical affirmations.*

## Thanksgiving

We know the grace of our Lord Jesus Christ, that though He was rich, yet for our sakes He became poor, that we through His poverty might become rich. (2 Corinthians 8:9)

Thanks be to God for His indescribable gift!
(2 Corinthians 9:15)

*Pause to offer your own expressions of thanksgiving.*

## Closing Prayer

I will not fear, for You are with me;
I will not be dismayed, for You are my God.
You will strengthen me and help me;
You will uphold me with Your righteous right hand.
For You are the Lord my God, who takes hold of my right hand
And says to me, "Do not fear; I will help you."
(Isaiah 41:10, 13)

I call this to mind,
And therefore I have hope:
The Lord's mercies never cease,
For His compassions never fail.
They are new every morning;
Great is Your faithfulness. (Lamentations 3:21–23)

Daily Prayer Guide

# THE FIRST MONTH
## DAY 7

### Adoration

The Lord my God is God in the heavens above and in the earth below. (Joshua 2:11)

The Lord stretches out the north over empty space;
He suspends the earth on nothing. (Job 26:7)

He who made the Pleiades and Orion
And turns deep darkness into morning
And darkens day into night,
Who calls for the waters of the sea
And pours them out over the face of the earth—
The Lord is His name. (Amos 5:8)

*Pause to express your thoughts of praise and worship.*

### Confession

Let the power of my Lord be great, just as You have spoken, saying, "The Lord is slow to anger and abounding in mercy, forgiving iniquity and transgression." (Numbers 14:17–18)

*Ask the Spirit to search your heart and reveal any areas of unconfessed sin. Acknowledge these to the Lord and thank Him for His forgiveness.*

First Month, Day 7

## Renewal

May the name of the Lord Jesus be magnified in my life. (Acts 19:17)

In view of God's mercy, may I present my body as a living sacrifice, holy and pleasing to God, which is my reasonable service. (Romans 12:1)

*Pause to add your own prayers for personal renewal.*

## Petition

May I do no injustice in judgment, nor show partiality to the poor or favoritism to the great, but judge my neighbor fairly. (Leviticus 19:15)

- **Personal Concerns**
    - Spiritual warfare
        - The world
        - The flesh
        - The devil
    - Growth in character
    - Personal disciplines
    - Physical health and strength
- My activities for this day
- Special concerns

## Intercession

O Lord, be gracious to us; we have hoped in You.

Be our strength every morning,
Our salvation in time of distress. (Isaiah 33:2)

## World Affairs

- The poor and hungry
- The oppressed and persecuted
- Those in authority
- Peace among nations
- Current events and concerns

## Affirmation

Blessed is the man who finds wisdom,
And the man who gains understanding,
For its profit is greater than that of silver,
And its gain than fine gold.
She is more precious than jewels,
And nothing I desire can compare with her.
Long life is in her right hand;
In her left hand are riches and honor.
Her ways are pleasant ways,
And all her paths are peace.
She is a tree of life to those who embrace her,
And happy are those who hold her fast. (Proverbs 3:13–18)

Wisdom is foremost; therefore I will get wisdom,
And though it costs all I have, I will get understanding.
I will esteem her, and she will exalt me;
I will embrace her, and she will honor me. (Proverbs 4:7–8)

*Pause to reflect upon these biblical affirmations.*

## Thanksgiving

Has any other people heard the voice of God speaking out of the midst of the fire, as the children of Israel have, and lived? Has any god ever tried to take for himself one nation from the midst of another nation, by trials, by miraculous signs and wonders, by war, by a mighty hand and an outstretched arm, and by great and awesome deeds, like all the things the Lord God did for Israel in Egypt before their very eyes? The Israelites were shown these things so that they might know that the Lord, He is God; there is no other besides Him. Out of heaven You made the children of Israel hear Your voice to discipline them. On earth You showed them Your great fire, and they heard Your words out of the midst of the fire. Because You loved their fathers, You chose their descendants after them, and You brought them out of Egypt by Your presence and Your great power; You drove out from before the Israelites nations greater and mightier than they, to bring them in and to give them their land as an inheritance. (Deuteronomy 4:33–38)

*Pause to offer your own expressions of thanksgiving.*

## Closing Prayer

Lord Jesus, I have nowhere else to go; You have the words of eternal life. I believe and know that You are the Holy One of God. (John 6:68–69)

You are the resurrection and the life. He who believes in You will live, even though he dies, and whoever lives and believes in You will never die. (John 11:25–26)

Daily Prayer Guide

# THE FIRST MONTH
# DAY 8

## Adoration

You, the Lord, alone have declared
What is to come from the distant past.
There is no God apart from You,
A righteous God and a Savior;
There is none besides You.
You are God, and there is no other. (Isaiah 45:21–22)

You are my hope, O Lord God;
You are my trust from my youth.
As for me, I will always have hope;
I will praise You more and more. (Psalm 71:5, 14)

*Pause to express your thoughts of praise and worship.*

## Confession

You are not a God who takes pleasure in wickedness;
Evil cannot dwell with You. (Psalm 5:4)

*Ask the Spirit to search your heart and reveal any areas of unconfessed sin. Acknowledge these to the Lord and thank Him for His forgiveness.*

## Renewal

Like Enoch, may I walk with God. (Genesis 5:24)

Like Noah, may I find favor in the eyes of the Lord. (Genesis 6:8)

*Pause to add your own prayers for personal renewal.*

## Petition

May I consider the members of my earthly body as dead to immorality, impurity, passion, evil desires, and greed, which is idolatry. Because of these, the wrath of God is coming, and in them I once walked when I lived in them. (Colossians 3:5–7)

- **Growth in Christ**
    - Greater desire to know and please Him
    - Greater love and commitment to Him
    - Grace to practice His presence
    - Grace to glorify Him in my life
- My activities for this day
- Special concerns

## Intercession

Just as we have many members in one body, but all the members do not have the same function, so we who are many are one body in Christ and individually members of one another. And we have different gifts, according to the grace given to us. (Romans 12:4–6)

Daily Prayer Guide

## Churches and Ministries

- My local church
- Other churches
- Evangelism and discipleship ministries
- Educational ministries
- Special concerns

## Affirmation

I believe that it is through the grace of our Lord Jesus that I am saved. (Acts 15:11)

I trusted in Christ when I heard the word of truth, the gospel of my salvation. Having believed, I was sealed in Him with the Holy Spirit of promise, who is a deposit guaranteeing my inheritance until the redemption of those who are God's possession, to the praise of His glory. (Ephesians 1:13–14)

*Pause to reflect upon these biblical affirmations.*

## Thanksgiving

I will sing of the mercies of the Lord forever;
With my mouth I will make Your faithfulness known through
  all generations.
I will declare that Your lovingkindness will be built up forever,
That You will establish Your faithfulness in the heavens.
And the heavens will praise Your wonders, O Lord,
Your faithfulness also in the assembly of the holy ones.
For who in the heavens can be compared with the Lord?

First Month, Day 8

Who is like the Lord among the sons of the mighty?
God is greatly feared in the council of the holy ones,
And more awesome than all who surround Him.
O Lord God of hosts, who is like You, O mighty Lord?
Your faithfulness also surrounds You. (Psalm 89:1–2, 5–8)

*Pause to offer your own expressions of thanksgiving.*

## Closing Prayer

You are the living bread that came down from heaven. If anyone eats of this bread, he will live forever. This bread is Your flesh, which You have given for the life of the world. (John 6:51)

You are the light of the world. He who follows You will not walk in the darkness but will have the light of life. (John 8:12)

# THE FIRST MONTH
## DAY 9

### Adoration

Lord, You have been our dwelling place throughout all
  generations.
Before the mountains were born
Or You brought forth the earth and the world,
From everlasting to everlasting, You are God.
You turn men back into dust,
And say, "Return, O children of men."
For a thousand years in Your sight
Are like yesterday when it passes by
Or like a watch in the night. (Psalm 90:1–4)

Jesus Christ is the same yesterday, today, and forever.
(Hebrews 13:8)

*Pause to express your thoughts of praise and worship.*

### Confession

God fashions the hearts of all
And understands all their works. (Psalm 33:15)

*Ask the Spirit to search your heart and reveal any areas of unconfessed sin. Acknowledge these to the Lord and thank Him for His forgiveness.*

## Renewal

Has a nation changed its gods
Which were not gods?
But my people have exchanged their Glory
For that which is worthless.
By Your grace may I not forsake You,
The fountain of living waters,
To dig my own cisterns,
Broken cisterns that can hold no water. (Jeremiah 2:11, 13)

As one who shares in the heavenly calling, may I fix my thoughts on Jesus, the Apostle and High Priest of my confession. (Hebrews 3:1)

*Pause to add your own prayers for personal renewal.*

## Petition

May I be strong and courageous, being careful to obey Your word; may I not turn from it to the right or to the left, that I may act wisely wherever I go. (Joshua 1:7)

- **Growth in Wisdom**
    - Developing an eternal perspective
    - Renewing my mind with truth
    - Greater skill in each area of life
- My activities for this day
- Special concerns

## Intercession

We should bear with one another in love and make every effort to keep the unity of the Spirit in the bond of peace. (Ephesians 4:2–3)

### Family

- My immediate family
- My relatives
- Spiritual concerns
- Emotional and physical concerns
- Other concerns

## Affirmation

Naked I came from my mother's womb,
And naked I will depart.
The Lord gives, and the Lord takes away;
Blessed be the name of the Lord. (Job 1:21)

Godliness with contentment is great gain. For I brought nothing into the world, and I can take nothing out of it. But if I have food and clothing, with these I will be content. (1 Timothy 6:6–8)

*Pause to reflect upon these biblical affirmations.*

First Month, Day 9

## Thanksgiving

I called to the Lord in my distress,
And He answered me.
From the depths of the grave, I called for help,
And You heard my voice. (Jonah 2:2)

I will exult in the Lord;
I will rejoice in the God of my salvation.
The Lord God is my strength;
He makes my feet like the feet of a deer
And enables me to go on the heights. (Habakkuk 3:18–19)

*Pause to offer your own expressions of thanksgiving.*

## Closing Prayer

You are the door; whoever enters through You will be saved and will come in and go out and find pasture. The thief comes only to steal and kill and destroy; You have come that we may have life and have it abundantly. (John 10:9–10)

Your sheep hear Your voice, and You know them, and they follow You. You give them eternal life, and they shall never perish; no one can snatch them out of Your hand. The Father, who has given them to You, is greater than all; no one can snatch them out of the Father's hand. You and the Father are one. (John 10:27–30)

## THE FIRST MONTH
## DAY 10

### Adoration

I will exalt You, my God and King;
I will bless Your name for ever and ever.
Every day I will bless You,
And I will praise Your name for ever and ever.
Great is the Lord and most worthy of praise;
His greatness is unsearchable. (Psalm 145:1–3)

Out of the north He comes in golden splendor;
With God is awesome majesty.
The Almighty is beyond our reach;
He is exalted in power
And in His justice and great righteousness,
He does not oppress. (Job 37:22–23)

*Pause to express your thoughts of praise and worship.*

### Confession

God will not always strive with us,
Nor will He harbor His anger forever;
He does not treat us as our sins deserve
Or repay us according to our iniquities.
For as high as the heavens are above the earth,
So great is His love for those who fear Him;

First Month, Day 10

As far as the east is from the west,
So far has He removed our transgressions from us.
As a father has compassion on his children,
So the Lord has compassion on those who fear Him.
(Psalm 103:9–13)

*Ask the Spirit to search your heart and reveal any areas of unconfessed sin. Acknowledge these to the Lord and thank Him for His forgiveness.*

## Renewal

May I let the fear of the Lord be upon me, and be careful in what I do, for with the Lord my God there is no injustice or partiality or bribery. (2 Chronicles 19:7)

May I meditate on Your precepts
And consider Your ways.
May I delight in Your statutes,
And not forget Your word.
Deal bountifully with Your servant,
That I may live and keep Your word.
Open my eyes that I may see
Wonderful things from Your law. (Psalm 119:15–18)

*Pause to add your own prayers for personal renewal.*

## Petition

May I not enter the path of the wicked
Or walk in the way of evil men. (Proverbs 4:14)

- **Spiritual Insight**
  - Understanding and insight into the Word
  - Understanding my identity in Christ
    - Who I am
    - Where I came from
    - Where I'm going
  - Understanding God's purpose for my life
- My activities for this day
- Special concerns

## Intercession

The Spirit helps me in my weakness, for I do not know what I ought to pray for, but the Spirit Himself intercedes for me with groans that words cannot express. And He who searches the hearts knows the mind of the Spirit, because the Spirit intercedes for the saints according to the will of God. (Romans 8:26–27)

### Believers

- Personal friends
- Those in ministry
- Those who are oppressed and in need
- Special concerns

## Affirmation

Jesus rejoiced in the Holy Spirit, and said, "I praise You, Father, Lord of heaven and earth, because You have hidden these things from the wise and learned, and revealed them to

First Month, Day 10

little children. Yes, Father, for this was well-pleasing in Your sight. All things have been delivered to Me by My Father. No one knows the Son except the Father, and no one knows the Father except the Son and those to whom the Son chooses to reveal Him." (Matthew 11:25–27; Luke 10:21–22)

The foolishness of God is wiser than men, and the weakness of God is stronger than men. But God chose the foolish things of the world to shame the wise, and God chose the weak things of the world to shame the strong; and the lowly things of this world and the despised things God has chosen, and the things that are not, to nullify the things that are, so that no one may boast before Him. (1 Corinthians 1:25, 27–29)

*Pause to reflect upon these biblical affirmations.*

## Thanksgiving

Rejoice greatly, O daughter of Zion!
Shout, O daughter of Jerusalem!
Behold, Your King is coming to you;
He is just and having salvation,
Humble and riding on a donkey,
On a colt, the foal of a donkey.
He will proclaim peace to the nations;
His dominion will extend from sea to sea
And from the River to the ends of the earth. (Zechariah 9:9–10)

*Pause to offer your own expressions of thanksgiving.*

## Closing Prayer

The Lord bless you and keep you;
The Lord make His face shine upon you
And be gracious to you;
The Lord turn His face toward you
And give you peace. (Numbers 6:24–26)

# THE FIRST MONTH
# **DAY 11**

## Adoration

O Lord, God of Israel, there is no God like You in heaven above or on earth below; You keep Your covenant and mercy with Your servants who walk before You with all their heart. (1 Kings 8:23; 2 Chronicles 6:14)

I know that You alone, whose name is the Lord,
Are the Most High over all the earth. (Psalm 83:18)

*Pause to express your thoughts of praise and worship.*

## Confession

A person's wickedness will punish him;
His backsliding will reprove him.
I know therefore and see that it is evil and bitter
To forsake the Lord my God
And have no fear of Him. (Jeremiah 2:19)

*Ask the Spirit to search your heart and reveal any areas of unconfessed sin. Acknowledge these to the Lord and thank Him for His forgiveness.*

## Renewal

May I be anxious for nothing, but in everything by prayer and petition with thanksgiving, may I let my requests be known to God. And the peace of God, which transcends all understanding, will guard my heart and my mind in Christ Jesus. (Philippians 4:6–7)

May I prepare my mind for action and be self-controlled, setting my hope fully on the grace to be brought to me at the revelation of Jesus Christ. (1 Peter 1:13)

*Pause to add your own prayers for personal renewal.*

## Petition

May I not be ashamed to testify about our Lord, but join with others in suffering for the gospel according to the power of God. (2 Timothy 1:8)

- **Relationships with Others**
    - Greater love and compassion for others
    - Loved ones
    - Those who do not know Christ
    - Those in need
- My activities for this day
- Special concerns

First Month, Day 11

## Intercession

The god of this age has blinded the minds of unbelievers, so that they cannot see the light of the gospel of the glory of Christ, who is the image of God. (2 Corinthians 4:4)

## Evangelism

- Friends
- Relatives
- Neighbors
- Coworkers
- Special opportunities

## Affirmation

Christ has been raised from the dead, the firstfruits of those who have fallen asleep. For since death came through a man, the resurrection of the dead comes also through a Man. For as in Adam all die, so in Christ all will be made alive. But each in his own order: Christ, the firstfruits; afterward, those who are Christ's at His coming. Then the end will come, when He delivers the kingdom to God the Father, when He has abolished all rule and all authority and power. For He must reign until He has put all His enemies under His feet. The last enemy that will be destroyed is death. (1 Corinthians 15:20–26)

The first man is of the dust of the earth; the second Man is from heaven. As was the earthly man, so are those who are of the earth; and as is the Man from heaven, so also are those who are of heaven. And just as we have borne the image of the earthly man, so shall we bear the likeness of the heavenly Man. (1 Corinthians 15:47–49)

*Pause to reflect upon these biblical affirmations.*

## Thanksgiving

The Son of Man did not come to be served, but to serve, and to give His life as a ransom for many. (Matthew 20:28)

Jesus took bread, gave thanks, and broke it, and gave it to His disciples, saying, "Take and eat; this is My body." Then He took the cup, gave thanks, and offered it to them, saying, "Drink from it, all of you. This is My blood of the new covenant, which is poured out for many for the forgiveness of sins." (Matthew 26:26–28)

*Pause to offer your own expressions of thanksgiving.*

## Closing Prayer

I will arise and bless the Lord, my God,
Who is from everlasting to everlasting.
Blessed be Your glorious name,
Which is exalted above all blessing and praise! (Nehemiah 9:5)

As for me, I will see Your face in righteousness;
When I awake, I will be satisfied with Your likeness.
(Psalm 17:15)

# THE FIRST MONTH
## DAY 12

### Adoration

God is jealous and the Lord avenges;
The Lord takes vengeance and is filled with wrath.
The Lord takes vengeance on His adversaries,
And He reserves wrath against His enemies.
The Lord is slow to anger and great in power
And will not leave the guilty unpunished.
His way is in the whirlwind and the storm,
And clouds are the dust of His feet. (Nahum 1:2–3)

Are You a God nearby,
And not a God far away?
Can anyone hide in secret places
So that You cannot see him?
Do You not fill heaven and earth? (Jeremiah 23:23–24)

*Pause to express your thoughts of praise and worship.*

### Confession

The fear of the Lord is to hate evil;
Wisdom hates pride and arrogance
And the evil way and the perverse mouth. (Proverbs 8:13)

*Ask the Spirit to search your heart and reveal any areas of unconfessed sin. Acknowledge these to the Lord and thank Him for His forgiveness.*

## Renewal

May I not trust in myself or in my own righteousness, nor view others with contempt. (Luke 18:9)

May I not be like the man who did not make God his strength but trusted in the abundance of his wealth and strengthened himself in his evil desires. (Psalm 52:7)

*Pause to add your own prayers for personal renewal.*

## Petition

Turn to me and be gracious to me,
For I am lonely and afflicted.
The troubles of my heart have multiplied;
Free me from my distresses.
Look on my affliction and my pain,
And forgive all my sins. (Psalm 25:16–18)

- **Faithfulness as a Steward**
    - Of time
    - Of talents
    - Of treasure
    - Of truth
    - Of relationships

First Month, Day 12

- My activities for this day
- Special concerns

## Intercession

May I remind others to be subject to rulers and authorities, to be obedient, to be ready for every good work, to slander no one, to be peaceable and gentle, and to show true humility toward all men. (Titus 3:1–2)

### Government

- Spiritual revival
- Local government
- State government
- National government
- Current events and concerns

## Affirmation

I am always of good courage and know that as long as I am at home in the body, I am away from the Lord. For I live by faith, not by sight. I am of good courage and would prefer to be absent from the body and to be at home with the Lord. (2 Corinthians 5:6–8)

Now I am a child of God, and what I shall be has not yet been revealed. I know that when He is revealed, I shall be like Him, for I shall see Him as He is. And everyone who has this hope in Him purifies himself, just as He is pure. (1 John 3:2–3)

*Pause to reflect upon these biblical affirmations.*

## Thanksgiving

Blessed be the Lord, the God of Israel,
Because He has visited us and has redeemed His people.
He has raised up a horn of salvation for us
In the house of His servant David
(As He spoke by the mouth of His holy prophets of long ago),
Salvation from our enemies
And from the hand of all who hate us—
To show mercy to our fathers
And to remember His holy covenant,
The oath He swore to our father Abraham,
To rescue us from the hand of our enemies,
And to enable us to serve Him without fear
In holiness and righteousness before Him all our days.
(Luke 1:68–75)

*Pause to offer your own expressions of thanksgiving.*

## Closing Prayer

The law of the Lord is perfect, restoring the soul.
The testimony of the Lord is sure, making wise the simple.
The precepts of the Lord are right, rejoicing the heart.
The commandment of the Lord is pure, enlightening the eyes.
The fear of the Lord is clean, enduring forever.
The judgments of the Lord are true and altogether righteous.
They are more desirable than gold, than much pure gold;
They are sweeter than honey, than honey from the comb.
Moreover, by them is Your servant warned;
In keeping them there is great reward. (Psalm 19:7–11)

# THE FIRST MONTH
## DAY 13

### Adoration

O Lord, You have searched me and You know me.
You know when I sit down and when I rise up;
You understand my thoughts from afar.
You scrutinize my path and my lying down
And are acquainted with all my ways.
Before a word is on my tongue,
O Lord, You know it completely.
You have enclosed me behind and before,
And laid Your hand upon me.
Such knowledge is too wonderful for me;
It is too lofty for me to attain. (Psalm 139:1–6)

*Pause to express your thoughts of praise and worship.*

### Confession

O Lord, be gracious to me;
Heal my soul, for I have sinned against You. (Psalm 41:4)

*Ask the Spirit to search your heart and reveal any areas of unconfessed sin. Acknowledge these to the Lord and thank Him for His forgiveness.*

## Renewal

May I not worry about my life, what I will eat or what I will drink; or about my body, what I will wear. Life is more than food, and the body more than clothes. The birds of the air do not sow or reap or gather into barns, and yet my heavenly Father feeds them. Am I not much more valuable than they? Who by worrying can add a single hour to his life? And why do I worry about clothes? I will consider how the lilies of the field grow; they neither labor nor spin, yet not even Solomon in all his splendor was dressed like one of these. But if God so clothes the grass of the field, which is here today and tomorrow is thrown into the fire, will He not much more clothe me? So may I not worry, saying, "What shall I eat?" or "What shall I drink?" or "What shall I wear?" For the pagans run after all these things, and my heavenly Father knows that I need them. But may I seek first Your kingdom and Your righteousness, and all these things will be added to me. (Matthew 6:25–33; Luke 12:22–31)

May I be more concerned about the things of God than the things of men. (Mark 8:33)

*Pause to add your own prayers for personal renewal.*

## Petition

May I follow Your commands and precepts and be careful to observe them, for this is my wisdom and understanding in the sight of others. (Deuteronomy 4:5–6)

First Month, Day 13

- **Family and Ministry**
    - Family
    - Ministry
        - Sharing Christ with others
        - Helping others grow in Him
    - Career
- My activities for this day
- Special concerns

## Intercession

But let all who take refuge in You be glad;
Let them ever sing for joy,
Because You defend them.
And let those who love Your name be joyful in You.
(Psalm 5:11)

## Missions

- Local missions
- National missions
- World missions
- The fulfillment of the Great Commission
- Special concerns

## Affirmation

The fear of the Lord, that is wisdom,
And to depart from evil is understanding. (Job 28:28)

Who is the man that fears the Lord?
He will instruct him in the way he should choose. (Psalm 25:12)

Blessed is everyone who fears the Lord,
Who walks in His ways. (Psalm 128:1)

The Lord takes pleasure in those who fear Him,
Who put their hope in His unfailing love. (Psalm 147:11)

*Pause to reflect upon these biblical affirmations.*

## Thanksgiving

And now therefore you have sorrow; but I will see you again and your heart will rejoice, and no one will take your joy from you. And in that day you will not ask Me any question. I tell you the truth, whatever you ask the Father in My name He will give you. Until now you have asked for nothing in My name; ask, and you will receive, that your joy may be full. (John 16:22–24)

The Father Himself loves me because I have loved Jesus and have believed that He came forth from God. (John 16:27)

*Pause to offer your own expressions of thanksgiving.*

## Closing Prayer

You have shown me what is good;
And what does the Lord require of me
But to act justly and to love mercy
And to walk humbly with my God? (Micah 6:8)

We will all stand before the judgment seat of God. For it is written,

"As I live, says the Lord, every knee will bow before Me,
And every tongue will confess to God."

So then, each of us will give an account of himself to God. (Romans 14:10b–12)

# THE FIRST MONTH
## DAY 14

### Adoration

Where can I go from Your Spirit?
Or where can I flee from Your presence?
If I ascend to heaven, You are there;
If I make my bed in Sheol, You are there.
If I take the wings of the dawn,
If I dwell in the furthest part of the sea,
Even there Your hand will lead me;
Your right hand will lay hold of me.
If I say, "Surely the darkness will cover me,"
Even the night will be light around me.
The darkness is not dark to You,
And the night shines as the day;
Darkness and light are alike to You. (Psalm 139:7–12)

*Pause to express your thoughts of praise and worship.*

### Confession

Those whom You love You rebuke and discipline. Therefore may I be zealous and repent. (Revelation 3:19)

*Ask the Spirit to search your heart and reveal any areas of unconfessed sin. Acknowledge these to the Lord and thank Him for His forgiveness.*

First Month, Day 14

## Renewal

May I act in the fear of the Lord, faithfully and with a loyal heart. (2 Chronicles 19:9)

Teach me Your way, O Lord;
I will walk in Your truth;
Unite my heart to fear Your name. (Psalm 86:11)

The foremost commandment is this: "Hear, O Israel; the Lord our God, the Lord is one; and you shall love the Lord your God with all your heart and with all your soul and with all your mind and with all your strength." The second is this: "You shall love your neighbor as yourself." There is no commandment greater than these. To love God with all the heart and with all the understanding and with all the strength, and to love one's neighbor as himself are more important than all burnt offerings and sacrifices. (Mark 12:29–31, 33)

*Pause to add your own prayers for personal renewal.*

## Petition

May I be strong and courageous, and act. May I not be afraid or discouraged, for the Lord God is with me. He will not fail me or forsake me. (1 Chronicles 28:20)

- **Personal Concerns**
    - Spiritual warfare
        - The world
        - The flesh
        - The devil
    - Growth in character
    - Personal disciplines
    - Physical health and strength
- My activities for this day
- Special concerns

## Intercession

I know that the Lord will maintain the cause of the afflicted
And justice for the poor. (Psalm 140:12)

### World Affairs

- The poor and hungry
- The oppressed and persecuted
- Those in authority
- Peace among nations
- Current events and concerns

## Affirmation

Those God foreknew, He also predestined to be conformed to the likeness of His Son, that He might be the firstborn among many brothers. And those He predestined, He also called; those He called, He also justified; those He justified, He also glorified. (Romans 8:29–30)

If I confess with my mouth the Lord Jesus and believe in my heart that God raised Him from the dead, I will be saved. For it is with my heart that I believe unto righteousness, and it is with my mouth that I confess unto salvation. As the Scripture says, "Whoever trusts in Him will not be put to shame." (Romans 10:9–11)

*Pause to reflect upon these biblical affirmations.*

## Thanksgiving

When we were helpless, at the right time, Christ died for the ungodly. For rarely will anyone die for a righteous man, though perhaps for a good man someone would even dare to die. But God demonstrates His own love for us in that while we were still sinners, Christ died for us. (Romans 5:6–8)

Since I have been justified by Christ's blood, much more shall I be saved from God's wrath through Him. For if, when I was God's enemy, I was reconciled to Him through the death of His Son, much more, having been reconciled, shall I be saved through His life. And not only this, but I also rejoice in God through my Lord Jesus Christ, through whom I have now received the reconciliation. (Romans 5:9–11)

*Pause to offer your own expressions of thanksgiving.*

## Closing Prayer

You are the Alpha and the Omega, the Beginning and the End. To him who is thirsty, You will give to drink without cost from the spring of the water of life. He who overcomes will inherit all this, and You will be his God and he will be Your son. (Revelation 21:6–7)

Lord Jesus, You are coming quickly. Your reward is with You, and You will give to everyone according to what he has done. You are the Alpha and the Omega, the First and the Last, the Beginning and the End. Yes, You are coming quickly. Amen. Come, Lord Jesus! (Revelation 22:12–13, 20)

# THE FIRST MONTH
## DAY 15

### Adoration

You formed my inward parts;
You wove me together in my mother's womb.
I thank You because I am fearfully and wonderfully made;
Your works are wonderful,
And my soul knows it full well.
My frame was not hidden from You
When I was made in secret
And skillfully wrought in the depths of the earth.
Your eyes saw my embryo,
And all the days ordained for me
Were written in Your book
Before one of them came to be. (Psalm 139:13–16)

*Pause to express your thoughts of praise and worship.*

### Confession

I return to the Lord my God,
For I have stumbled because of my iniquity.
I take words with me and return to the Lord,
Saying, "Take away all iniquity and receive me graciously,
That I may offer the fruit of my lips." (Hosea 14:1–2)

*Ask the Spirit to search your heart and reveal any areas of unconfessed sin. Acknowledge these to the Lord and thank Him for His forgiveness.*

## Renewal

May God grant me, according to the riches of His glory, to be strengthened with power through His Spirit in my inner being, so that Christ may dwell in my heart through faith. And may I, being rooted and grounded in love, be able to comprehend with all the saints what is the width and length and height and depth of the love of Christ, and to know this love that surpasses knowledge, that I may be filled to all the fullness of God. (Ephesians 3:16–19)

May I be strong in the grace that is in Christ Jesus.
(2 Timothy 2:1)

*Pause to add your own prayers for personal renewal.*

## Petition

I was once darkness, but now I am light in the Lord. May I walk as a child of light (for the fruit of the light consists in all goodness and righteousness and truth), learning what is pleasing to the Lord. (Ephesians 5:8–10)

- **Growth in Christ**
    - Greater desire to know and please Him
    - Greater love and commitment to Him
    - Grace to practice His presence
    - Grace to glorify Him in my life

- My activities for this day
- Special concerns

## Intercession

How good and pleasant it is
When brothers live together in unity! (Psalm 133:1)

### Churches and Ministries

- My local church
- Other churches
- Evangelism and discipleship ministries
- Educational ministries
- Special concerns

## Affirmation

If anyone is in Christ, he is a new creation; the old things passed away; behold, they have become new. (2 Corinthians 5:17)

We are the true circumcision, who worship by the Spirit of God and glory in Christ Jesus and put no confidence in the flesh. (Philippians 3:3)

The mystery that has been kept hidden for ages and generations is now disclosed to the saints. To them God has chosen to make known among the Gentiles the glorious riches of this mystery, which is Christ in you, the hope of glory. (Colossians 1:26–27)

*Pause to reflect upon these biblical affirmations.*

## Thanksgiving

I am unworthy of all the lovingkindness and faithfulness You have shown Your servant. (Genesis 32:10)

You are the God who answered me in the day of my distress and have been with me wherever I have gone. (Genesis 35:3)

The Almighty is my shepherd, the Rock of Israel, who helps me and blesses me with blessings of the heavens above. (Genesis 49:24–25)

*Pause to offer your own expressions of thanksgiving.*

## Closing Prayer

The Lord is the great God,
The great King above all gods.
In His hand are the depths of the earth,
And the summits of the mountains are His also.
The sea is His, for He made it,
And His hands formed the dry land.
He is our God and we are the people of His pasture
And the sheep under His care. (Psalm 95:3–5, 7)

Shout joyfully to the Lord, all the earth.
Worship the Lord with gladness;
Come before Him with joyful singing.
The Lord, He is God.
It is He who made us, and not we ourselves;
We are His people and the sheep of His pasture.
(Psalm 100:1–3)

# THE FIRST MONTH
# **DAY 16**

## Adoration

How precious are Your thoughts to me, O God!
How vast is the sum of them!
If I should count them, they would outnumber the grains of sand.
When I awake, I am still with You. (Psalm 139:17–18)

To whom can I liken You or count You equal?
To whom can I compare You that You may be alike?
(Isaiah 46:5)

*Pause to express your thoughts of praise and worship.*

## Confession

My trespasses are multiplied before You,
And my sins testify against me.
For my transgressions are with me,
And I know my iniquities:
Transgressing and lying against the Lord,
And departing from my God,
Speaking oppression and revolt,
Uttering lies my heart has conceived. (Isaiah 59:12–13)

*Ask the Spirit to search your heart and reveal any areas of unconfessed sin. Acknowledge these to the Lord and thank Him for His forgiveness.*

## Renewal

May I fear the Lord and serve You in truth with all my heart, for I consider what great things You have done for me. (1 Samuel 12:24)

May I not transgress the commandments of the Lord, for I cannot prosper in disobedience. May I not forsake the Lord. (2 Chronicles 24:20)

*Pause to add your own prayers for personal renewal.*

## Petition

May I be worthy of respect, not double-tongued, not addicted to wine, not fond of dishonest gain, but holding the mystery of the faith with a clear conscience. (1 Timothy 3:8–9)

- **Growth in Wisdom**
    - Developing an eternal perspective
    - Renewing my mind with truth
    - Greater skill in each area of life
- My activities for this day
- Special concerns

## Intercession

Beloved, I pray that you may prosper in all things and be in good health, even as your soul prospers. (3 John 2)

### Family

- My immediate family
- My relatives
- Spiritual concerns
- Emotional and physical concerns
- Other concerns

## Affirmation

Christ has appeared once for all at the end of the ages to do away with sin by the sacrifice of Himself. And as it is appointed for man to die once and after that to face judgment, so Christ was offered once to bear the sins of many; and He will appear a second time, not to bear sin but to bring salvation to those who eagerly wait for Him. (Hebrews 9:26–28)

Christ was chosen before the creation of the world but was revealed in these last times for our sake. Through Him I believe in God, who raised Him from the dead and glorified Him, so that my faith and hope are in God. (1 Peter 1:20–21)

*Pause to reflect upon these biblical affirmations.*

## Thanksgiving

My heart rejoices in the Lord;
My horn is exalted in the Lord.
My mouth boasts over my enemies,
For I delight in Your salvation. (1 Samuel 2:1)

You reached down from on high and took hold of me;
You drew me out of deep waters.
You delivered me from my strong enemy,
From those who hated me,
For they were stronger than me. (2 Samuel 22:17–18)

*Pause to offer your own expressions of thanksgiving.*

## Closing Prayer

Who is like You, O Lord?
Who is like You—majestic in holiness,
Awesome in praises, working wonders? (Exodus 15:11)

There is no one holy like the Lord;
There is no one besides You;
Nor is there any Rock like our God. (1 Samuel 2:2)

# THE FIRST MONTH
## DAY 17

### Adoration

You are the high and lofty One
Who inhabits eternity, whose name is holy.
You live in a high and holy place
But also with him who is contrite and lowly in spirit,
To revive the spirit of the lowly
And to revive the heart of the contrite. (Isaiah 57:15)

The multitudes who went before Jesus and those who followed shouted,
"Hosanna to the Son of David!
Blessed is he who comes in the name of the Lord!
Hosanna in the highest!" (Matthew 21:9)

*Pause to express your thoughts of praise and worship.*

### Confession

We have sinned with our fathers;
We have committed iniquity and acted wickedly. (Psalm 106:6)

*Ask the Spirit to search your heart and reveal any areas of unconfessed sin. Acknowledge these to the Lord and thank Him for His forgiveness.*

## Renewal

As an obedient child, may I not conform myself to the former lusts I had when I lived in ignorance, but as He who called me is holy, so may I be holy in all my conduct, because it is written: "You shall be holy, for I am holy." (1 Peter 1:14–16)

You are the Lord my God; may I consecrate myself and be holy, because You are holy. You are the Lord who brought Your people up out of Egypt to be their God; therefore may I be holy, because You are holy. (Leviticus 11:44–45; 19:2)

*Pause to add your own prayers for personal renewal.*

## Petition

O Lord, I pray, let Your ear be attentive to the prayer of Your servant and to the prayer of Your servants who delight in revering Your name. (Nehemiah 1:11)

- **Spiritual Insight**
    - Understanding and insight into the Word
    - Understanding my identity in Christ
        - Who I am
        - Where I came from
        - Where I'm going
    - Understanding God's purpose for my life
- My activities for this day
- Special concerns

## Intercession

The Lord Jesus prayed these words for the unity of all who would believe in Him: "I ask that all of them may be one, Father, just as You are in Me and I am in You, that they also may be in Us, that the world may believe that You sent Me. And the glory which You gave Me I have given to them, that they may be one, just as We are one: I in them, and You in Me, that they may be perfected in one, that the world may know that You have sent Me and have loved them, even as You have loved Me." (John 17:21–23)

## Believers

- Personal friends
- Those in ministry
- Those who are oppressed and in need
- Special concerns

## Affirmation

A Shoot will come forth from the stump of Jesse;
From his roots a Branch will bear fruit.
The Spirit of the Lord will rest on Him—
The Spirit of wisdom and of understanding,
The Spirit of counsel and of power,
The Spirit of knowledge and of the fear of the Lord—
And He will delight in the fear of the Lord.
He will not judge by what He sees with His eyes,
Or decide by what He hears with His ears,
But with righteousness He will judge the poor
And decide with fairness for the meek of the earth.

And He will strike the earth with the rod of His mouth;
With the breath of His lips He will slay the wicked.
Righteousness will be His belt,
And faithfulness the sash around His waist. (Isaiah 11:1–5)

Behold, a virgin shall be with child and will give birth to a son, and they will call His name Immanuel, which means, "God with us." (Matthew 1:23)

*Pause to reflect upon these biblical affirmations.*

## Thanksgiving

This poor man cried out, and the Lord heard him,
And saved him out of all his troubles.
The angel of the Lord encamps around those who fear Him,
And delivers them. (Psalm 34:6–7)

I waited patiently for the Lord,
And He turned to me and heard my cry.
God lifted me out of the slimy pit, out of the mud and mire;
He set my feet on a rock and gave me a firm place to stand.
He put a new song in my mouth, a hymn of praise to our God.
Many will see and fear
And put their trust in the Lord. (Psalm 40:1–3)

*Pause to offer your own expressions of thanksgiving.*

## Closing Prayer

Let the words of my mouth and the meditation of my heart
Be pleasing in Your sight,
O Lord, my Rock and my Redeemer. (Psalm 19:14)

# THE FIRST MONTH
## DAY 18

### Adoration

Blessed are You, O Lord, God of Israel, our father, forever and ever. Yours, O Lord, is the greatness and the power and the glory and the victory and the majesty, for everything in heaven and earth is Yours. Yours, O Lord, is the kingdom, and You are exalted as head over all. Both riches and honor come from You, and You are the ruler of all things. In Your hand is power and might to exalt and to give strength to all. Therefore, my God, I give You thanks and praise Your glorious name. (1 Chronicles 29:10–13)

I will proclaim the name of the Lord and praise the greatness of my God. (Deuteronomy 32:3)

*Pause to express your thoughts of praise and worship.*

### Confession

O Lord, do not rebuke me in Your wrath,
And do not chasten me in Your anger.
For Your arrows have pierced me deeply,
And Your hand has pressed down upon me.
There is no health in my body because of Your wrath,
Nor peace in my bones because of my sin.
For my iniquities have gone over my head;
As a heavy burden, they weigh too much for me. (Psalm 38:1–4)

*Ask the Spirit to search your heart and reveal any areas of unconfessed sin. Acknowledge these to the Lord and thank Him for His forgiveness.*

## Renewal

As a servant of Christ and a steward of His possessions, it is required that I be found faithful. (1 Corinthians 4:1–2)

Those who want to get rich fall into temptation and a snare and into many foolish and harmful desires that plunge men into ruin and destruction. For the love of money is a root of all kinds of evil, and some by longing for it have wandered from the faith and pierced themselves with many sorrows. But let me flee from these things, and pursue righteousness, godliness, faith, love, patience, and gentleness. (1 Timothy 6:9–11)

*Pause to add your own prayers for personal renewal.*

## Petition

May I put away all of these things: anger, wrath, malice, slander, and abusive language from my mouth. (Colossians 3:8)

- **Relationships with Others**
    - Greater love and compassion for others
    - Loved ones
    - Those who do not know Christ
    - Those in need
- My activities for this day
- Special concerns

## Intercession

Grant that I may be used to open the eyes of others and to turn them from darkness to light, and from the power of Satan to God, so that they may receive forgiveness of sins and an inheritance among those who have been sanctified by faith in Jesus. (Acts 26:18)

### Evangelism

- Friends
- Relatives
- Neighbors
- Coworkers
- Special opportunities

## Affirmation

Blessed is the man who perseveres under trial, because when he has been approved, he will receive the crown of life that God has promised to those who love Him. (James 1:12)

Those who suffer according to the will of God should commit themselves to their faithful Creator in doing good. (1 Peter 4:19)

I am from God and am an overcomer, because He who is in me is greater than he who is in the world. (1 John 4:4)

*Pause to reflect upon these biblical affirmations.*

## Thanksgiving

Bless the Lord, O my soul;
And all that is within me, bless His holy name.
Bless the Lord, O my soul,
And forget not all His benefits;
Who forgives all your iniquities
And heals all your diseases;
Who redeems your life from the pit
And crowns you with love and compassion;
Who satisfies your desires with good things,
So that your youth is renewed like the eagle's. (Psalm 103:1–5)

*Pause to offer your own expressions of thanksgiving.*

## Closing Prayer

The Lord is my rock and my fortress and my deliverer;
My God is my rock; I will take refuge in Him,
My shield and the horn of my salvation,
My stronghold and my refuge—
My Savior, You save me from violence.
I call on the Lord, who is worthy of praise,
And I am saved from my enemies. (2 Samuel 22:2–4)

Daily Prayer Guide

# THE FIRST MONTH
# DAY 19

### Adoration

How great You are, O Sovereign Lord! There is no one like You, and there is no God besides You, according to all that I have heard with my ears. (2 Samuel 7:22; 1 Chronicles 17:20)

You alone are the Lord.
You made the heavens,
The heaven of heavens, and all their host,
The earth and all that is on it,
The seas and all that is in them.
You give life to all that is in them,
And the host of heaven worships You. (Nehemiah 9:6)

*Pause to express your thoughts of praise and worship.*

### Confession

Peter came to Jesus and asked, "Lord, how often shall my brother sin against me, and I forgive him? Up to seven times?" Jesus said to him, "I tell you, not seven times, but up to seventy times seven." (Matthew 18:21–22)

*Ask the Spirit to search your heart and reveal any areas of unconfessed sin. Acknowledge these to the Lord and thank Him for His forgiveness.*

## Renewal

May I not be like those who draw near to You with their mouths and honor You with their lips, but whose hearts are far from You, and whose reverence for You is made up only of rules taught by men. (Isaiah 29:13)

I desire not only to call You Lord but to do what You say. By Your grace, I will come to You, hear Your words, and put them into practice. Then I will be like a man building a house, who dug down deep and laid the foundation on rock, and when a flood came, the torrent struck that house but could not shake it, because it was well built. (Luke 6:46–48)

*Pause to add your own prayers for personal renewal.*

## Petition

Guard my soul and rescue me;
Let me not be ashamed, for I take refuge in You.
May integrity and uprightness protect me,
For I wait for You. (Psalm 25:20–21)

- **Faithfulness as a Steward**
    - Of time
    - Of talents
    - Of treasure
    - Of truth
    - Of relationships
- My activities for this day
- Special concerns

## Intercession

May I submit myself to the governing authorities. For there is no authority except from God, and the authorities that exist have been established by God. Consequently, he who resists authority has opposed the ordinance of God, and those who do so will bring judgment on themselves. (Romans 13:1–2)

### Government

- Spiritual revival
- Local government
- State government
- National government
- Current events and concerns

## Affirmation

Before I was afflicted I went astray,
But now I keep Your word.
It was good for me to be afflicted,
So that I might learn Your statutes.
I know, O Lord, that Your judgments are righteous,
And that in faithfulness You have afflicted me.
(Psalm 119:67, 71, 75)

I know that if my earthly house, or tent, is destroyed, I have a building from God, a house not made with hands, eternal in the heavens. For in this house I groan, longing to be clothed with my heavenly dwelling, because when I am clothed, I will not be found naked. For while I am in this tent, I groan, being burdened, because I do not want to be unclothed but to be clothed, so that what is mortal may be swallowed up by life. Now it is God who has made me for this very purpose and has given me the Spirit as a guarantee. (2 Corinthians 5:1–5)

*Pause to reflect upon these biblical affirmations.*

## Thanksgiving

Because the Lord God helps me,
I will not be disgraced.
Therefore I have set my face like flint,
And I know I will not be put to shame.
He who vindicates me is near;
Who will contend with me?
Surely the Lord God will help me;
Who is he that will condemn me? (Isaiah 50:7–9)

I did not receive a spirit of slavery again to fear, but I received the Spirit of adoption by whom I cry, "Abba, Father." The Spirit Himself testifies with my spirit that I am a child of God. (Romans 8:15–16)

*Pause to offer your own expressions of thanksgiving.*

## Closing Prayer

Lord Jesus, all that the Father gives You will come to You, and whoever comes to You, You will never cast out. For You have come down from heaven not to do Your own will, but the will of Him who sent You. And this is the will of Him who sent You, that You will lose none of all that He has given You, but raise them up at the last day. For Your Father's will is that everyone who looks to the Son and believes in Him may have eternal life, and You will raise him up at the last day. (John 6:37–40)

# THE FIRST MONTH
# **DAY 20**

## Adoration

Praise the Lord!
Praise God in His sanctuary;
Praise Him in His mighty heavens.
Praise Him for His mighty acts;
Praise Him according to His excellent greatness.
Praise Him with the sound of the trumpet;
Praise Him with the harp and lyre.
Praise Him with the timbrel and dancing;
Praise Him with stringed instruments and flutes.
Praise Him on the sounding cymbals;
Praise Him on the resounding cymbals.
Let everything that has breath praise the Lord.
Praise the Lord! (Psalm 150:1–6)

The Lord shall reign for ever and ever. (Exodus 15:18)

*Pause to express your thoughts of praise and worship.*

## Confession

Heal me, O Lord, and I will be healed;
Save me, and I will be saved,
For You are my praise. (Jeremiah 17:14)

*Ask the Spirit to search your heart and reveal any areas of unconfessed sin. Acknowledge these to the Lord and thank Him for His forgiveness.*

## Renewal

Since I call on the Father who judges each man's work impartially, may I conduct myself in fear during the time of my sojourn on earth. (1 Peter 1:17)

May I keep the commandments of the Lord my God, to walk in His ways and to fear Him. May I follow the Lord my God and fear Him; may I keep Your commandments, hear Your voice, serve You, and hold fast to You. (Deuteronomy 8:6; 13:4)

*Pause to add your own prayers for personal renewal.*

## Petition

May I be careful and watch myself closely lest I forget the things my eyes have seen or let them depart from my heart as long as I live. May I teach them to my children and to their children after them. (Deuteronomy 4:9)

- **Family and Ministry**
    - Family
    - Ministry
        - Sharing Christ with others
        - Helping others grow in Him
    - Career

- My activities for this day
- Special concerns

## Intercession

With all prayer and petition, we should pray always in the Spirit, and to this end we should be watchful with all perseverance and petition for all the saints. (Ephesians 6:18)

## Missions

- Local missions
- National missions
- World missions
- The fulfillment of the Great Commission
- Special concerns

## Affirmation

Many who are first will be last, and the last first. (Matthew 19:30; Mark 10:31)

Whoever wishes to become great among others must become their servant, and whoever wishes to be first among them must be their slave. (Matthew 20:26–27; Mark 10:43–44)

Whoever exalts himself will be humbled, and whoever humbles himself will be exalted. (Matthew 23:12; Luke 14:11; 18:14)

*Pause to reflect upon these biblical affirmations.*

Daily Prayer Guide

## Thanksgiving

Shout for joy, O heavens! Rejoice, O earth!
Break out into singing, O mountains!
For the Lord has comforted His people
And will have compassion on His afflicted. (Isaiah 49:13)

I will greatly rejoice in the Lord;
My soul will be joyful in my God.
For He has clothed me with garments of salvation
And arrayed me in a robe of righteousness,
As a bridegroom decks himself with ornaments,
And as a bride adorns herself with her jewels. (Isaiah 61:10)

*Pause to offer your own expressions of thanksgiving.*

## Closing Prayer

The Lord will command His lovingkindness by day,
And His song will be in the night—
A prayer to the God of my life. (Psalm 42:8)

Blessed be the Lord God, the God of Israel,
Who alone does wonderful things.
And blessed be His glorious name forever;
May the whole earth be filled with His glory.
Amen and Amen. (Psalm 72:18–19)

# THE FIRST MONTH
## DAY 21

### Adoration

In the year that King Uzziah died, I saw the Lord sitting on a throne, high and exalted, and the train of His robe filled the temple. Above it stood the seraphim; each one had six wings: with two they covered their faces, with two they covered their feet, and with two they flew. And one cried to the other and said,

"Holy, Holy, Holy is the Lord of hosts;
The whole earth is full of His glory!" (Isaiah 6:1–3)

The Lord God is the Alpha and the Omega, who is, and who was, and who is to come, the Almighty. (Revelation 1:8)

*Pause to express your thoughts of praise and worship.*

### Confession

I, even I, am He who blots out your transgressions for My own sake,
And I will not remember your sins. (Isaiah 43:25)

*Ask the Spirit to search your heart and reveal any areas of unconfessed sin. Acknowledge these to the Lord and thank Him for His forgiveness.*

## Renewal

"You shall love the Lord your God with all your heart and with all your soul and with all your mind." This is the first and great commandment. And the second is like it: "You shall love your neighbor as yourself." All the Law and the Prophets hang on these two commandments. (Matthew 22:37–40)

May I not love with words or tongue, but in deed and in truth. By this I will know that I am of the truth and will assure my heart before Him; for if my heart condemns me, God is greater than my heart, and knows all things. If my heart does not condemn me, I have confidence before God and receive from Him whatever I ask, because I keep His commandments and do the things that are pleasing in His sight. (1 John 3:18–22)

*Pause to add your own prayers for personal renewal.*

## Petition

May I not say, "Today or tomorrow I will go to this or that city, spend a year there, carry on business, and make a profit." For I do not even know what my life will be tomorrow. I am a vapor that appears for a little while and then vanishes away. Instead, let me say, "If the Lord wills, I will live and do this or that." Otherwise, I boast in my arrogance, and all such boasting is evil. (James 4:13–16)

- **Personal Concerns**
    - Spiritual warfare
        - The world
        - The flesh
        - The devil
    - Growth in character
    - Personal disciplines
    - Physical health and strength
- My activities for this day
- Special concerns

## Intercession

May I remember those in prison as though bound with them, and those who are mistreated, since I myself am also in the body. (Hebrews 13:3)

### World Affairs

- The poor and hungry
- The oppressed and persecuted
- Those in authority
- Peace among nations
- Current events and concerns

## Affirmation

Apart from the law the righteousness of God has been made known, being witnessed by the law and the prophets, even the righteousness of God through faith in Jesus Christ to all who believe. For there is no difference, for all have sinned and fall short of the glory of God, being justified freely by His grace through the redemption that is in Christ Jesus. (Romans 3:21–24)

What the law was powerless to do in that it was weakened through the flesh, God did by sending His own Son in the likeness of sinful flesh, on account of sin; He condemned sin in the flesh, in order that the requirement of the law might be fully met in us, who do not walk according to the flesh, but according to the Spirit. (Romans 8:3–4)

*Pause to reflect upon these biblical affirmations.*

## Thanksgiving

For those who revere Your name, the Sun of righteousness will rise with healing in His wings. And they will go out and leap like calves released from the stall. (Malachi 4:2)

Jesus fulfilled the words of the prophet Isaiah:

"The Spirit of the Lord is upon Me,
Because He has anointed Me to preach good news to the poor.
He has sent Me to proclaim freedom for the captives
And recovery of sight to the blind,
To set free those who are downtrodden,
To proclaim the acceptable year of the Lord." (Luke 4:18–19)

*Pause to offer your own expressions of thanksgiving.*

## Closing Prayer

I will enter Your gates with thanksgiving
And Your courts with praise;
I will give thanks to You and bless Your name.
For the Lord is good
And Your lovingkindness endures forever;
Your faithfulness continues through all generations.
(Psalm 100:4–5)

May the glory of the Lord endure forever;
May the Lord rejoice in His works. (Psalm 104:31)

Daily Prayer Guide

# THE FIRST MONTH
## DAY 22

### Adoration

A great multitude, which no one could number, from all nations and tribes and peoples and languages will stand before the throne and before the Lamb, clothed with white robes with palm branches in their hands, and will cry out with a loud voice, "Salvation belongs to our God, who sits on the throne, and to the Lamb!" (Revelation 7:9–10)

Blessed is the King who comes in the name of the Lord!
Peace in heaven and glory in the highest! (Luke 19:38)

*Pause to express your thoughts of praise and worship.*

### Confession

The eyes of the Lord are everywhere,
Keeping watch on the evil and the good. (Proverbs 15:3)

*Ask the Spirit to search your heart and reveal any areas of unconfessed sin. Acknowledge these to the Lord and thank Him for His forgiveness.*

## Renewal

Like Abraham, may I call upon the name of the Lord, the Everlasting God. (Genesis 13:4; 21:33)

May I listen carefully to the voice of the Lord my God and do what is right in Your sight; may I pay attention to Your commandments and keep all Your statutes. (Exodus 15:26)

May I rejoice in my tribulations, knowing that tribulation produces perseverance; and perseverance, character; and character, hope. And hope does not disappoint, because the love of God has been poured out into my heart through the Holy Spirit who was given to me. (Romans 5:3–5)

*Pause to add your own prayers for personal renewal.*

## Petition

May Your merciful kindness be my comfort,
According to Your promise to Your servant. (Psalm 119:76)

- **Growth in Christ**
  - Greater desire to know and please Him
  - Greater love and commitment to Him
  - Grace to practice His presence
  - Grace to glorify Him in my life
- My activities for this day
- Special concerns

## Intercession

Is this not the fast You have chosen:
To loose the bonds of wickedness,
To undo the cords of the yoke,
And to let the oppressed go free
And break every yoke?
Is it not to share our food with the hungry
And to provide the poor wanderer with shelter;
When we see the naked, to clothe him,
And not to turn away from our own flesh?
Then our light will break forth like the dawn,
And our healing will quickly appear,
And our righteousness will go before us;
The glory of the Lord will be our rear guard.
Then we will call, and the Lord will answer;
We will cry, and He will say, "Here I am."
If we put away the yoke from our midst,
The pointing of the finger and malicious talk,
And if we extend our souls to the hungry
And satisfy the afflicted soul,
Then our light will rise in the darkness,
And our gloom will become like the noonday. (Isaiah 58:6–10)

## Churches and Ministries

- My local church
- Other churches
- Evangelism and discipleship ministries
- Educational ministries
- Special concerns

## Affirmation

By the will of God, I have been sanctified through the offering of the body of Jesus Christ once for all. And every priest stands daily ministering and offering again and again the same sacrifices, which can never take away sins. But when this Priest had offered for all time one sacrifice for sins, He sat down at the right hand of God, waiting from that time for His enemies to be made a footstool for His feet. For by one offering, He has made perfect forever those who are being sanctified. (Hebrews 10:10–14)

Christ suffered for me, leaving me an example that I should follow in His steps. "He committed no sin, and no deceit was found in his mouth." When He was reviled, He did not retaliate; when He suffered, He made no threats, but entrusted Himself to Him who judges righteously; and He himself bore our sins in His body on the tree, so that I might die to sins and live for righteousness; by His wounds I have been healed. For I was like a sheep going astray, but now I have returned to the Shepherd and Overseer of my soul. (1 Peter 2:21–25)

*Pause to reflect upon these biblical affirmations.*

## Thanksgiving

From Christ's fullness we have all received, and grace upon grace. For the law was given through Moses; grace and truth came through Jesus Christ. (John 1:16–17)

Jesus is the Lamb of God, who takes away the sin of the world. (John 1:29)

*Pause to offer your own expressions of thanksgiving.*

## Closing Prayer

The Lord will keep me from all evil;
He will preserve my soul.
The Lord will watch over my coming and going
From this time forth and forever. (Psalm 121:7–8)

# THE FIRST MONTH
## DAY 23

### Adoration

Great is the Lord and most worthy of praise;
He is to be feared above all gods.
For all the gods of the nations are idols,
But the Lord made the heavens.
Splendor and majesty are before Him;
Strength and beauty are in His sanctuary.
I will ascribe to the Lord glory and strength.
I will ascribe to the Lord the glory due His name
And worship the Lord in the beauty of holiness. (Psalm 96:4–8)

Blessed is the man who fears the Lord,
Who finds great delight in His commands. (Psalm 112:1)

*Pause to express your thoughts of praise and worship.*

### Confession

I confess my iniquity;
I am troubled by my sin.
O Lord, do not forsake me;
O my God, be not far from me!
Make haste to help me,
O Lord my salvation. (Psalm 38:18, 21–22)

*Ask the Spirit to search your heart and reveal any areas of unconfessed sin. Acknowledge these to the Lord and thank Him for His forgiveness.*

## Renewal

May I be a faithful person who fears God. (Nehemiah 7:2)

I have hope in God, that there will be a resurrection of both the righteous and the wicked. In view of this, may I strive always to keep my conscience blameless before God and men. (Acts 24:15–16)

*Pause to add your own prayers for personal renewal.*

## Petition

May I not take revenge, but leave room for the wrath of God, for it is written: "Vengeance is Mine; I will repay," says the Lord. May I not be overcome by evil, but overcome evil with good. (Romans 12:19, 21)

- **Growth in Wisdom**
    - Developing an eternal perspective
    - Renewing my mind with truth
    - Greater skill in each area of life
- My activities for this day
- Special concerns

## Intercession

May Your commandments be upon my heart, so that I may teach them diligently to my children and talk about them when I sit in my house and when I walk along the way and when I lie down and when I rise up. (Deuteronomy 6:6–7)

### Family

- My immediate family
- My relatives
- Spiritual concerns
- Emotional and physical concerns
- Other concerns

## Affirmation

Jesus is the way and the truth and the life. No one comes to the Father except through Him. (John 14:6)

Through Jesus the forgiveness of sins is proclaimed, that through Him everyone who believes is justified from all things from which they could not be justified by the law of Moses. (Acts 13:38–39)

Through faith I am guarded by the power of God for salvation that is ready to be revealed in the last time. (1 Peter 1:5)

*Pause to reflect upon these biblical affirmations.*

## Thanksgiving

Lord Jesus, You were oppressed and afflicted,
Yet You did not open Your mouth;
You were led like a lamb to the slaughter,
And as a sheep before her shearers is silent,
So You did not open Your mouth.
By oppression and judgment You were taken away.
And who can speak of Your descendants?
For You were cut off from the land of the living;
You were stricken for the transgression of God's people.
You were assigned a grave with the wicked,
Yet with a rich man in Your death,
Though You had done no violence,
Nor was any deceit in Your mouth.
Yet it was the Lord's will
To crush You and cause You to suffer.
When You make Your soul a guilt offering,
You will see Your offspring and prolong Your days,
And the pleasure of the Lord will prosper in Your hand.
You will see the fruit of the travail of Your soul and be satisfied;
By Your knowledge, God's righteous Servant, You will
   justify many,
And You will bear their iniquities.
Therefore God will give You a portion among the great,
And You will divide the spoils with the strong,
Because You poured out Your life unto death,
And were numbered with the transgressors.
For You bore the sin of many,
And made intercession for the transgressors. (Isaiah 53:7–12)

*Pause to offer your own expressions of thanksgiving.*

## Closing Prayer

Trust in the Lord with all your heart
And lean not on your own understanding;
In all your ways acknowledge Him,
And He will make your paths straight.
Do not be wise in your own eyes,
But fear the Lord and depart from evil. (Proverbs 3:5–7)

# THE FIRST MONTH
## DAY 24

### Adoration

The Son of Man will come with the clouds of heaven. In the presence of the Ancient of Days, He will be given dominion and glory and a kingdom, so that all peoples, nations, and men of every language will worship Him. His dominion is an everlasting dominion that will not pass away, and His kingdom is one that will never be destroyed. (Daniel 7:13–14)

Jesus is my Lord and my God. (John 20:28)

*Pause to express your thoughts of praise and worship.*

### Confession

Who may ascend the hill of the Lord?
Who may stand in His holy place?
He who has clean hands and a pure heart,
Who has not lifted up his soul to an idol
Or sworn by what is false. (Psalm 24:3–4)

*Ask the Spirit to search your heart and reveal any areas of unconfessed sin. Acknowledge these to the Lord and thank Him for His forgiveness.*

First Month, Day 24

## Renewal

May the Lord my God be with me as You were with our fathers; may You never leave me nor forsake me. Incline my heart to You, to walk in all Your ways and to keep Your commands and Your statutes and Your judgments, which You commanded our fathers. May all the peoples of the earth know that the Lord is God; there is no other. Let my heart be fully committed to the Lord my God, to walk in Your statutes and keep Your commandments, as at this day. (1 Kings 8:57–58, 60–61)

As one who knows righteousness, who has Your law in my heart, may I not fear the reproach of men or be terrified by their revilings. (Isaiah 51:7)

*Pause to add your own prayers for personal renewal.*

## Petition

Joseph said to his brothers, "Do not be grieved or angry with yourselves for selling me here, for God sent me before you to save lives. He sent me ahead of you to preserve for you a remnant on earth and to save your lives by a great deliverance. So it was not you who sent me here, but God." (Genesis 45:5, 7–8)

*Like Joseph, may I seek your perspective on the circumstances of my life.*

- **Spiritual Insight**
  - Understanding and insight into the Word
  - Understanding my identity in Christ
    - Who I am
    - Where I came from
    - Where I'm going
  - Understanding God's purpose for my life
- My activities for this day
- Special concerns

## Intercession

May we be devoted to one another in brotherly love, honoring one another above ourselves. (Romans 12:10)

### Believers

- Personal friends
- Those in ministry
- Those who are oppressed and in need
- Special concerns

## Affirmation

No one can serve two masters; for either he will hate the one and love the other, or he will be devoted to the one and despise the other. I cannot serve God and wealth. (Matthew 6:24; Luke 16:13)

First Month, Day 24

Those who are rich in this present world should not be arrogant or set their hope on the uncertainty of riches but on God, who richly provides us with everything for our enjoyment. They should do good, be rich in good works, and be generous and willing to share. In this way they will lay up treasure for themselves as a firm foundation for the future, so that they may lay hold of true life. (1 Timothy 6:17–19)

*Pause to reflect upon these biblical affirmations.*

## Thanksgiving

I will sing to the Lord and give praise to the Lord,
For He has rescued the life of the needy
From the hands of evildoers. (Jeremiah 20:13)

The Lord is good,
A refuge in times of trouble;
He knows those who trust in Him. (Nahum 1:7)

*Pause to offer your own expressions of thanksgiving.*

## Closing Prayer

Thus says the Lord: "Let not the wise man boast of his wisdom, and let not the strong man boast of his strength, and let not the rich man boast of his riches; but let him who boasts boast about this: that he understands and knows Me, that I am the Lord, who exercises lovingkindness, justice, and righteousness on earth; for in these I delight," declares the Lord. (Jeremiah 9:23–24)

"The Lord is my portion," says my soul,
"Therefore I will wait for Him."
The Lord is good to those who wait for Him,
To the soul who seeks Him.
It is good to hope silently
For the salvation of the Lord. (Lamentations 3:24–26)

# THE FIRST MONTH
## DAY 25

### Adoration

Where were you when I laid the foundations of the earth?
Tell Me, if you have understanding.
Who determined its measurements?
Surely you know!
Or who stretched the line across it?
On what were its bases sunk,
Or who laid its cornerstone,
When the morning stars sang together
And all the sons of God shouted for joy? (Job 38:4–7)

You revealed Yourself to Moses as "I AM WHO I AM." (Exodus 3:14)

*Pause to express your thoughts of praise and worship.*

### Confession

You have been just in all that has happened to me; You have acted faithfully, while I did wrong. (Nehemiah 9:33)

*Ask the Spirit to search your heart and reveal any areas of unconfessed sin. Acknowledge these to the Lord and thank Him for His forgiveness.*

## Renewal

If I abide in You, and Your words abide in me, I can ask whatever I wish, and it will be done for me. As I ask in Your name, I will receive, that my joy may be full. (John 15:7; 16:24)

As I walk in the Spirit, I will not fulfill the desires of the flesh. For the flesh desires what is contrary to the Spirit, and the Spirit what is contrary to the flesh; for they oppose each other, so that I may not do the things that I wish. But if I am led by the Spirit, I am not under the law. (Galatians 5:16–18)

*Pause to add your own prayers for personal renewal.*

## Petition

May I be above reproach, temperate, sensible, respectable, hospitable, able to teach, not given to drunkenness, not violent but gentle, not quarrelsome, not a lover of money, one who manages his own family well, and who keeps his children under control with proper respect. Grant me a good reputation with outsiders, so that I will not fall into disgrace and the snare of the devil. (1 Timothy 3:2–4, 7)

- **Relationships with Others**
  - Greater love and compassion for others
  - Loved ones
  - Those who do not know Christ
  - Those in need
- My activities for this day
- Special concerns

## Intercession

Knowing the fear of the Lord, may I seek to persuade men. (2 Corinthians 5:11)

## Evangelism

- Friends
- Relatives
- Neighbors
- Coworkers
- Special opportunities

## Affirmation

The Lord is righteous; He loves righteousness;
The upright will see His face. (Psalm 11:7)

Lord, who may dwell in Your tabernacle?
Who may live on Your holy mountain?
He who walks uprightly and works righteousness
And speaks the truth in his heart;
He does not slander with his tongue
Nor does evil to his neighbor
Nor takes up a reproach against his friend;
He despises the reprobate
But honors those who fear the Lord.
He keeps his oath even when it hurts,
Lends his money without interest,
And does not accept a bribe against the innocent.
He who does these things will never be shaken. (Psalm 15:1–5)

*Pause to reflect upon these biblical affirmations.*

## Thanksgiving

Lord, You completed the heavens and the earth in all their vast array. By the seventh day You finished the work which You had done, and rested on the seventh day from all Your creative work. (Genesis 2:1–2)

Lord God, You formed man from the dust of the ground and breathed into his nostrils the breath of life; and man became a living being. (Genesis 2:7)

*Pause to offer your own expressions of thanksgiving.*

## Closing Prayer

Who shall separate me from the love of Christ? Shall tribulation, or distress, or persecution, or famine, or nakedness, or danger, or sword? As it is written:

> "For Your sake we face death all day long;
> We are considered as sheep to be slaughtered."

Yet in all these things I am more than a conqueror through Him who loved me. (Romans 8:35–37)

# THE FIRST MONTH
## DAY 26

### Adoration

You are the living God,
And there is no god besides You.
You put to death and You bring to life,
You have wounded and You will heal,
And no one can deliver from Your hand. (Deuteronomy 32:39)

I will recall to mind the former things, those of long ago;
You are God, and there is no other;
You are God, and there is none like You. (Isaiah 46:9)

*Pause to express your thoughts of praise and worship.*

### Confession

When I sin against the Lord, I may be sure that my sin will find me out. (Numbers 32:23)

*Ask the Spirit to search your heart and reveal any areas of unconfessed sin. Acknowledge these to the Lord and thank Him for His forgiveness.*

## Renewal

May I not be conformed to the pattern of this world but be transformed by the renewing of my mind, that I may prove that the will of God is good and acceptable and perfect. (Romans 12:2)

May the God of my Lord Jesus Christ, the Father of glory, give me a spirit of wisdom and of revelation in the full knowledge of Him, and may the eyes of my heart be enlightened, in order that I may know what is the hope of His calling, what are the riches of His glorious inheritance in the saints, and what is the incomparable greatness of His power toward us who believe. (Ephesians 1:17–19)

*Pause to add your own prayers for personal renewal.*

## Petition

Whatever I do, may I do all to the glory of God.
(1 Corinthians 10:31)

- **Faithfulness as a Steward**
    - Of time
    - Of talents
    - Of treasure
    - Of truth
    - Of relationships
- My activities for this day
- Special concerns

## Intercession

We should offer petitions, prayers, intercessions, and thanksgivings on behalf of all men, for kings and all those who are in authority, that we may live peaceful and quiet lives in all godliness and reverence. This is good and acceptable in the sight of God our Savior, who desires all men to be saved and to come to the knowledge of the truth. (1 Timothy 2:1–4)

### Government

- Spiritual revival
- Local government
- State government
- National government
- Current events and concerns

## Affirmation

There is a time for everything, and a season for every activity under heaven. (Ecclesiastes 3:1)

God has made everything beautiful in its time. He has also set eternity in the hearts of men; yet they cannot fathom what God has done from beginning to end. (Ecclesiastes 3:11)

*Pause to reflect upon these biblical affirmations.*

## Thanksgiving

I do not lose heart; even though my outward man is perishing, yet my inner man is being renewed day by day. For this light affliction which is momentary is working for me a far more exceeding and eternal weight of glory, while I do not look at the things which are seen but at the things which are unseen. For the things which are seen are temporary, but the things which are unseen are eternal. (2 Corinthians 4:16–18)

*Pause to offer your own expressions of thanksgiving.*

## Closing Prayer

Glory in the holy name of the Lord;
Let the hearts of those who seek the Lord rejoice.
Seek the Lord and His strength;
Seek His face always.
Remember the wonderful works He has done,
His miracles, and the judgments He pronounced.
(1 Chronicles 16:10–12)

The Lord reigns forever;
He has established His throne for judgment.
He will judge the world in righteousness,
And He will govern the peoples with justice.
The Lord will also be a refuge for the oppressed,
A stronghold in times of trouble.
Those who know Your name will trust in You,
For You, Lord, have never forsaken those who seek You.
(Psalm 9:7–10)

# THE FIRST MONTH
## DAY 27

### Adoration

Praise the Lord!
Praise, O servants of the Lord,
Praise the name of the Lord.
Blessed be the name of the Lord
Both now and forever.
From the rising of the sun to its setting,
The name of the Lord is to be praised.
The Lord is high above all nations,
His glory above the heavens.
Who is like the Lord our God,
The One who is enthroned on high,
Who humbles Himself to behold
The things that are in the heavens and in the earth?
(Psalm 113:1–6)

*Pause to express your thoughts of praise and worship.*

### Confession

"For a brief moment I forsook you,
But with great compassion I will gather you.
In a flood of anger I hid My face from you for a moment,
But I will have compassion on you with everlasting kindness,"
Says the Lord your Redeemer. (Isaiah 54:7–8)

Daily Prayer Guide

*Ask the Spirit to search your heart and reveal any areas of unconfessed sin. Acknowledge these to the Lord and thank Him for His forgiveness.*

## Renewal

Like Job, may I be blameless and upright, fearing God and shunning evil. (Job 1:1)

May I be careful to lead a blameless life.
May I walk in the integrity of my heart in the midst of
  my house.
May I set no wicked thing before my eyes.
I hate the work of those who fall away;
May it not cling to me. (Psalm 101:2–3)

*Pause to add your own prayers for personal renewal.*

## Petition

Even when I am old and gray, do not forsake me, O God,
Until I declare Your strength to the next generation,
Your power to all who are to come. (Psalm 71:18)

- **Family and Ministry**
    - Family
    - Ministry
        - Sharing Christ with others
        - Helping others grow in Him
    - Career
- My activities for this day
- Special concerns

## Intercession

God be gracious to us and bless us,
And make His face shine upon us;
That Your way may be known on earth,
Your salvation among all nations. (Psalm 67:1–2)

## Missions

- Local missions
- National missions
- World missions
- The fulfillment of the Great Commission
- Special concerns

## Affirmation

The wolf will dwell with the lamb,
And the leopard will lie down with the goat,
And the calf and the lion and the yearling together,
And a little child will lead them.
The cow will feed with the bear;
Their young will lie down together,
And the lion will eat straw like the ox.
The infant will play near the hole of the cobra,
And the young child will put his hand into the viper's hole.
They will neither harm nor destroy on all My holy mountain,
For the earth will be full of the knowledge of the Lord
As the waters cover the sea. (Isaiah 11:6–9)

As the earth brings forth its sprouts
And as a garden causes that which is sown to spring up,

So the Lord God will make righteousness
And praise spring up before all nations. (Isaiah 61:11)

*Pause to reflect upon these biblical affirmations.*

## Thanksgiving

By grace I have been saved through faith, and this not of myself; it is the gift of God, not of works, so that no one can boast. (Ephesians 2:8–9)

I am confident of this, that He who began a good work in me will carry it on to completion until the day of Christ Jesus. (Philippians 1:6)

*Pause to offer your own expressions of thanksgiving.*

## Closing Prayer

Blessed are those who have learned to acclaim You,
Who walk in the light of Your presence, O Lord.
They rejoice in Your name all day long,
And they are exalted in Your righteousness. (Psalm 89:15–16)

# THE FIRST MONTH
## DAY 28

### Adoration

Who has measured the waters in the hollow of His hand,
Or marked off the heavens with the breadth of His hand?
Who has calculated the dust of the earth in a measure,
Or weighed the mountains in the balance
And the hills in scales? (Isaiah 40:12)

You are the Lord, and there is no other;
Apart from You there is no God.
From the rising to the setting of the sun,
We know there is none besides You.
You are the Lord, and there is no other. (Isaiah 45:5–6)

*Pause to express your thoughts of praise and worship.*

### Confession

When my soul was fainting away,
I remembered the Lord,
And my prayer went up to You, to Your holy temple.
Those who cling to worthless idols
Forsake Your lovingkindness.
But I will sacrifice to You
With the voice of thanksgiving.
I will fulfill what I have vowed.
Salvation is from the Lord. (Jonah 2:7–9)

*Ask the Spirit to search your heart and reveal any areas of unconfessed sin. Acknowledge these to the Lord and thank Him for His forgiveness.*

## Renewal

I am the salt of the earth, but if the salt loses its flavor, how can it be made salty again? It is no longer good for anything, except to be thrown out and trampled underfoot by men. I am the light of the world. A city set on a hill cannot be hidden. Neither do people light a lamp and put it under a basket, but on a lampstand, and it gives light to all who are in the house. In the same way, I must let my light shine before men, that they may see my good deeds and praise my Father in heaven. (Matthew 5:13–16)

I want to walk in a way that is worthy of the calling with which I was called, with all humility and meekness and patience. (Ephesians 4:1–2)

*Pause to add your own prayers for personal renewal.*

## Petition

May I be strong and courageous; may I not be afraid or discouraged, for the Lord my God will be with me wherever I go. (Joshua 1:9)

First Month, Day 28

- **Personal Concerns**
    - Spiritual warfare
        - The world
        - The flesh
        - The devil
    - Growth in character
    - Personal disciplines
    - Physical health and strength
- My activities for this day
- Special concerns

## Intercession

O Lord, the great and awesome God, who keeps His covenant and lovingkindness with those who love Him and with those who obey His commandments, we have sinned and committed iniquity; we have been wicked and have rebelled, even turning away from Your commandments and from Your judgments. To the Lord our God belong mercy and forgiveness, even though we have rebelled against Him. We have not obeyed the voice of the Lord our God to walk in His laws which He set before us through His servants the prophets. (Daniel 9:4–5, 9–10)

## World Affairs

- The poor and hungry
- The oppressed and persecuted
- Those in authority
- Peace among nations
- Current events and concerns

## Affirmation

Cursed is the one who trusts in man,
Who depends on flesh for his strength
And whose heart turns away from the Lord.
But blessed is the man who trusts in the Lord,
Whose confidence is in Him. (Jeremiah 17:5, 7)

Jesus knew all men, and had no need for anyone's testimony about man, for He knew what was in man. (John 2:24–25)

God will judge the secrets of men through Jesus Christ, according to the gospel. (Romans 2:16)

*Pause to reflect upon these biblical affirmations.*

## Thanksgiving

May I rejoice in the Lord always. (Philippians 4:4)

I have been called by God my Savior, and Christ Jesus is my hope. (1 Timothy 1:1)

*Pause to offer your own expressions of thanksgiving.*

## Closing Prayer

Praise the Lord!
Praise the Lord from the heavens;
Praise Him in the heights.
Praise Him, all His angels;
Praise Him, all His hosts.

Praise Him, sun and moon;
Praise Him, all you shining stars.
Praise Him, you highest heavens
And you waters above the heavens.
Let them praise the name of the Lord,
For He commanded and they were created.
He established them for ever and ever;
He gave a decree that will not pass away. (Psalm 148:1–6)

Daily Prayer Guide

# THE FIRST MONTH
# DAY 29

## Adoration

John looked and heard the voice of many angels encircling the throne and the living creatures and the elders; and their number was myriads of myriads, and thousands of thousands, saying with a loud voice,

> "Worthy is the Lamb, who was slain,
> To receive power and riches and wisdom
> And strength and honor and glory and blessing!"
> (Revelation 5:11–12)

The Lord Jesus Christ received honor and glory from God the Father when the voice came to Him from the Majestic Glory who said, "This is My beloved Son, with whom I am well pleased." (2 Peter 1:17)

*Pause to express your thoughts of praise and worship.*

## Confession

I will not forget the exhortation that addresses me as a son:

> "My son, do not despise the Lord's discipline,
> Nor lose heart when you are rebuked by Him,
> For whom the Lord loves He disciplines,
> And He chastises every son whom He receives."
> (Hebrews 12:5–6)

First Month, Day 29

*Ask the Spirit to search your heart and reveal any areas of unconfessed sin. Acknowledge these to the Lord and thank Him for His forgiveness.*

## Renewal

May I fear God and keep His commandments, for this applies to every person. (Ecclesiastes 12:13)

Give me understanding, and I will keep Your law
And observe it with all my heart.
Make me walk in the path of Your commands,
For there I find delight.
Incline my heart to Your testimonies
And not to selfish gain.
Turn my eyes away from worthless things,
And revive me in Your way. (Psalm 119:34–37)

*Pause to add your own prayers for personal renewal.*

## Petition

Like Ezra, I want to set my heart to study the word of the Lord, and to do it, and to teach it to others. (Ezra 7:10)

- **Growth in Christ**
    - Greater desire to know and please Him
    - Greater love and commitment to Him
    - Grace to practice His presence
    - Grace to glorify Him in my life

- My activities for this day
- Special concerns

## Intercession

Since we were called into fellowship with the Lord Jesus Christ, all of us should agree with one another, so that there may be no divisions among us, and that we may be perfectly joined together in the same mind and in the same judgment. (1 Corinthians 1:9–10)

### Churches and Ministries

- My local church
- Other churches
- Evangelism and discipleship ministries
- Educational ministries
- Special concerns

## Affirmation

I will not lay up for myself treasures on earth, where moth and rust destroy and where thieves break in and steal. But I will lay up for myself treasures in heaven, where moth and rust do not destroy and where thieves do not break in and steal. For where my treasure is, there my heart will be also. (Matthew 6:19–21; Luke 12:34)

God's divine power has given me all things that pertain to life and godliness, through the knowledge of Him who called me by His own glory and virtue. Through these He has given me

His very great and precious promises, so that through them I may be a partaker of the divine nature, having escaped the corruption that is in the world by lust. (2 Peter 1:3–4)

*Pause to reflect upon these biblical affirmations.*

## Thanksgiving

Surely the Lord's hand is not too short to save,
Nor His ear too dull to hear.
But our iniquities have separated us from our God;
Our sins have hidden His face from us, so that He will
  not hear.
Yet the Lord saw that there was no one to intervene;
So His own arm worked salvation for Him,
And His righteousness sustained Him.
He put on righteousness as His breastplate,
And the helmet of salvation on His head;
He put on the garments of vengeance
And wrapped Himself in zeal as a cloak.
From the west, men will fear the name of the Lord,
And from the rising of the sun, they will revere His glory.
For He will come like a flood
That the breath of the Lord drives along.
(Isaiah 59:1–2, 16–19)

*Pause to offer your own expressions of thanksgiving.*

## Closing Prayer

I am convinced that neither death nor life, nor angels nor principalities, nor things present nor things to come, nor powers, nor height nor depth, nor anything else in all creation, will be able to separate me from the love of God that is in Christ Jesus my Lord. (Romans 8:38–39)

# THE FIRST MONTH
# **DAY 30**

## Adoration

May I fear You, the Lord my God; may I serve You, hold fast to You, and take my oaths in Your name. For You are my praise, and You are my God, who performed for me these great and awesome wonders which I have seen with my own eyes. (Deuteronomy 10:20–21)

You are the great, the mighty, and the awesome God, who keeps His covenant of lovingkindness. (Nehemiah 9:32)

*Pause to express your thoughts of praise and worship.*

## Confession

From within, out of the hearts of men, proceed evil thoughts, sexual immorality, thefts, murders, adulteries, greed, wickedness, deceit, lewdness, envy, slander, arrogance, and folly. All these evil things come from within and defile a man. (Mark 7:21–23)

*Ask the Spirit to search your heart and reveal any areas of unconfessed sin. Acknowledge these to the Lord and thank Him for His forgiveness.*

## Renewal

I will not let sin reign in my mortal body that I should obey its lusts. Nor will I present the members of my body to sin, as instruments of wickedness, but I will present myself to God as one who is alive from the dead and my members as instruments of righteousness to God. (Romans 6:12–13)

May I put away all filthiness and the overflow of wickedness, and in meekness accept the word planted in me, which is able to save my soul. (James 1:21)

*Pause to add your own prayers for personal renewal.*

## Petition

I have called on You, O God, for You will answer me;
Incline Your ear to me and hear my prayer.
Show Your wonderful lovingkindness,
O Savior of those who take refuge at Your right hand
From those who rise up against them.
Keep me as the apple of Your eye;
Hide me in the shadow of Your wings. (Psalm 17:6–8)

- **Growth in Wisdom**
    - Developing an eternal perspective
    - Renewing my mind with truth
    - Greater skill in each area of life
- My activities for this day
- Special concerns

## Intercession

No one should seek his own good, but the good of others. (1 Corinthians 10:24)

### Family

- My immediate family
- My relatives
- Spiritual concerns
- Emotional and physical concerns
- Other concerns

## Affirmation

The day of the Lord will come like a thief, in which the heavens will pass away with a roar, and the elements will be destroyed by intense heat, and the earth and its works will be laid bare. The day of God will bring about the destruction of the heavens by fire, and the elements will melt with intense heat. (2 Peter 3:10, 12)

There will be a new heaven and a new earth, for the first heaven and the first earth will pass away, and there will no longer be any sea. (Revelation 21:1)

*Pause to reflect upon these biblical affirmations.*

## Thanksgiving

Lord, You said, "Let there be lights in the expanse of the heavens to separate the day from the night, and let them serve as signs to mark seasons and days and years, and let them be lights in the expanse of the heavens to give light on the earth"; and it was so. You made two great lights—the greater light to govern the day and the lesser light to govern the night. You also made the stars; You set them in the expanse of the heavens to give light on the earth, and to govern the day and the night, and to separate the light from the darkness. And You saw that it was good. (Genesis 1:14–18)

You made the earth and created man upon it.
Your own hands stretched out the heavens,
And You ordered their starry hosts. (Isaiah 45:12)

*Pause to offer your own expressions of thanksgiving.*

## Closing Prayer

All Your works will praise you, O Lord,
And Your saints will bless You.
They will speak of the glory of Your kingdom
And talk of Your power,
So that all men may know of Your mighty acts
And the glorious majesty of Your kingdom.
Your kingdom is an everlasting kingdom,
And Your dominion endures through all generations.
(Psalm 145:10–13)

Be exalted, O God, above the heavens,
And Your glory above all the earth. (Psalm 108:5)

# THE FIRST MONTH
# DAY 31

## Adoration

The word of the Lord is upright,
And all His work is done in faithfulness.
He loves righteousness and justice;
The earth is full of the lovingkindness of the Lord.
(Psalm 33:4–5)

Once God has spoken;
Twice I have heard this:
That power belongs to God,
And that You, O Lord, are loving.
For You reward each person according to what he has done.
(Psalm 62:11–12)

*Pause to express your thoughts of praise and worship.*

## Confession

When I have sinned against You, hear from heaven and forgive my sin and restore me. Teach me the good way in which I should walk. When I sin against You—for there is no one who does not sin—may I return to You with all my heart and with all my soul. (1 Kings 8:33–34, 36, 46, 48)

*Ask the Spirit to search your heart and reveal any areas of unconfessed sin. Acknowledge these to the Lord and thank Him for His forgiveness.*

## Renewal

Like Noah, may I be a righteous person, blameless among the people of my time, and one who walks with God. (Genesis 6:9)

Like Moses, may I do according to all that the Lord commands me. (Exodus 39:42; 40:16)

*Pause to add your own prayers for personal renewal.*

## Petition

But You, O Lord, be not far off;
O my Strength, come quickly to help me. (Psalm 22:19)

- **Spiritual Insight**
    - Understanding and insight into the Word
    - Understanding my identity in Christ
        - Who I am
        - Where I came from
        - Where I'm going
    - Understanding God's purpose for my life
- My activities for this day
- Special concerns

First Month, Day 31

## Intercession

We should bear one another's burdens and so fulfill the law of Christ. (Galatians 6:2)

### Believers

- Personal friends
- Those in ministry
- Those who are oppressed and in need
- Special concerns

## Affirmation

You are my lamp, O Lord;
The Lord turns my darkness into light.
With Your help I can advance against a troop;
With my God I can leap over a wall. (2 Samuel 22:29–30)

You know the way that I take;
When You have tested me, I shall come forth as gold.
My feet have held fast to Your steps;
I have kept to Your way without turning aside. (Job 23:10–11)

*Pause to reflect upon these biblical affirmations.*

## Thanksgiving

In the beginning You created the heavens and the earth. When the earth was formless and empty, and darkness was over the surface of the deep, Your Spirit hovered over the face of the waters. And You said, "Let there be light," and there was light.

Then You said, "Let there be an expanse in the midst of the waters, and let it separate the waters from the waters." So You made the expanse and separated the waters under the expanse from the waters above it, and it was so. Then You said, "Let the waters under the heavens be gathered into one place, and let dry ground appear"; and it was so. And You saw that it was good. (Genesis 1:1–10)

*Pause to offer your own expressions of thanksgiving.*

## Closing Prayer

Come and listen, all you who fear God,
And I will tell you what He has done for my soul.
I cried out to Him with my mouth,
And He was extolled with my tongue.
If I had regarded iniquity in my heart,
The Lord would not have heard.
But God has surely heard;
He has attended to the voice of my prayer.
Blessed be God, who has not turned away my prayer
Nor His love from me! (Psalm 66:16–20)

Daily Prayer Guide

# The Second Month

# THE SECOND MONTH
# DAY 1

## Adoration

The Lord covers Himself in light as with a garment;
He stretches out the heavens like a tent curtain
And lays the beams of His upper chambers in the waters.
He makes the clouds His chariot
And walks on the wings of the wind.
He makes the winds His messengers,
Flames of fire His servants.
He set the earth on its foundations,
So that it can never be moved.
You covered it with the deep as with a garment;
The waters stood above the mountains.
At Your rebuke the waters fled;
At the sound of Your thunder they hurried away.
They flowed over the mountains
And went down into the valleys
To the place You assigned for them.
You set a boundary they cannot cross,
That they will not return to cover the earth.
O Lord, how manifold are Your works!
In wisdom You made them all;
The earth is full of Your possessions. (Psalm 104:2–9, 24)

*Pause to express your thoughts of praise and worship.*

## Confession

God is wise in heart and mighty in strength.
Who has resisted Him without harm? (Job 9:4)

*Ask the Spirit to search your heart and reveal any areas of unconfessed sin. Acknowledge these to the Lord and thank Him for His forgiveness.*

## Renewal

Examine me, O Lord, and try me;
Purify my mind and my heart;
For Your lovingkindness is ever before me,
And I have walked in Your truth. (Psalm 26:2–3)

May I sow righteousness,
Reap the fruit of unfailing love,
And break up my fallow ground;
For it is time to seek the Lord,
Until He comes and rains righteousness on me. (Hosea 10:12)

*Pause to add your own prayers for personal renewal.*

## Petition

O Lord, hear my prayer;
Listen to the voice of my supplications.
In the day of my trouble I will call upon You,
For You will answer me.
You are great and do wondrous deeds;
You alone are God. (Psalm 86:6–7, 10)

Second Month, Day 1

- **Relationships with Others**
  - Greater love and compassion for others
  - Loved ones
  - Those who do not know Christ
  - Those in need
- My activities for this day
- Special concerns

## Intercession

May I sanctify Christ as Lord in my heart, always being ready to make a defense to everyone who asks me to give the reason for the hope that is in me, but with gentleness and respect. (1 Peter 3:15)

## Evangelism

- Friends
- Relatives
- Neighbors
- Coworkers
- Special opportunities

## Affirmation

Sin shall not be my master, because I am not under law, but under grace. I have been set free from sin and have become a slave of righteousness. (Romans 6:14, 18)

He who has Your commandments and obeys them, he is the one who loves You; and he who loves You will be loved by Your

Father, and You will love him and manifest Yourself to him. (John 14:21)

*Pause to reflect upon these biblical affirmations.*

## Thanksgiving

Lord, You said, "Let Us make man in Our image, in Our likeness, and let them rule over the fish of the sea and the birds of the air and over the livestock and over all the earth and over all the creatures that creep on the earth." So You created man in Your own image; male and female You created them. Then You blessed them and said to them, "Be fruitful and multiply; fill the earth and subdue it; and rule over the fish of the sea and the birds of the air and over every living creature that moves on the earth." Then You said, "Behold, I have given you every seed-bearing plant on the face of the whole earth and every tree that has fruit with seed in it; they will be yours for food. And to all the beasts of the earth and all the birds of the air and all the creatures that move on the ground, in which there is life, I have given every green plant for food"; and it was so. You saw all that You had made, and it was very good. (Genesis 1:26–31)

*Pause to offer your own expressions of thanksgiving.*

## Closing Prayer

May the favor of the Lord our God rest upon us,
And establish the work of our hands for us—
Yes, confirm the work of our hands. (Psalm 90:17)

# THE SECOND MONTH
## DAY 2

### Adoration

As the deer pants for the water brooks,
So my soul pants for You, O God.
My soul thirsts for God, for the living God.
When shall I come and appear before God? (Psalm 42:1–2)

My soul yearns for You in the night;
My spirit within me diligently seeks You.
When Your judgments come upon the earth,
The inhabitants of the world learn righteousness. (Isaiah 26:9)

*Pause to express your thoughts of praise and worship.*

### Confession

You are the righteous God, who searches the hearts and secret thoughts. (Psalm 7:9)

The spirit of a man is the lamp of the Lord,
Searching the inward depths of his being. (Proverbs 20:27)

*Ask the Spirit to search your heart and reveal any areas of unconfessed sin. Acknowledge these to the Lord and thank Him for His forgiveness.*

## Renewal

With regard to my former way of life, may I put off my old self, which is being corrupted by its deceitful desires, and be renewed in the spirit of my mind; and may I put on the new self, which was created according to God in righteousness and true holiness. (Ephesians 4:22–24)

May I be diligent to add to my faith, virtue; and to virtue, knowledge; and to knowledge, self-control; and to self-control, perseverance; and to perseverance, godliness; and to godliness, brotherly kindness; and to brotherly kindness, love. For if these qualities are mine in increasing measure, they will keep me from being barren and unfruitful in the full knowledge of our Lord Jesus Christ. (2 Peter 1:5–8)

*Pause to add your own prayers for personal renewal.*

## Petition

May I discipline myself to godliness. For physical exercise profits a little, but godliness is profitable for all things, since it holds promise for both the present life and the life to come. (1 Timothy 4:7–8)

- **Faithfulness as a Steward**
    - Of time
    - Of talents
    - Of treasure
    - Of truth
    - Of relationships

Second Month, Day 2

- My activities for this day
- Special concerns

## Intercession

May I give to all what they are due: taxes to whom taxes are due, custom to whom custom, respect to whom respect, honor to whom honor. (Romans 13:7)

## Government

- Spiritual revival
- Local government
- State government
- National government
- Current events and concerns

## Affirmation

He who pursues righteousness and love
Finds life, righteousness, and honor. (Proverbs 21:21)

He who heeds the word prospers,
And blessed is he who trusts in the Lord. (Proverbs 16:20)

*Pause to reflect upon these biblical affirmations.*

## Thanksgiving

You are the Lord our God, who brought Your people out of Egypt, out of the land of slavery. (Exodus 20:2)

Was it not You who dried up the sea,
The waters of the great deep;
Who made the depths of the sea a road
So that the redeemed might cross over? (Isaiah 51:10)

*Pause to offer your own expressions of thanksgiving.*

## Closing Prayer

The Lord who created the heavens, He is God.
He fashioned and made the earth and established it;
He did not create it to be empty
But formed it to be inhabited.
He is the Lord, and there is no other. (Isaiah 45:18)

The Lord is in His holy temple;
Let all the earth be silent before Him. (Habakkuk 2:20)

# THE SECOND MONTH
## DAY 3

### Adoration

Not to us, O Lord, not to us,
But to Your name give glory,
Because of Your lovingkindness and truth. (Psalm 115:1)

Praise the Lord!
For it is good to sing praises to our God,
Because praise is pleasant and beautiful. (Psalm 147:1)

*Pause to express your thoughts of praise and worship.*

### Confession

You have set our iniquities before You,
Our secret sins in the light of Your presence. (Psalm 90:8)

*Ask the Spirit to search your heart and reveal any areas of unconfessed sin. Acknowledge these to the Lord and thank Him for His forgiveness.*

### Renewal

May I fight the good fight of faith and lay hold of the eternal life to which I was called when I made the good confession in the presence of many witnesses. In the sight of God, who gives life to all things, and of Christ Jesus, who testified the good

Daily Prayer Guide

confession before Pontius Pilate, may I keep this command without blemish or reproach until the appearing of our Lord Jesus Christ, which God will bring about in His own time. (1 Timothy 6:12–15a)

May I be diligent to present myself approved to God, a workman who does not need to be ashamed and who correctly handles the word of truth. (2 Timothy 2:15)

*Pause to add your own prayers for personal renewal.*

## Petition

You, O Sovereign Lord, deal well with me for Your name's sake;
Because of the goodness of Your mercy, deliver me.
(Psalm 109:21)

- **Family and Ministry**
    - Family
    - Ministry
        - Sharing Christ with others
        - Helping others grow in Him
    - Career
- My activities for this day
- Special concerns

## Intercession

This is pure and undefiled religion before our God and Father: to visit orphans and widows in their affliction and to keep oneself unspotted from the world. (James 1:27)

## Missions

- Local missions
- National missions
- World missions
- The fulfillment of the Great Commission
- Special concerns

## Affirmation

Unless one is born again, he cannot see the kingdom of God; unless one is born of water and the Spirit, he cannot enter into the kingdom of God. That which is born of the flesh is flesh, and that which is born of the Spirit is spirit. The wind blows wherever it pleases, and we hear its sound, but we cannot tell where it comes from, or where it is going. So it is with everyone born of the Spirit. (John 3:3, 5–6, 8)

Through the Spirit, by faith, I eagerly await the righteousness for which I hope. (Galatians 5:5)

*Pause to reflect upon these biblical affirmations.*

## Thanksgiving

I will give thanks to the Lord, call upon His name,
And make known to others what He has done.
I will sing to Him, sing praises to Him,
And tell of all His wonderful acts. (1 Chronicles 16:8–9)

I know that the Lord has set apart the godly for Himself;
The Lord hears when I call to Him. (Psalm 4:3)

*Pause to offer your own expressions of thanksgiving.*

## Closing Prayer

God highly exalted Christ Jesus and gave Him the name that is above every name, that at the name of Jesus every knee should bow, in heaven and on earth and under the earth, and every tongue should confess that Jesus Christ is Lord, to the glory of God the Father. (Philippians 2:9–11)

Christ is the head of the body, the church; He is the beginning and the firstborn from among the dead, so that in everything He might have the supremacy. (Colossians 1:18)

# THE SECOND MONTH
# DAY 4

### Adoration

Who has directed the Spirit of the Lord,
Or instructed Him as His counselor?
Whom did the Lord consult to enlighten Him,
And who taught Him the path of justice?
Who taught Him knowledge
Or showed Him the way of understanding?
Surely the nations are like a drop in a bucket
And are regarded as dust on the scales;
He weighs the islands as though they were fine dust.
Before Him all the nations are as nothing;
They are regarded by Him as less than nothing and worthless.
To whom, then, will I compare God?
Or what likeness will I compare with Him?
(Isaiah 40:13–15, 17–18)

*Pause to express your thoughts of praise and worship.*

### Confession

Who among us fears the Lord
And obeys the word of His Servant?
Let him who walks in darkness and has no light
Trust in the name of the Lord and rely upon his God.
(Isaiah 50:10)

*Ask the Spirit to search your heart and reveal any areas of unconfessed sin. Acknowledge these to the Lord and thank Him for His forgiveness.*

## Renewal

By Your grace, I want to observe Your judgments and keep Your statutes, to walk in them; You are the Lord my God. May I keep Your statutes and Your judgments, by which a man may live if he does them; You are the Lord. (Leviticus 18:4–5)

May I fear the Lord and serve and obey Him and not rebel against the command of the Lord. (1 Samuel 12:14)

*Pause to add your own prayers for personal renewal.*

## Petition

May I not imitate what is evil but what is good. The one who does good is of God; the one who does evil has not seen God. (3 John 11)

- **Personal Concerns**
    - Spiritual warfare
        - The world
        - The flesh
        - The devil
    - Growth in character
    - Personal disciplines
    - Physical health and strength

Second Month, Day 4

- My activities for this day
- Special concerns

## Intercession

Lord, there is no one besides You to help the powerless against the mighty. Help us, O Lord our God, for we rest in You. O Lord, You are our God; do not let man prevail against You. (2 Chronicles 14:11)

## World Affairs

- The poor and hungry
- The oppressed and persecuted
- Those in authority
- Peace among nations
- Current events and concerns

## Affirmation

You will keep in perfect peace him whose mind is stayed
   on You,
Because he trusts in You. (Isaiah 26:3)

I will seek the Lord while He may be found
And call upon Him while He is near. (Isaiah 55:6)

*Pause to reflect upon these biblical affirmations.*

## Thanksgiving

I will give thanks to the Lord according to His righteousness
And will sing praise to the name of the Lord Most High.
(Psalm 7:17)

The Lord is my light and my salvation;
Whom shall I fear?
The Lord is the strength of my life;
Of whom shall I be afraid? (Psalm 27:1)

*Pause to offer your own expressions of thanksgiving.*

## Closing Prayer

I will sing to the Lord as long as I live;
I will sing praise to my God while I have my being.
May my meditation be pleasing to Him;
I will be glad in the Lord. (Psalm 104:33–34)

God gives strength to the weary
And increases the power of the weak.
Even youths grow tired and weary,
And young men stumble and fall;
But those who wait for the Lord
Will renew their strength;
They will mount up with wings like eagles;
They will run and not grow weary;
They will walk and not be faint. (Isaiah 40:29–31)

# THE SECOND MONTH
# DAY 5

## Adoration

The Lord is the true God;
He is the living God and the everlasting King.
At His wrath, the earth trembles,
And the nations cannot endure His indignation.
(Jeremiah 10:10)

How great are God's signs,
And how mighty are His wonders!
His kingdom is an eternal kingdom;
His dominion endures from generation to generation.
(Daniel 4:3)

*Pause to express your thoughts of praise and worship.*

## Confession

May I produce fruit worthy of repentance. (Matthew 3:8)

*Ask the Spirit to search your heart and reveal any areas of unconfessed sin. Acknowledge these to the Lord and thank Him for His forgiveness.*

## Renewal

Teach me to number my days,
That I may gain a heart of wisdom. (Psalm 90:12)

May I let my eyes look straight ahead,
And fix my gaze straight before me.
May I ponder the path of my feet
So that all my ways will be established.
May I not turn to the right or to the left
But keep my foot from evil. (Proverbs 4:25–27)

*Pause to add your own prayers for personal renewal.*

## Petition

Hear my prayer, O Lord,
Give ear to my supplications!
Answer me in Your faithfulness and righteousness. (Psalm 143:1)

- **Growth in Christ**
  - Greater desire to know and please Him
  - Greater love and commitment to Him
  - Grace to practice His presence
  - Grace to glorify Him in my life
- My activities for this day
- Special concerns

## Intercession

There are different kinds of gifts, but the same Spirit. And there are different kinds of service, but the same Lord. And there are different kinds of working, but the same God works all of them in all people. But to each one the manifestation of the Spirit is given for the common good. (1 Corinthians 12:4–7)

### Churches and Ministries

- My local church
- Other churches
- Evangelism and discipleship ministries
- Educational ministries
- Special concerns

## Affirmation

No one can lay a foundation other than the one already laid, which is Jesus Christ. (1 Corinthians 3:11)

It is by faith that I stand firm. (2 Corinthians 1:24)

Knowing that a man is not justified by the works of the law, but through faith in Christ Jesus, I have believed in Christ Jesus, that I may be justified through faith in Christ and not by the works of the law; for by the works of the law, no flesh will be justified. (Galatians 2:16)

*Pause to reflect upon these biblical affirmations.*

## Thanksgiving

Many, O Lord my God, are the wonders You have done,
And Your thoughts toward us no one can recount to You;
Were I to speak and tell of them,
They would be too many to declare. (Psalm 40:5)

I will praise You forever for what You have done;
I will hope in Your name, for it is good.
I will praise You in the presence of Your saints. (Psalm 52:9)

*Pause to offer your own expressions of thanksgiving.*

## Closing Prayer

I know that all things work together for good to those who love God, to those who have been called according to His purpose. (Romans 8:28)

If God is for me, who can be against me? He who did not spare His own Son, but delivered Him up for us all, how will He not, also with Him, freely give us all things? (Romans 8:31–32)

# THE SECOND MONTH
# DAY 6

## Adoration

"To whom will you compare Me?
Or who is My equal?" says the Holy One.
Lift your eyes to the heavens
And see who has created them,
He who brings out the starry host by number
And calls them each by name.
Because of His great might and the strength of His power,
Not one of them is missing.
Do you not know? Have you not heard?
The everlasting God, the Lord, the Creator of the ends of the earth,
Does not grow tired or weary.
No one can fathom His understanding. (Isaiah 40:25–26, 28)

You, O Lord, remain forever;
Your throne endures from generation to generation.
(Lamentations 5:19)

*Pause to express your thoughts of praise and worship.*

## Confession

Why should any living man complain
When punished for his sins?

Let us search out and examine our ways,
And let us return to the Lord. (Lamentations 3:39–40)

*Ask the Spirit to search your heart and reveal any areas of unconfessed sin. Acknowledge these to the Lord and thank Him for His forgiveness.*

## Renewal

May I apply my heart to instruction
And my ears to words of knowledge. (Proverbs 23:12)

May I watch and pray so that I will not fall into temptation; the spirit is willing, but the flesh is weak. (Matthew 26:41)

*Pause to add your own prayers for personal renewal.*

## Petition

May I keep Your statutes and Your commandments and be careful to do as the Lord my God has commanded me; may I not turn aside to the right or to the left. (Deuteronomy 4:40; 5:32)

**Growth in Wisdom**

- o Developing an eternal perspective
- o Renewing my mind with truth
- o Greater skill in each area of life
- My activities for this day
- Special concerns

## Intercession

If I speak in the tongues of men and of angels, but have not love, I am only a resounding gong or a clanging cymbal. And if I have the gift of prophecy and understand all mysteries and all knowledge, and if I have all faith so as to remove mountains, but have not love, I am nothing. And if I give all my possessions to the poor, and if I deliver my body to be burned, but have not love, it profits me nothing. (1 Corinthians 13:1–3)

### Family

- My immediate family
- My relatives
- Spiritual concerns
- Emotional and physical concerns
- Other concerns

## Affirmation

I am no longer a stranger and alien, but a fellow citizen with God's people and a member of God's household, built on the foundation of the apostles and prophets, with Christ Jesus Himself as the chief cornerstone. (Ephesians 2:19–20)

I have been called, having been loved by God the Father and kept by Jesus Christ. (Jude 1)

*Pause to reflect upon these biblical affirmations.*

## Thanksgiving

You answer us with awesome deeds of righteousness,
O God of our salvation,
You who are the hope of all the ends of the earth
And of the farthest seas;
You formed the mountains by Your strength,
Having armed Yourself with power;
And You stilled the roaring of the seas,
The roaring of their waves,
And the tumult of the peoples. (Psalm 65:5–7)

*Pause to offer your own expressions of thanksgiving.*

## Closing Prayer

Better is one day in Your courts than a thousand elsewhere;
I would rather be a doorkeeper in the house of my God
Than dwell in the tents of the wicked.
For the Lord God is a sun and shield;
The Lord will give grace and glory;
No good thing does He withhold
From those who walk in integrity.
O Lord of hosts,
Blessed is the man who trusts in You! (Psalm 84:10–12)

# THE SECOND MONTH
## DAY 7

### Adoration

In the beginning was the Word, and the Word was with God, and the Word was God. He was in the beginning with God. (John 1:1–2)

There is but one God, the Father, from whom all things came and for whom I live; and there is but one Lord, Jesus Christ, through whom all things came and through whom I live. (1 Corinthians 8:6)

*Pause to express your thoughts of praise and worship.*

### Confession

I know that You are a gracious and compassionate God, slow to anger and abounding in lovingkindness, a God who relents from sending calamity. (Jonah 4:2)

*Ask the Spirit to search your heart and reveal any areas of unconfessed sin. Acknowledge these to the Lord and thank Him for His forgiveness.*

### Renewal

May I not be like those rocky places on whom seed was thrown, who hear the word and at once receive it with joy, but since they have no root, last only a short time; when affliction or persecution comes because of the word, they quickly fall away. And may I not be like those among the thorns on whom seed was sown, who hear the word, but the worries of this world, the deceitfulness of riches and pleasures, and the desires for other things come in and choke the word, making it immature and unfruitful. Instead, may I be like the good soil on whom seed was sown, who with a noble and good heart hear the word, understand and accept it, and with perseverance bear fruit, yielding thirty, sixty, or a hundred times what was sown. (Matthew 13:20–23; Mark 4:16–20; Luke 8:13–15)

*Pause to add your own prayers for personal renewal.*

## Petition

If a man dies, will he live again?
All the days of my hard service
I will wait for my renewal to come. (Job 14:14)

- **Spiritual Insight**
    - Understanding and insight into the Word
    - Understanding my identity in Christ
        - Who I am
        - Where I came from
        - Where I'm going
    - Understanding God's purpose for my life
- My activities for this day
- Special concerns

## Intercession

All of us have become like one who is unclean,
And all our righteous acts are like filthy rags;
We all shrivel up like a leaf,
And our iniquities, like the wind, sweep us away.
But now, O Lord, You are our Father.
We are the clay; You are the potter;
We are all the work of Your hand. (Isaiah 64:6, 8)

### Believers

- Personal friends
- Those in ministry
- Those who are oppressed and in need
- Special concerns

## Affirmation

Like Abram, when I believe in Your promises, You will credit it to me as righteousness. (Genesis 15:5–6)

Whatever things were written in the past were written for our learning, so that through endurance and the encouragement of the Scriptures we might have hope. (Romans 15:4)

Like Abraham, I am looking for a city which has foundations, whose architect and builder is God. (Hebrews 11:10)

*Pause to reflect upon these biblical affirmations.*

Daily Prayer Guide

## Thanksgiving

I will praise You, O Lord my God, with all my heart,
And I will glorify Your name forever.
For great is Your love toward me,
And You have delivered my soul from the depths of the grave.
(Psalm 86:12–13)

Rejoice in the Lord, you who are righteous,
And give thanks at the remembrance of His holy name.
(Psalm 97:12)

*Pause to offer your own expressions of thanksgiving.*

## Closing Prayer

I love You, O Lord, my strength.
The Lord is my rock and my fortress and my deliverer;
My God is my rock, in whom I take refuge.
He is my shield and the horn of my salvation, my stronghold.
I call upon the Lord, who is worthy of praise,
And I am saved from my enemies. (Psalm 18:1–3)

Many are the sorrows of the wicked,
But he who trusts in the Lord, lovingkindness shall surround
    him. (Psalm 32:10)

# THE SECOND MONTH
## **DAY 8**

### Adoration

Can you bind the cluster of the Pleiades?
Can you loose the cords of Orion?
Can you bring forth the constellations in their seasons
Or guide the Bear with its cubs?
Do you know the ordinances of the heavens?
Can you set their dominion over the earth? (Job 38:31–33)

I know that You can do all things
And that no purpose of Yours can be thwarted. (Job 42:2)

*Pause to express your thoughts of praise and worship.*

### Confession

I know, O Lord, that a man's way is not his own;
It is not in a man who walks to direct his steps.
O Lord, correct me, but with justice—
Not in Your anger, lest You reduce me to nothing.
(Jeremiah 10:23–24)

*Ask the Spirit to search your heart and reveal any areas of unconfessed sin. Acknowledge these to the Lord and thank Him for His forgiveness.*

## Renewal

May I receive the words of wisdom
And treasure her commands within me,
Turning my ear to wisdom
And applying my heart to understanding.
If I cry for discernment
And lift up my voice for understanding,
If I seek her as silver
And search for her as for hidden treasures,
Then I will understand the fear of the Lord
And find the knowledge of God.
Then I will understand righteousness and justice and
　honesty—
Every good path.
For wisdom will enter my heart,
And knowledge will be pleasant to my soul.
Discretion will protect me,
And understanding will guard me. (Proverbs 2:1–5, 9–11)

*Pause to add your own prayers for personal renewal.*

## Petition

Hear, O Lord, and be merciful to me;
O Lord, be my helper.
You turned my mourning into dancing;
You removed my sackcloth and clothed me with gladness,
That my heart may sing praise to You and not be silent.
O Lord my God, I will give thanks to You forever.
(Psalm 30:10–12)

- **Relationships with Others**
    - Greater love and compassion for others
    - Loved ones
    - Those who do not know Christ
    - Those in need
- My activities for this day
- Special concerns

## Intercession

The harvest is plentiful, but the workers are few. Therefore, I will pray that the Lord of the harvest will send out workers into His harvest. (Matthew 9:37–38; Luke 10:2)

## Evangelism

- Friends
- Relatives
- Neighbors
- Coworkers
- Special opportunities

## Affirmation

You are my hiding place and my shield;
I have put my hope in Your word. (Psalm 119:114)

Every word of God is tested;
He is a shield to those who take refuge in Him. (Proverbs 30:5)

Daily Prayer Guide

The earnest expectation of the creation eagerly waits for the revealing of the sons of God. (Romans 8:19)

*Pause to reflect upon these biblical affirmations.*

## Thanksgiving

All the kings of the earth will give thanks to You, O Lord,
When they hear the words of Your mouth.
Yes, they sing of the ways of the Lord,
For the glory of the Lord is great.
Though the Lord is on high,
Yet He looks upon the lowly,
But the proud He knows from afar. (Psalm 138:4–6)

*Pause to offer your own expressions of thanksgiving.*

## Closing Prayer

My days are like a lengthened shadow,
And I wither away like grass.
But You, O Lord, will endure forever,
And the remembrance of Your name to all generations.
Of old, You laid the foundations of the earth,
And the heavens are the work of Your hands.
They will perish, but You will endure;
They will all wear out like a garment.
Like clothing, You will change them, and they will be
   discarded.
But You are the same,
And Your years will have no end. (Psalm 102:11–12, 25–27)

# THE SECOND MONTH
## DAY 9

### Adoration

The earth is the Lord's, and everything in it,
The world and all who dwell in it.
For He founded it upon the seas
And established it upon the waters. (Psalm 24:1–2)

God sits enthroned above the circle of the earth,
And its inhabitants are like grasshoppers.
He stretches out the heavens like a curtain
And spreads them out like a tent to dwell in.
He reduces rulers to nothing
And makes the judges of this world meaningless.
(Isaiah 40:22–23)

*Pause to express your thoughts of praise and worship.*

### Confession

The refining pot is for silver and the furnace for gold,
But the Lord tests the hearts. (Proverbs 17:3)

*Ask the Spirit to search your heart and reveal any areas of unconfessed sin. Acknowledge these to the Lord and thank Him for His forgiveness.*

## Renewal

May I know God and serve Him with a whole heart and with a willing mind; for the Lord searches all hearts and understands every motive behind the thoughts. (1 Chronicles 28:9)

May I be an imitator of God as a beloved child, and walk in love, just as Christ loved me and gave Himself up for me as a fragrant offering and sacrifice to God. (Ephesians 5:1–2)

*Pause to add your own prayers for personal renewal.*

## Petition

May I not love the world or the things in the world. If anyone loves the world, the love of the Father is not in him. For all that is in the world—the lust of the flesh, the lust of the eyes, and the pride of life—is not of the Father but of the world. And the world and its lusts are passing away, but the one who does the will of God abides forever. (1 John 2:15–17)

- **Faithfulness as a Steward**
    - Of time
    - Of talents
    - Of treasure
    - Of truth
    - Of relationships
- My activities for this day
- Special concerns

## Intercession

The Lord has said, "If My people who are called by My name will humble themselves and pray and seek My face and turn from their wicked ways, then I will hear from heaven and will forgive their sin and heal their land." (2 Chronicles 7:14)

### Government

- Spiritual revival
- Local government
- State government
- National government
- Current events and concerns

## Affirmation

The righteous will live by his faith. (Habakkuk 2:4)

I am not ashamed of the gospel, for it is the power of God for salvation to everyone who believes, to the Jew first, and also to the Gentile. For in it the righteousness of God is revealed from faith to faith, just as it is written: "The righteous will live by faith." (Romans 1:16–17)

Clearly no one is justified before God by the law, for "The righteous will live by faith." (Galatians 3:11)

Before faith in Christ came, we were guarded by the law, confined for the faith which was later to be revealed. So the law has become our tutor to lead us to Christ, that we might be justified by faith. Now that faith has come, we are no longer under a tutor. (Galatians 3:23–25)

*Pause to reflect upon these biblical affirmations.*

## Thanksgiving

The Lord upholds all who fall
And lifts up all who are bowed down.
The eyes of all look to You,
And You give them their food at the proper time.
You open Your hand
And satisfy the desire of every living thing. (Psalm 145:14–16)

*Pause to offer your own expressions of thanksgiving.*

## Closing Prayer

The Lord Jesus is the first and the last, and the Living One; He was dead, and behold He is alive forevermore and holds the keys of death and of Hades. (Revelation 1:17–18)

Worthy is the Lamb, who was slain,
To receive power and riches and wisdom
And strength and honor and glory and blessing!
(Revelation 5:12)

# THE SECOND MONTH
## DAY 10

### Adoration

You are He; You are the first,
And You are also the last. (Isaiah 48:12)

The God and Father of the Lord Jesus is blessed forever. (2 Corinthians 11:31)

The Son is the radiance of God's glory and the exact representation of His being, upholding all things by His powerful word. After He cleansed our sins, He sat down at the right hand of the Majesty on high, having become as much superior to angels as the name He has inherited is more excellent than theirs. (Hebrews 1:3–4)

*Pause to express your thoughts of praise and worship.*

### Confession

The ways of a man are before the eyes of the Lord,
And He examines all his paths. (Proverbs 5:21)

*Ask the Spirit to search your heart and reveal any areas of unconfessed sin. Acknowledge these to the Lord and thank Him for His forgiveness.*

## Renewal

Since I live in the Spirit, may I also walk in the Spirit. (Galatians 5:25)

May God fill me with the knowledge of His will through all spiritual wisdom and understanding, so that I may walk worthy of the Lord and please Him in every way, bearing fruit in every good work, and growing in the knowledge of God; strengthened with all power according to His glorious might, so that I may have great endurance and patience with joy. (Colossians 1:9–11)

*Pause to add your own prayers for personal renewal.*

## Petition

I cry out to You, O Lord,
And say, "You are my refuge,
My portion in the land of the living." (Psalm 142:5)

- **Family and Ministry**
    - Family
    - Ministry
        - Sharing Christ with others
        - Helping others grow in Him
    - Career
- My activities for this day
- Special concerns

Second Month, Day 10

## Intercession

As the Father sent the Son into the world, He also has sent us into the world. And He has prayed for those who will believe in Him through our message. (John 17:18, 20)

### Missions

- Local missions
- National missions
- World missions
- The fulfillment of the Great Commission
- Special concerns

## Affirmation

Like Jesus, my food is to do the will of Him who sent me and to accomplish His work. (John 4:34)

This is love: that I walk in obedience to God's commandments. And this is the commandment: that as I have heard from the beginning, I should walk in love. (2 John 6)

*Pause to reflect upon these biblical affirmations.*

## Thanksgiving

The Lord God will swallow up death forever,
And He will wipe away the tears from all faces;
He will remove the reproach of His people from all the earth.
For the Lord has spoken.

And it will be said in that day,
"Behold, this is our God;
We have waited for Him, and He will save us.
This is the Lord;
We have trusted in Him.
Let us rejoice and be glad in His salvation." (Isaiah 25:8–9)

The Holy City, new Jerusalem, will come down out of heaven from God, prepared as a bride adorned for her husband. A loud voice from the throne will say, "Behold, the tabernacle of God is with men, and He will dwell with them, and they will be His people, and God Himself will be with them and be their God, and He will wipe every tear from their eyes. There will be no more death or mourning or crying or pain, for the first things have passed away." He who is seated on the throne will say, "Behold, I make all things new." (Revelation 21:2–5)

*Pause to offer your own expressions of thanksgiving.*

## Closing Prayer

You have sworn by Yourself;
The word has gone out of Your mouth in righteousness
And will not return.
Every knee will bow before You,
And every tongue will acknowledge You. (Isaiah 45:23)

You are worthy to take the scroll
And to open its seals,
Because You were slain,

Second Month, Day 10

And with Your blood You purchased men for God
From every tribe and language and people and nation.
You have made them to be a kingdom and priests to serve
 our God,
And they will reign on the earth. (Revelation 5:9–10)

Daily Prayer Guide

# THE SECOND MONTH
# DAY 11

## Adoration

Your testimonies, which You have commanded,
Are righteous and trustworthy.
Your righteousness is everlasting,
And Your law is truth. (Psalm 119:138, 142)

My heart is steadfast, O God;
I will sing praises with all my soul.
Awake, harp and lyre!
I will awaken the dawn.
I will praise You, O Lord, among the peoples;
I will sing of You among the nations.
Your merciful love is higher than the heavens,
And Your truth reaches to the skies. (Psalm 108:1–4)

*Pause to express your thoughts of praise and worship.*

## Confession

Blessed is the man You discipline, O Lord,
The man You teach from Your word. (Psalm 94:12)

*Ask the Spirit to search your heart and reveal any areas of unconfessed sin. Acknowledge these to the Lord and thank Him for His forgiveness.*

Second Month, Day 11

## Renewal

You are God Almighty; may I walk before You and be blameless. (Genesis 17:1)

May I love my enemies, do good to them, and lend to them, expecting nothing in return. Then my reward will be great, and I will be a child of the Most High; for He is kind to the ungrateful and evil. May I be merciful just as my Father is merciful. (Luke 6:35–36)

*Pause to add your own prayers for personal renewal.*

## Petition

May I not be dishonest in judgment, in measurement of weight or quantity. May I be honest and just in my business affairs. (Leviticus 19:35–36)

- **Personal Concerns**
    - Spiritual warfare
        - The world
        - The flesh
        - The devil
    - Growth in character
    - Personal disciplines
    - Physical health and strength
- My activities for this day
- Special concerns

## Intercession

Defend the weak and the fatherless;
Do justice to the afflicted and destitute.
Rescue the poor and needy;
Deliver them from the hand of the wicked. (Psalm 82:3–4)

### World Affairs

- The poor and hungry
- The oppressed and persecuted
- Those in authority
- Peace among nations
- Current events and concerns

## Affirmation

I am not trying to win the approval of men, but of God. If I were still trying to please men, I would not be a servant of Christ. (Galatians 1:10)

The fear of man brings a snare,
But he who trusts in the Lord is set on high. (Proverbs 29:25)

My help is in the name of the Lord,
Who made heaven and earth. (Psalm 124:8)

*Pause to reflect upon these biblical affirmations.*

## Thanksgiving

Since God's children have partaken of flesh and blood, He too shared in their humanity so that by His death He might destroy him who holds the power of death, that is, the devil, and free those who all their lives were held in slavery by their fear of death. (Hebrews 2:14–15)

Christ had to be made like His brothers in every way, in order that He might become a merciful and faithful high priest in things pertaining to God, to make propitiation for the sins of the people. Because He Himself suffered when He was tempted, He is able to help those who are being tempted. (Hebrews 2:17–18)

*Pause to offer your own expressions of thanksgiving.*

## Closing Prayer

Blessed is the man who does not walk in the counsel of
  the wicked
Or stand in the way of sinners
Or sit in the seat of scorners.
But his delight is in the law of the Lord,
And in His law he meditates day and night.
And he shall be like a tree planted by streams of water,
Which yields its fruit in its season
And whose leaf does not wither;
And whatever he does will prosper. (Psalm 1:1–3)

Daily Prayer Guide

# THE SECOND MONTH
# DAY 12

## Adoration

Great is the Lord, and most worthy of praise
In the city of our God, His holy mountain.
We have meditated on Your unfailing love, O God,
In the midst of Your temple.
As is Your name, O God,
So is Your praise to the ends of the earth;
Your right hand is filled with righteousness. (Psalm 48:1, 9–10)

O come, let us worship and bow down,
Let us kneel before the Lord our Maker. (Psalm 95:6)

*Pause to express your thoughts of praise and worship.*

## Confession

Who can discern his errors?
Cleanse me from hidden faults.
Keep Your servant also from presumptuous sins;
Let them not rule over me.
Then will I be blameless,
And innocent of great transgression. (Psalm 19:12–13)

*Ask the Spirit to search your heart and reveal any areas of unconfessed sin. Acknowledge these to the Lord and thank Him for His forgiveness.*

## Renewal

Love is patient, love is kind, it does not envy; love does not boast, it is not arrogant, it does not behave rudely; it does not seek its own, it is not provoked, it keeps no record of wrongs; it does not rejoice in unrighteousness but rejoices with the truth; it bears all things, believes all things, hopes all things, endures all things. Love never fails. (1 Corinthians 13:4–8)

May my love abound more and more in full knowledge and depth of insight, so that I may be able to approve the things that are excellent, in order to be sincere and blameless until the day of Christ—having been filled with the fruit of righteousness that comes through Jesus Christ, to the glory and praise of God. (Philippians 1:9–11)

*Pause to add your own prayers for personal renewal.*

## Petition

Since I died with Christ to the basic principles of this world, may I not submit to its regulations as though I still belonged to it. (Colossians 2:20)

- **Growth in Christ**
    - Greater desire to know and please Him
    - Greater love and commitment to Him
    - Grace to practice His presence
    - Grace to glorify Him in my life
- My activities for this day
- Special concerns

## Intercession

There should be no division in the body, but its members should have the same concern for each other. If one member suffers, all the members suffer with it; if one member is honored, all the members rejoice with it. Now we are the body of Christ, and each one of us is a member of it. (1 Corinthians 12:25–27)

### Churches and Ministries

- My local church
- Other churches
- Evangelism and discipleship ministries
- Educational ministries
- Special concerns

## Affirmation

I am not competent in myself to claim anything for myself, but my competence comes from God. He has made me competent as a minister of a new covenant, not of the letter, but of the Spirit; for the letter kills, but the Spirit gives life. (2 Corinthians 3:5–6)

It is because of God that I am in Christ Jesus, who has become for me wisdom from God and righteousness and sanctification and redemption. (1 Corinthians 1:30)

*Pause to reflect upon these biblical affirmations.*

Second Month, Day 12

## Thanksgiving

It is in You, Lord Jesus, that I have peace. In this world I will have tribulation, but I will be of good cheer, because You have overcome the world. (John 16:33)

I have been set apart for the gospel of God—I am among those who are called to belong to Jesus Christ. (Romans 1:1, 6)

*Pause to offer your own expressions of thanksgiving.*

## Closing Prayer

The Lord is my shepherd;
I shall not be in want.
He makes me lie down in green pastures;
He leads me beside quiet waters;
He restores my soul.
He guides me in the paths of righteousness
For His name's sake.
Even though I walk through the valley of the shadow of death,
I will fear no evil, for You are with me;
Your rod and Your staff, they comfort me.
You prepare a table before me in the presence of my enemies.
You anoint my head with oil;
My cup overflows.
Surely goodness and mercy will follow me all the days of
  my life,
And I will dwell in the house of the Lord forever.
(Psalm 23:1–6)

Daily Prayer Guide

# THE SECOND MONTH
# DAY 13

### Adoration

The Lord God of hosts—
He who touches the earth and it melts,
And all who live in it mourn;
He who builds His staircase in the heavens
And founded the expanse over the earth;
He who calls for the waters of the sea
And pours them out over the face of the earth—
The Lord is His name. (Amos 9:5–6)

Be silent, all flesh, before the Lord, for He is aroused from His holy dwelling place. (Zechariah 2:13)

*Pause to express your thoughts of praise and worship.*

### Confession

Have mercy on me, O God,
According to Your loyal love;
According to the greatness of Your compassion
Blot out my transgressions.
Wash me completely from my iniquity
And cleanse me from my sin.

For I know my transgressions,
And my sin is ever before me.
Against You, You only, have I sinned
And done what is evil in Your sight,
So that You are justified when You speak
And blameless when You judge. (Psalm 51:1–4)

*Ask the Spirit to search your heart and reveal any areas of unconfessed sin. Acknowledge these to the Lord and thank Him for His forgiveness.*

## Renewal

May I not work for the food that perishes, but for the food that endures to eternal life, which the Son of Man gives me, for God the Father has set His seal on Him. (John 6:27)

Whatever was gain to me I now consider loss for the sake of Christ. What is more, I consider all things loss compared to the surpassing greatness of knowing Christ Jesus my Lord, for whose sake I have suffered the loss of all things and consider them rubbish, that I may gain Christ and be found in Him, not having a righteousness of my own that comes from the law, but that which is through faith in Christ—the righteousness that comes from God on the basis of faith. (Philippians 3:7–9)

*Pause to add your own prayers for personal renewal.*

Daily Prayer Guide

## Petition

Rise up, O Lord!
May Your enemies be scattered,
And may those who hate You flee before You. (Numbers 10:35)

- **Growth in Wisdom**
    - Developing an eternal perspective
    - Renewing my mind with truth
    - Greater skill in each area of life
- My activities for this day
- Special concerns

## Intercession

May we keep the feast of Christ, our Passover, not with old leaven, or with the leaven of malice and wickedness, but with the unleavened bread of sincerity and truth. (1 Corinthians 5:7–8)

### Family

- My immediate family
- My relatives
- Spiritual concerns
- Emotional and physical concerns
- Other concerns

## Affirmation

A natural man does not receive the things of the Spirit, for they are foolishness to him, and he cannot understand them, because they are spiritually discerned. "For who has known the mind of the Lord that he may instruct Him?" But we have the mind of Christ. (1 Corinthians 2:14, 16)

Now I see dimly, as in a mirror, but then I shall see face to face. Now I know in part, but then I shall know fully, even as I am fully known. (1 Corinthians 13:12)

*Pause to reflect upon these biblical affirmations.*

## Thanksgiving

God will keep me strong to the end, so that I will be blameless on the day of our Lord Jesus Christ. God is faithful, through whom I was called into fellowship with His Son, Jesus Christ our Lord. (1 Corinthians 1:8–9)

Eye has not seen, ear has not heard, nor have entered the heart of man the things that God has prepared for those who love Him. (1 Corinthians 2:9)

*Pause to offer your own expressions of thanksgiving.*

## Closing Prayer

Lord, make me to know my end
And what is the measure of my days;
Let me know how fleeting is my life. (Psalm 39:4)

You know how I am formed;
You remember that I am dust.
As for man, his days are like grass;

He flourishes like a flower of the field.
The wind passes over it and it is gone,
And its place remembers it no more.
But the lovingkindness of the Lord is from everlasting
  to everlasting
On those who fear Him,
And His righteousness with their children's children,
To those who keep His covenant
And remember to obey His precepts. (Psalm 103:14–18)

# THE SECOND MONTH
## DAY 14

### Adoration

The Lord reigns; He is clothed with majesty;
The Lord is robed in majesty and is armed with strength.
Indeed, the world is firmly established; it cannot be moved.
Your throne is established from of old;
You are from everlasting.
Your testimonies stand firm;
Holiness adorns Your house,
O Lord, forever. (Psalm 93:1–2, 5)

Bless the Lord, O my soul.
O Lord, my God, You are very great;
You are clothed with splendor and majesty. (Psalm 104:1)

*Pause to express your thoughts of praise and worship.*

### Confession

If I claim to be without sin, I deceive myself, and the truth is not in me. If I confess my sins, He is faithful and just and will forgive me my sins and purify me from all unrighteousness. If I claim I have not sinned, I make Him a liar and His word is not in me. (1 John 1:8–10)

*Ask the Spirit to search your heart and reveal any areas of unconfessed sin. Acknowledge these to the Lord and thank Him for His forgiveness.*

## Renewal

Teach me to do Your will,
For You are my God;
May Your good Spirit lead me on level ground. (Psalm 143:10)

May I listen to counsel and accept instruction,
That I may be wise in my latter days. (Proverbs 19:20)

*Pause to add your own prayers for personal renewal.*

## Petition

May I be strong and courageous; may I not be afraid or discouraged because of my adversaries, for there is a greater power with me than with them, for the Lord my God is with me to help me. (2 Chronicles 32:7–8)

- **Spiritual Insight**
    - Understanding and insight into the Word
    - Understanding my identity in Christ
        - Who I am
        - Where I came from
        - Where I'm going
    - Understanding God's purpose for my life
- My activities for this day
- Special concerns

## Intercession

I was called to freedom, but may I not use my freedom to indulge the flesh, but through love let me serve others. For the whole law is summed up in this word: "You shall love your neighbor as yourself." (Galatians 5:13–14)

### Believers

- Personal friends
- Those in ministry
- Those who are oppressed and in need
- Special concerns

## Affirmation

Who will bring a charge against those whom God has chosen? It is God who justifies. Who is he who condemns? It is Christ Jesus who died, who was furthermore raised to life, who is at the right hand of God and is also interceding for me. (Romans 8:33–34)

An hour is coming, and now is, when the dead will hear the voice of the Son of God; and those who hear will live. For as the Father has life in Himself, so He has granted the Son to have life in Himself, and He has given Him authority to execute judgment, because He is the Son of Man. (John 5:25–27)

*Pause to reflect upon these biblical affirmations.*

## Thanksgiving

The Lord is close to the brokenhearted
And saves those who are crushed in spirit.
Many are the afflictions of the righteous,
But the Lord delivers him out of them all. (Psalm 34:18–19)

God is my refuge and strength,
An ever-present help in trouble.
Therefore I will not fear, though the earth changes
And the mountains slip into the heart of the sea. (Psalm 46:1–2)

*Pause to offer your own expressions of thanksgiving.*

## Closing Prayer

The Lord is for me; I will not fear.
What can man do to me?
It is better to take refuge in the Lord
Than to trust in man.
It is better to take refuge in the Lord
Than to trust in princes. (Psalm 118:6, 8–9)

I lift up my eyes to the hills—
Where does my help come from?
My help comes from the Lord,
Who made heaven and earth.
He will not allow my foot to slip;
He who watches over me will not slumber.
The Lord is my keeper;
The Lord is my shade at my right hand.
The sun will not harm me by day,
Nor the moon by night. (Psalm 121:1–3, 5–6)

# THE SECOND MONTH
## DAY 15

### Adoration

The works of the Lord's hands are truth and justice;
All His precepts are trustworthy.
They stand firm for ever and ever,
Done in faithfulness and uprightness.
He sent redemption to His people;
He has ordained His covenant forever;
Holy and awesome is His name. (Psalm 111:7–9)

Your name, O Lord, endures forever,
Your renown, O Lord, through all generations. (Psalm 135:13)

*Pause to express your thoughts of praise and worship.*

### Confession

No temptation has overtaken me except what is common to man. And God is faithful, who will not let me be tempted beyond what I am able, but with the temptation will also provide a way out, so that I may be able to endure it. (1 Corinthians 10:13)

*Ask the Spirit to search your heart and reveal any areas of unconfessed sin. Acknowledge these to the Lord and thank Him for His forgiveness.*

## Renewal

May I have no other gods before You. (Exodus 20:3; Deuteronomy 5:7)

May I not make for myself an idol in any form. (Exodus 20:4; Deuteronomy 5:8)

May I not take the name of the Lord my God in vain, for the Lord will not hold anyone guiltless who misuses His name. (Exodus 20:7; Deuteronomy 5:11)

*Pause to add your own prayers for personal renewal.*

## Petition

Hear, O Lord, my voice when I call;
Be merciful to me and answer me.
My heart said of You, "Seek His face!"
Your face, Lord, I will seek. (Psalm 27:7–8)

- **Relationships with Others**
    - Greater love and compassion for others
    - Loved ones
    - Those who do not know Christ
    - Those in need
- My activities for this day
- Special concerns

## Intercession

All things are for our sakes, so that the grace that is reaching more and more people may cause thanksgiving to abound to the glory of God. (2 Corinthians 4:15)

### Evangelism

- Friends
- Relatives
- Neighbors
- Coworkers
- Special opportunities

## Affirmation

Is the law opposed to the promises of God? Certainly not! For if a law had been given that could impart life, then righteousness would indeed have been by the law. But the Scripture has confined all under sin, so that the promise by faith in Jesus Christ might be given to those who believe. (Galatians 3:21–22)

In Christ I was circumcised with a circumcision made without hands, in the removal of the body of the flesh by the circumcision of Christ, having been buried with Him in baptism and raised with Him through faith in the working of God, who raised Him from the dead. (Colossians 2:11–12)

*Pause to reflect upon these biblical affirmations.*

## Thanksgiving

We give thanks to You, O God, we give thanks,
For Your name is near;
Men tell of Your wonderful works. (Psalm 75:1)

Lovingkindness and truth have met together;
Righteousness and peace have kissed each other.
Truth shall spring forth from the earth,
And righteousness looks down from heaven. (Psalm 85:10–11)

*Pause to offer your own expressions of thanksgiving.*

## Closing Prayer

O Lord, my heart is not proud, nor have my eyes been arrogant;
Neither do I concern myself with great matters
Or things too wonderful for me.
Surely I have stilled and quieted my soul;
Like a weaned child with its mother,
Like a weaned child is my soul within me. (Psalm 131:1–2)

# THE SECOND MONTH
## DAY 16

### Adoration

The Most High is sovereign over the kingdoms of men
And gives them to whomever He wishes
And sets over them the lowliest of men.
I will bless the Most High
And praise and honor Him who lives forever.
His dominion is an eternal dominion,
And His kingdom endures from generation to generation.
He regards all the inhabitants of the earth as nothing,
And does as He pleases with the host of heaven
And the inhabitants of the earth.
No one can hold back His hand
Or say to Him: "What have You done?"
I praise, exalt, and honor the King of heaven,
For all His works are true, and all His ways are just,
And He is able to humble those who walk in pride.
(Daniel 4:17, 34–35, 37)

*Pause to express your thoughts of praise and worship.*

### Confession

I will cleanse them from all their iniquity they have committed against Me, and I will pardon all their iniquities which they have committed against Me, and by which they have transgressed against Me. (Jeremiah 33:8)

*Ask the Spirit to search your heart and reveal any areas of unconfessed sin. Acknowledge these to the Lord and thank Him for His forgiveness.*

## Renewal

May I honor my father and my mother. (Exodus 20:12; Deuteronomy 5:16)

May I not murder. (Exodus 20:13; Deuteronomy 5:17)

May I not commit adultery. (Exodus 20:14; Deuteronomy 5:18)

*Pause to add your own prayers for personal renewal.*

## Petition

In You, O Lord, I have taken refuge;
Let me never be put to shame.
In Your righteousness deliver me and rescue me;
Turn Your ear to me and save me.
Be my rock of refuge, to which I can always go;
You have given the commandment to save me,
For You are my rock and my fortress. (Psalm 71:1–3)

- **Faithfulness as a Steward**
    - Of time
    - Of talents
    - Of treasure
    - Of truth
    - Of relationships

- My activities for this day
- Special concerns

## Intercession

O Lord God of Israel, You are righteous, for we are left this day as a remnant. Here we are before You in our guilt, though no one can stand in Your presence because of this. (Ezra 9:15)

## Government

- Spiritual revival
- Local government
- State government
- National government
- Current events and concerns

## Affirmation

The grace of God has appeared, bringing salvation to all men, teaching us to deny ungodliness and worldly passions and to live sensibly, righteously, and godly in the present age. (Titus 2:11–12)

Whoever would love life and see good days must keep his tongue from evil and his lips from speaking guile. He must turn from evil and do good; he must seek peace and pursue it. For the eyes of the Lord are on the righteous, and His ears attend to their prayer, but the face of the Lord is against those who do evil. (1 Peter 3:10–12)

*Pause to reflect upon these biblical affirmations.*

## Thanksgiving

I will give thanks to the Lord, for He is good;
His lovingkindness endures forever.
I will give thanks to the Lord for His unfailing love
And His wonderful acts to the children of men,
For He satisfies the thirsty soul
And fills the hungry soul with good things. (Psalm 107:1, 8–9)

*Pause to offer your own expressions of thanksgiving.*

## Closing Prayer

Thus says the Lord, my Redeemer, the Holy One of Israel:
"I am the Lord your God, who teaches you to profit,
Who leads you in the way you should go." (Isaiah 48:17)

Lord, You have said, "Come to Me, all you who labor and are heavy laden, and I will give you rest. Take My yoke upon you and learn from Me, for I am gentle and humble in heart, and you will find rest for your souls. For My yoke is easy, and My burden is light." (Matthew 11:28–30)

# THE SECOND MONTH
## DAY 17

### Adoration

Through Christ all things were made, and without Him nothing was made that has been made. In Him was life, and the life was the light of men. (John 1:3–4)

The Lord Jesus, who is holy and true, holds the key of David. What He opens no one can shut, and what He shuts no one can open. (Revelation 3:7)

*Pause to express your thoughts of praise and worship.*

### Confession

Let the wicked forsake his way
And the unrighteous man his thoughts;
Let him return to the Lord,
And He will have mercy on him,
And to our God, for He will abundantly pardon. (Isaiah 55:7)

*Ask the Spirit to search your heart and reveal any areas of unconfessed sin. Acknowledge these to the Lord and thank Him for His forgiveness.*

## Renewal

May I not steal. (Exodus 20:15; Deuteronomy 5:19)

May I not bear false witness against my neighbor. (Exodus 20:16; Deuteronomy 5:20)

May I not covet my neighbor's house, my neighbor's wife, his manservant or maidservant, his ox or donkey, or anything that belongs to my neighbor. (Exodus 20:17; Deuteronomy 5:21)

*Pause to add your own prayers for personal renewal.*

## Petition

Out of the depths I have called to You, O Lord.
O Lord, hear my voice,
And let Your ears be attentive
To the voice of my supplications. (Psalm 130:1–2)

- **Family and Ministry**
    - Family
    - Ministry
        - Sharing Christ with others
        - Helping others grow in Him
    - Career
- My activities for this day
- Special concerns

## Intercession

The Holy Spirit convicts the world concerning sin and righteousness and judgment. (John 16:8)

## Missions

- Local missions
- National missions
- World missions
- The fulfillment of the Great Commission
- Special concerns

## Affirmation

Whoever is wise and understanding will show it by his good conduct and works done in the humility that comes from wisdom. If I harbor bitter envy and selfish ambition in my heart, I should not boast and lie against the truth. This wisdom does not come down from above, but is earthly, natural, demonic. For where there is envy and selfish ambition, there is disorder and every evil practice. (James 3:13–16)

The wisdom that comes from above is first pure, then peaceable, gentle, submissive, full of mercy and good fruits, without partiality and hypocrisy. And the fruit of righteousness is sown in peace by those who make peace. (James 3:17–18)

*Pause to reflect upon these biblical affirmations.*

## Thanksgiving

The angel said to the shepherds, "Do not be afraid. I bring you good news of great joy that will be for all the people. For today in the city of David a Savior has been born to you, who is Christ the Lord." (Luke 2:10–11)

The Son of Man came to seek and to save that which was lost. (Luke 19:10)

As many as received Christ, to them He gave the right to become children of God, to those who believe in His name, who were born not of blood, nor of the will of the flesh, nor of the will of man, but of God. (John 1:12–13)

*Pause to offer your own expressions of thanksgiving.*

## Closing Prayer

If anyone wishes to come after You, he must deny himself and take up his cross and follow You. For whoever wants to save his life will lose it, but whoever loses his life for Your sake and the gospel's will find it. For what is a man profited if he gains the whole world, yet forfeits his soul? Or what will a man give in exchange for his soul? (Matthew 16:24–26; Mark 8:34–37; Luke 9:23–25)

I shall know the truth, and the truth shall set me free. Everyone who commits sin is a slave of sin. And a slave has no permanent place in the family, but a son belongs to it forever. So if the Son sets me free, I shall be free indeed. (John 8:32, 34–36)

# THE SECOND MONTH
## DAY 18

### Adoration

Praise the Lord!
Give thanks to the Lord, for He is good;
For His loving mercy endures forever.
Who can express the mighty acts of the Lord
Or fully declare His praise? (Psalm 106:1–2)

You endowed the heart with wisdom
And gave understanding to the mind. (Job 38:36)

*Pause to express your thoughts of praise and worship.*

### Confession

Search me, O God, and know my heart;
Try me and know my anxious thoughts,
And see if there is any wicked way in me,
And lead me in the way everlasting. (Psalm 139:23–24)

*Ask the Spirit to search your heart and reveal any areas of unconfessed sin. Acknowledge these to the Lord and thank Him for His forgiveness.*

## Renewal

Blessed are the poor in spirit, for theirs is the kingdom of heaven. Blessed are those who mourn, for they will be comforted. Blessed are the meek, for they will inherit the earth. Blessed are those who hunger and thirst for righteousness, for they shall be satisfied. Blessed are the merciful, for they shall obtain mercy. (Matthew 5:3–7)

*May these beatitudes become a reality in my life.*

*Pause to add your own prayers for personal renewal.*

## Petition

May I not wear myself out to get rich;
Give me the understanding to cease.
May I not set my desire on what flies away,
For wealth surely sprouts wings
And flies into the heavens like an eagle. (Proverbs 23:4–5)

- **Personal Concerns**
    - Spiritual warfare
        - The world
        - The flesh
        - The devil
    - Growth in character
    - Personal disciplines
    - Physical health and strength
- My activities for this day
- Special concerns

## Intercession

May I learn to do good,
Seek justice,
Remove the oppressor,
Defend the orphan,
And plead for the widow. (Isaiah 1:17)

## World Affairs

- The poor and hungry
- The oppressed and persecuted
- Those in authority
- Peace among nations
- Current events and concerns

## Affirmation

If anyone loves You, he will keep Your word; and Your Father will love him, and You and Your Father will come to him and make Your home with him. (John 14:23)

If anyone serves You, he must follow You; and where You are, Your servant also will be. If anyone serves You, the Father will honor him. (John 12:26)

*Pause to reflect upon these biblical affirmations.*

## Thanksgiving

Blessed is the one You choose and bring near
To live in Your courts.
We will be satisfied with the goodness of Your house,
Of Your holy temple. (Psalm 65:4)

He who dwells in the shelter of the Most High
Will rest in the shadow of the Almighty.
I will say of the Lord, "He is my refuge and my fortress,
My God, in whom I trust." (Psalm 91:1–2)

*Pause to offer your own expressions of thanksgiving.*

## Closing Prayer

May the God who gives endurance and encouragement grant us to be of the same mind toward one another according to Christ Jesus, so that with one accord and one mouth we may glorify the God and Father of our Lord Jesus Christ. (Romans 15:5–6)

May the God of peace Himself sanctify us completely, and may our whole spirit, soul, and body be preserved blameless at the coming of our Lord Jesus Christ. He who calls us is faithful, who also will do it. (1 Thessalonians 5:23–24)

# THE SECOND MONTH
## DAY 19

### Adoration

Your throne, O God, is forever and ever;
A scepter of righteousness is the scepter of Your kingdom.
You love righteousness and hate wickedness;
Therefore God, Your God, has anointed You
With the oil of gladness more than your companions.
(Psalm 45:6–7)

One generation shall praise Your works to another,
And shall declare Your mighty acts.
I will meditate on the glorious splendor of Your majesty
And on Your wonderful works.
Men shall speak of the might of Your awesome works,
And I will proclaim Your great deeds. (Psalm 145:4–6)

*Pause to express your thoughts of praise and worship.*

### Confession

Purge me with hyssop, and I will be clean;
Wash me, and I will be whiter than snow.
Cause me to hear joy and gladness,
That the bones You have crushed may rejoice.
Hide Your face from my sins
And blot out all my iniquities.

Create in me a clean heart, O God,
And renew a steadfast spirit within me.
Do not cast me from Your presence
Or take Your Holy Spirit from me.
Restore to me the joy of Your salvation
And uphold me with a willing spirit.
Then I will teach transgressors Your ways,
And sinners will be converted to You. (Psalm 51:7–13)

*Ask the Spirit to search your heart and reveal any areas of unconfessed sin. Acknowledge these to the Lord and thank Him for His forgiveness.*

## Renewal

Blessed are the pure in heart, for they shall see God. Blessed are the peacemakers, for they shall be called sons of God. Blessed are those who are persecuted for the sake of righteousness, for theirs is the kingdom of heaven. Blessed are you when people insult you, persecute you, and falsely say all kinds of evil against you because of Me. Rejoice and be glad, because great is your reward in heaven, for in the same way they persecuted the prophets who were before you. (Matthew 5:8–12)

*May these beatitudes become a reality in my life.*

*Pause to add your own prayers for personal renewal.*

Second Month, Day 19

## Petition

I called on Your name, O Lord,
From the depths of the pit.
You have heard my voice:
"Do not hide Your ear from my cry for relief,
From my cry for help."
You drew near when I called on You,
And You said, "Do not fear!"
O Lord, You pleaded the cause of my soul;
You redeemed my life. (Lamentations 3:55–58)

- **Growth in Christ**
  - Greater desire to know and please Him
  - Greater love and commitment to Him
  - Grace to practice His presence
  - Grace to glorify Him in my life
- My activities for this day
- Special concerns

## Intercession

We were all baptized by one Spirit into one body—whether Jews or Greeks, slave or free—and we were all given the one Spirit to drink. (1 Corinthians 12:13)

### Churches and Ministries

- My local church
- Other churches
- Evangelism and discipleship ministries

- Educational ministries
- Special concerns

## Affirmation

Surely Your salvation is near to those who fear You.
(Psalm 85:9)

The fear of the Lord is the beginning of knowledge,
But fools despise wisdom and discipline. (Proverbs 1:7)

The fear of the Lord is a fountain of life,
To turn one away from the snares of death. (Proverbs 14:27)

The secret of the Lord is with those who fear Him,
And He will make them know His covenant. (Psalm 25:14)

*Pause to reflect upon these biblical affirmations.*

## Thanksgiving

Surely the righteous will give thanks to Your name;
The upright will dwell in Your presence. (Psalm 140:13)

The Lord is near to all who call upon Him,
To all who call upon Him in truth.
He fulfills the desire of those who fear Him;
He hears their cry and saves them.
The Lord preserves all who love Him,
But all the wicked He will destroy. (Psalm 145:18–20)

*Pause to offer your own expressions of thanksgiving.*

## Closing Prayer

By common confession, great is the mystery of godliness:
He who was revealed in the flesh,
Vindicated in the Spirit,
Seen by angels,
Preached among the nations,
Believed on in the world,
Taken up in glory. (1 Timothy 3:16)

Daily Prayer Guide

# THE SECOND MONTH
# DAY 20

### Adoration

I will regard the Lord of hosts as holy;
He shall be my fear,
And He shall be my dread. (Isaiah 8:13)

You are the stability of our times,
A wealth of salvation, wisdom, and knowledge;
The fear of the Lord is the key to this treasure. (Isaiah 33:6)

*Pause to express your thoughts of praise and worship.*

### Confession

I will sing praises to the Lord
And give thanks at the remembrance of His holy name.
For His anger lasts only a moment,
But His favor is for a lifetime;
Weeping may endure for a night,
But joy comes in the morning. (Psalm 30:4–5)

*Ask the Spirit to search your heart and reveal any areas of unconfessed sin. Acknowledge these to the Lord and thank Him for His forgiveness.*

Second Month, Day 20

## Renewal

May I be righteous before God, walking blamelessly in all the commandments and ordinances of the Lord. (Luke 1:6)

May I love my enemies, do good to those who hate me, bless those who curse me, and pray for those who mistreat me. Just as I want others to do to me, may I do to them in the same way. (Luke 6:27–28, 31)

*Pause to add your own prayers for personal renewal.*

## Petition

I look to You for my daily bread, to forgive me my debts as I also have forgiven my debtors, and to lead me not into temptation, but to deliver me from the evil one. For Yours is the kingdom and the power and the glory forever. (Matthew 6:11–13)

- **Growth in Wisdom**
    - Developing an eternal perspective
    - Renewing my mind with truth
    - Greater skill in each area of life
- My activities for this day
- Special concerns

## Intercession

Oh, that they would always have such a heart to fear Me and keep all My commandments, so that it might be well with them and with their children forever! (Deuteronomy 5:29)

## Family

- My immediate family
- My relatives
- Spiritual concerns
- Emotional and physical concerns
- Other concerns

## Affirmation

I know that whatever God does will remain forever; nothing can be added to it and nothing taken from it. God does it so that men will revere Him. (Ecclesiastes 3:14)

God will bring every work into judgment, including every hidden thing, whether it is good or evil. (Ecclesiastes 12:14)

*Pause to reflect upon these biblical affirmations.*

## Thanksgiving

Because I love You, You will deliver me;
You will protect me, for I acknowledge Your name.
I will call upon You, and You will answer me;
You will be with me in trouble,
You will deliver me and honor me.
With long life You will satisfy me
And show me Your salvation. (Psalm 91:14–16)

*Pause to offer your own expressions of thanksgiving.*

## Closing Prayer

The word of God is living and active and sharper than any double-edged sword, piercing even to the dividing of soul and spirit and of joints and marrow, and it judges the thoughts and attitudes of the heart. And there is no creature hidden from His sight, but everything is uncovered and laid bare before the eyes of Him to whom we must give account. (Hebrews 4:12–13)

Being built up in the most holy faith and praying in the Holy Spirit, may I keep myself in the love of God as I wait for the mercy of our Lord Jesus Christ to eternal life. (Jude 20–21)

# THE SECOND MONTH
## DAY 21

### Adoration

The Lord made the earth by His power;
He established the world by His wisdom
And stretched out the heavens by His understanding.
(Jeremiah 10:12; 51:15)

The Lord gives the sun for light by day,
And decrees the moon and stars for light by night;
He stirs up the sea so that its waves roar;
The Lord of hosts is His name. (Jeremiah 31:35)

*Pause to express your thoughts of praise and worship.*

### Confession

O Lord, God of heaven, You are the great and awesome God, keeping Your covenant of loyal love with those who love You and obey Your commands. Let Your ear be attentive and Your eyes open so that You may hear the prayer Your servant is praying before You day and night. I confess the sins I have committed against You. (Nehemiah 1:5–6)

*Ask the Spirit to search your heart and reveal any areas of unconfessed sin. Acknowledge these to the Lord and thank Him for His forgiveness.*

## Renewal

Just as I presented the members of my body as slaves to impurity and to ever-increasing lawlessness, so I now present my members as slaves to righteousness, leading to holiness. (Romans 6:19)

Those who live according to the flesh set their minds on the things of the flesh; but those who live according to the Spirit set their minds on the things of the Spirit. The mind of the flesh is death, but the mind of the Spirit is life and peace. (Romans 8:5–6)

*Pause to add your own prayers for personal renewal.*

## Petition

May I watch carefully how I walk, not as the unwise but as wise, making the most of every opportunity, because the days are evil. May I not be foolish, but understand what the will of the Lord is. (Ephesians 5:15–17)

- **Spiritual Insight**
    - Understanding and insight into the Word
    - Understanding my identity in Christ
        - Who I am
        - Where I came from
        - Where I'm going
    - Understanding God's purpose for my life
- My activities for this day
- Special concerns

## Intercession

We ought always to thank God for other believers and pray that their faith would grow more and more, and that the love each of them has toward one another would increase. (2 Thessalonians 1:3)

### Believers

- Personal friends
- Those in ministry
- Those who are oppressed and in need
- Special concerns

## Affirmation

All men are like grass, and all their glory is like the flower
  of the field.
The grass withers and the flower fades,
Because the breath of the Lord blows on it.
Surely the people are grass.
The grass withers and the flower fades,
But the word of our God stands forever. (Isaiah 40:6–8)

Heaven and earth will pass away, but the words of the Lord Jesus will never pass away. (Matthew 24:35; Luke 21:33)

*Pause to reflect upon these biblical affirmations.*

## Thanksgiving

Surely God is my salvation;
I will trust and not be afraid.
For the Lord God is my strength and my song,
And He has become my salvation. (Isaiah 12:2)

I will trust in the Lord forever,
For in Yahweh, the Lord, I have an everlasting Rock.
(Isaiah 26:4)

*Pause to offer your own expressions of thanksgiving.*

## Closing Prayer

The eyes of the Lord move to and fro throughout the whole earth to strengthen those whose hearts are fully committed to Him. (2 Chronicles 16:9)

I have set the Lord always before me;
Because He is at my right hand, I will not be shaken.
Therefore my heart is glad, and my glory rejoices;
My body also will rest in hope.
You will make known to me the path of life;
In Your presence is fullness of joy;
In Your right hand are pleasures forever. (Psalm 16:8–9, 11)

Daily Prayer Guide

# THE SECOND MONTH
# DAY 22

### Adoration

O Lord, the God of our fathers, are You not the God who is in heaven? Are You not the ruler over all the kingdoms of the nations? Power and might are in Your hand, and no one is able to withstand You. (2 Chronicles 20:6)

I will praise You, O Lord, with all my heart;
I will tell of all Your wonders.
I will be glad and rejoice in You;
I will sing praise to Your name, O Most High. (Psalm 9:1–2)

*Pause to express your thoughts of praise and worship.*

### Confession

Has the Lord as much delight in burnt offerings and sacrifices
As in obeying the voice of the Lord?
To obey is better than sacrifice,
And to heed is better than the fat of rams.
For rebellion is like the sin of divination,
And stubbornness is as iniquity and idolatry. (1 Samuel 15:22–23)

*Ask the Spirit to search your heart and reveal any areas of unconfessed sin. Acknowledge these to the Lord and thank Him for His forgiveness.*

## Renewal

May I put away all bitterness and anger and wrath and shouting and slander, along with all malice. And may I be kind and compassionate to others, forgiving them just as God in Christ also forgave me. (Ephesians 4:31–32)

May I do all things without complaining or arguing, so that I may become blameless and pure, a child of God without fault in the midst of a crooked and perverse generation, among whom I shine as a light in the world, holding fast the word of life. (Philippians 2:14–16)

*Pause to add your own prayers for personal renewal.*

## Petition

As one who has been chosen of God, holy and beloved, may I put on a heart of compassion, kindness, humility, gentleness, and patience, bearing with others and forgiving others even as the Lord forgave me; and above all these things, may I put on love, which is the bond of perfection. (Colossians 3:12–14)

- **Relationships with Others**
    - Greater love and compassion for others
    - Loved ones
    - Those who do not know Christ
    - Those in need
- My activities for this day
- Special concerns

## Intercession

Do you not say, "Four months more and then comes the harvest"? Behold, I say to you, lift up your eyes and look at the fields, for they are white for harvest. Even now the reaper draws his wages, and gathers fruit for eternal life, that he who sows and he who reaps may rejoice together. (John 4:35–36)

### Evangelism

- Friends
- Relatives
- Neighbors
- Coworkers
- Special opportunities

## Affirmation

He who is faithful with very little is also faithful with much, and whoever is dishonest with very little will also be dishonest with much. If one is not faithful in handling worldly wealth, who will trust him with true riches? And if one is not faithful with someone else's property, who will give him property of his own? (Luke 16:10–12)

This is a trustworthy saying: If we died with Him, we will also live with Him; if we endure, we will also reign with Him. If we deny Him, He will also deny us; if we are faithless, He will remain faithful, for He cannot deny Himself. (2 Timothy 2:11–13)

*Pause to reflect upon these biblical affirmations.*

Second Month, Day 22

## Thanksgiving

The Lord has bared His holy arm
In the sight of all the nations,
And all the ends of the earth will see
The salvation of our God. (Isaiah 52:10)

The Lord has performed mighty deeds with His arm;
He has scattered those who are proud in the thoughts of
 their heart.
He has brought down rulers from their thrones
And has lifted up the humble. (Luke 1:51–52)

*Pause to offer your own expressions of thanksgiving.*

## Closing Prayer

God is the maker of the Bear and Orion, the Pleiades,
And the constellations of the south.
He does great things that cannot be fathomed
And wonderful works that cannot be counted. (Job 9:9–10)

When I consider Your heavens, the work of Your fingers,
The moon and the stars, which You have set in place,
What is man that You are mindful of him,
And the son of man that You care for him?
You made him a little lower than the heavenly beings
And crowned him with glory and honor.
You made him ruler over the works of Your hands,
And You put everything under his feet. (Psalm 8:3–6)

# THE SECOND MONTH
## DAY 23

### Adoration

Rejoice in the Lord, O you righteous;
Praise is becoming to the upright. (Psalm 33:1)

Walking in the way of Your laws,
O Lord, I wait for You;
Your name and Your memory are the desire of my soul.
(Isaiah 26:8)

*Pause to express your thoughts of praise and worship.*

### Confession

Woe to me, for I am undone!
Because I am a man of unclean lips,
And I live among a people of unclean lips;
For my eyes have seen the King,
The Lord of hosts. (Isaiah 6:5)

*Ask the Spirit to search your heart and reveal any areas of unconfessed sin. Acknowledge these to the Lord and thank Him for His forgiveness.*

## Renewal

If I have found grace in Your sight, teach me Your ways, so I may know You and continue to find favor with You. (Exodus 33:13)

May I consecrate myself and be holy, because You are the Lord my God. May I keep Your statutes and practice them, for You are the Lord who sanctifies me. (Leviticus 20:7–8)

*Pause to add your own prayers for personal renewal.*

## Petition

May I examine all things, hold fast to the good, and abstain from every form of evil. (1 Thessalonians 5:21–22)

- **Faithfulness as a Steward**
    - Of time
    - Of talents
    - Of treasure
    - Of truth
    - Of relationships
- My activities for this day
- Special concerns

## Intercession

O Lord, God of our fathers Abraham, Isaac, and Israel, keep this desire in the hearts of Your people forever, and keep their hearts loyal to You. (1 Chronicles 29:18)

## Government

- Spiritual revival
- Local government
- State government
- National government
- Current events and concerns

## Affirmation

Where is the wise man? Where is the scholar? Where is the disputer of this age? Has not God made foolish the wisdom of the world? But to those whom God has called, both Jews and Greeks, Christ is the power of God and the wisdom of God. (1 Corinthians 1:20, 24)

If anyone thinks he is something when he is nothing, he deceives himself. (Galatians 6:3)

Let him who boasts, boast in the Lord. (1 Corinthians 1:31)

*Pause to reflect upon these biblical affirmations.*

## Thanksgiving

Concerning the lost, Jesus said, "What man among you, if he has a hundred sheep and loses one of them, does not leave the ninety-nine in the open country and go after the one that is lost until he finds it? And when he finds it, he lays it on his shoulders, rejoicing. And when he comes into his house, he calls his friends and neighbors together and says to them,

'Rejoice with me, for I have found my sheep which was lost!' I tell you that in the same way there will be more joy in heaven over one sinner who repents than over ninety-nine righteous persons who need no repentance. There is joy in the presence of the angels of God over one sinner who repents." (Luke 15:4–7, 10)

*Pause to offer your own expressions of thanksgiving.*

## Closing Prayer

Now I know that the Lord saves His anointed;
He answers him from His holy heaven
With the saving strength of His right hand.
Some trust in chariots and some in horses,
But I will remember the name of the Lord my God.
(Psalm 20:6–7)

Love the Lord, all you His saints!
The Lord preserves the faithful,
And fully repays the proud doer.
Be of good courage and He will strengthen your heart,
All you who hope in the Lord. (Psalm 31:23–24)

## THE SECOND MONTH
# DAY 24

### Adoration

"My thoughts are not your thoughts,
Neither are your ways My ways," declares the Lord.
"As the heavens are higher than the earth,
So are My ways higher than your ways,
And My thoughts than your thoughts." (Isaiah 55:8–9)

You are the Lord, the God of all mankind. Nothing is too difficult for You. (Jeremiah 32:27)

*Pause to express your thoughts of praise and worship.*

### Confession

The heart is deceitful above all things
And incurably sick.
Who can understand it?
You, the Lord, search the heart
And test the mind
To reward a man according to his ways,
According to the fruit of his deeds. (Jeremiah 17:9–10)

*Ask the Spirit to search your heart and reveal any areas of unconfessed sin. Acknowledge these to the Lord and thank Him for His forgiveness.*

Second Month, Day 24

## Renewal

May I not profane Your holy name, but acknowledge You as holy before others. You are the Lord, who sanctifies me. (Leviticus 22:32)

The Lord my God, the Lord is one. May I love the Lord my God with all my heart and with all my soul and with all my strength. (Deuteronomy 6:4–5)

*Pause to add your own prayers for personal renewal.*

## Petition

May I fight the good fight, finish the race, and keep the faith, so that there will be laid up for me the crown of righteousness, which the Lord, the righteous Judge, will award to me on that day; and not only to me, but also to all who have longed for His appearing. (2 Timothy 4:7–8)

- **Family and Ministry**
    - Family
    - Ministry
        - Sharing Christ with others
        - Helping others grow in Him
    - Career
- My activities for this day
- Special concerns

## Intercession

The Lord told the apostles, "You will receive power when the Holy Spirit comes upon you; and you will be My witnesses in Jerusalem, and in all Judea and Samaria, and to the ends of the earth." (Acts 1:8)

### Missions

- Local missions
- National missions
- World missions
- The fulfillment of the Great Commission
- Special concerns

## Affirmation

Whoever is wise understands these things;
Whoever is discerning knows them.
The ways of the Lord are right;
The righteous will walk in them,
But transgressors will stumble in them. (Hosea 14:9)

You have called the humble of the earth who have upheld Your justice to seek the Lord, to seek righteousness, and to seek humility. (Zephaniah 2:3)

*Pause to reflect upon these biblical affirmations.*

## Thanksgiving

God sent His word to the children of Israel, telling the good news of peace through Jesus Christ, who is Lord of all. He commanded the apostles to preach to the people and to testify that He is the One whom God appointed as judge of the living and the dead. To Him all the prophets witness that through His name, everyone who believes in Him receives forgiveness of sins. (Acts 10:36, 42–43)

I have been loved by God and called to be a saint; grace and peace have been given to me from God our Father and the Lord Jesus Christ. (Romans 1:7)

*Pause to offer your own expressions of thanksgiving.*

## Closing Prayer

Why are you downcast, O my soul?
Why are you disturbed within me?
Hope in God, for I will yet praise Him
For the help of His presence.
O my God, my soul is downcast within me;
Therefore I will remember You.
Why are you downcast, O my soul?
Why are you disturbed within me?
Hope in God, for I will yet praise Him,
The help of my countenance and my God. (Psalm 42:5–6, 11)

Daily Prayer Guide

# THE SECOND MONTH
# DAY 25

## Adoration

As I looked, thrones were set in place,
And the Ancient of Days took His seat.
His clothing was as white as snow,
And the hair of His head was like pure wool.
His throne was ablaze with flames,
And its wheels were a burning fire.
A river of fire was flowing
And coming out from before Him.
A thousand thousands attended Him;
Ten thousand times ten thousand stood before Him.
The court was seated,
And the books were opened. (Daniel 7:9–10)

O Lord, God of Israel, enthroned between the cherubim, You alone are God over all the kingdoms of the earth. You have made heaven and earth. (2 Kings 19:15)

*Pause to express your thoughts of praise and worship.*

## Confession

"Even now," declares the Lord,
"Return to Me with all your heart,
With fasting and weeping and mourning.
So rend your heart and not your garments."

Second Month, Day 25

Return to the Lord your God,
For He is gracious and compassionate,
Slow to anger and abounding in lovingkindness,
And He relents from sending calamity. (Joel 2:12–13)

*Ask the Spirit to search your heart and reveal any areas of unconfessed sin. Acknowledge these to the Lord and thank Him for His forgiveness.*

## Renewal

May I preserve sound wisdom and discretion,
Not letting them out of my sight;
They will be life to my soul. (Proverbs 3:21–22)

May I not let Your word depart from my mouth, but meditate on it day and night, so that I may be careful to do according to all that is written in it; for then I will make my way prosperous, and I will act wisely. (Joshua 1:8)

*Pause to add your own prayers for personal renewal.*

## Petition

By God's grace I want to live to the end in faith, knowing that I will not receive the promises on earth, but seeing them and welcoming them from a distance, I confess that I am a stranger and a pilgrim on the earth. Instead, I long for a better country, a heavenly one. In this way, God will not be ashamed to be called my God, for He has prepared a city for me. Like Moses, may I esteem reproach for the sake of Christ as of greater value than the treasures of this world, because I am looking to the reward. (Hebrews 11:13, 16, 26)

- **Personal Concerns**
    - Spiritual warfare
        - The world
        - The flesh
        - The devil
    - Growth in character
    - Personal disciplines
    - Physical health and strength
- My activities for this day
- Special concerns

## Intercession

Hear from heaven, Your dwelling place, and forgive and deal with each man according to all he does, since You know his heart (for You alone know the hearts of men). (2 Chronicles 6:30)

## World Affairs

- The poor and hungry
- The oppressed and persecuted
- Those in authority
- Peace among nations
- Current events and concerns

Second Month, Day 25

## Affirmation

From the rising to the setting of the sun, Your name will be great among the nations. In every place incense and pure offerings will be brought to Your name, for Your name will be great among the nations. (Malachi 1:11)

All authority in heaven and on earth has been given to the Son of God. (Matthew 28:18)

Jesus Christ is coming with the clouds, and every eye will see Him, even those who pierced Him; and all the peoples of the earth will mourn because of Him. Even so, Amen. (Revelation 1:7)

*Pause to reflect upon these biblical affirmations.*

## Thanksgiving

The salvation of the righteous comes from the Lord;
He is their stronghold in time of trouble.
The Lord helps them and delivers them;
He delivers them from the wicked and saves them,
Because they take refuge in Him. (Psalm 37:39–40)

*Pause to offer your own expressions of thanksgiving.*

## Closing Prayer

Be exalted, O God, above the heavens;
Let Your glory be over all the earth.
I will praise You, O Lord, among the peoples;
I will sing to You among the nations.
For Your mercy reaches to the heavens,
And Your faithfulness reaches to the clouds.
Be exalted, O God, above the heavens;
Let Your glory be above all the earth. (Psalm 57:5, 9–11)

# THE SECOND MONTH
## DAY 26

### Adoration

Behold, He who forms the mountains and creates the wind,
And reveals His thoughts to man,
He who turns dawn to darkness,
And treads the high places of the earth—
The Lord God of hosts is His name. (Amos 4:13)

In Your majesty, You dwell in the likeness of a throne of sapphire above the expanse that is over the cherubim. (Ezekiel 10:1)

*Pause to express your thoughts of praise and worship.*

### Confession

Our fathers disciplined us for a little while as they thought best, but God disciplines us for our good, that we may share in His holiness. No discipline seems pleasant at the time, but painful; later on, however, it produces the peaceable fruit of righteousness for those who have been trained by it. Therefore, let us strengthen the hands that are weary and the feeble knees, and make straight paths for our feet, so that what is lame may not be disabled, but rather healed. (Hebrews 12:10–13)

*Ask the Spirit to search your heart and reveal any areas of unconfessed sin. Acknowledge these to the Lord and thank Him for His forgiveness.*

## Renewal

May I not be afraid of those who kill the body and after that can do no more. But I will fear the One who, after killing, has authority to cast into hell. (Luke 12:4–5)

May I fear only the Lord my God and serve Him and take my oaths in His name. (Deuteronomy 6:13)

May I be very careful to love the Lord my God, to walk in all His ways, to obey His commands, to hold fast to Him, and to serve Him with all my heart and all my soul. (Joshua 22:5)

*Pause to add your own prayers for personal renewal.*

## Petition

May I submit myself for the Lord's sake to every human authority, whether to a king as being supreme, or to governors as sent by him to punish evildoers and to praise those who do right; for it is the will of God that by doing good I may silence the ignorance of foolish men. (1 Peter 2:13–15)

- **Growth in Christ**
  - Greater desire to know and please Him
  - Greater love and commitment to Him
  - Grace to practice His presence
  - Grace to glorify Him in my life
- My activities for this day
- Special concerns

Second Month, Day 26

## Intercession

We should not get drunk on wine, for that is dissipation. Instead, we should be filled with the Spirit, speaking to one another with psalms, hymns, and spiritual songs; singing and making music in our hearts to the Lord, always giving thanks to God the Father for everything, in the name of our Lord Jesus Christ. (Ephesians 5:18–20)

### Churches and Ministries

- My local church
- Other churches
- Evangelism and discipleship ministries
- Educational ministries
- Special concerns

## Affirmation

Lord Jesus, You have said that unless I am converted and become like a little child, I will never enter the kingdom of heaven. Therefore, whoever humbles himself like a child is the greatest in the kingdom of heaven. (Matthew 18:3–4)

You did not want the little children to be hindered from coming to You, for of such is the kingdom of heaven. (Matthew 19:14)

*Pause to reflect upon these biblical affirmations.*

## Thanksgiving

Blessed be the Lord; day by day He bears our burdens,
The God of our salvation.
Our God is the God of salvation,
And to God the Lord belongs escape from death.
(Psalm 68:19–20)

It is good to give thanks to the Lord
And to sing praises to Your name, O Most High,
To declare Your lovingkindness in the morning
And Your faithfulness at night. (Psalm 92:1–2)

*Pause to offer your own expressions of thanksgiving.*

## Closing Prayer

When I remember You on my bed,
I meditate on You through the watches of the night.
Because You have been my help,
I will rejoice in the shadow of Your wings.
My soul clings to You;
Your right hand upholds me. (Psalm 63:6–8)

# THE SECOND MONTH
## DAY 27

### Adoration

Heaven is Your throne,
And the earth is Your footstool.
Your hand made all these things,
And so they came into being. (Isaiah 66:1–2a)

Your hand laid the foundations of the earth,
And Your right hand spread out the heavens;
When You summon them, they all stand up together.
(Isaiah 48:13)

*Pause to express your thoughts of praise and worship.*

### Confession

Surely You desire truth in the inner parts,
And in the hidden part You make me know wisdom.
(Psalm 51:6)

*Ask the Spirit to search your heart and reveal any areas of unconfessed sin. Acknowledge these to the Lord and thank Him for His forgiveness.*

## Renewal

Like Josiah, may I do what is right in the sight of the Lord and walk in all the ways of David, not turning aside to the right or to the left. May I turn to the Lord with all my heart and with all my soul and with all my might, in accordance with all of Your Word. (2 Kings 22:1–2; 23:25)

These are the things I want to do: speak the truth to others, judge with truth and justice for peace, not plot evil against my neighbor, and not love a false oath; for all these things the Lord hates. (Zechariah 8:16–17)

*Pause to add your own prayers for personal renewal.*

## Petition

May I not be afraid of my adversaries, but remember the Lord, who is great and awesome. (Nehemiah 4:14)

- **Growth in Wisdom**
    - Developing an eternal perspective
    - Renewing my mind with truth
    - Greater skill in each area of life
- My activities for this day
- Special concerns

## Intercession

May I do nothing out of selfish ambition or vain conceit, but in humility may I esteem others as more important than myself. Let me look not only to my own interests, but also to the interests of others. (Philippians 2:3–4)

**Family**

- My immediate family
- My relatives
- Spiritual concerns
- Emotional and physical concerns
- Other concerns

## Affirmation

Jesus will be great and will be called the Son of the Most High. The Lord God will give Him the throne of His father David, and He will reign over the house of Jacob forever, and His kingdom will never end. (Luke 1:32–33)

The heavens will vanish like smoke;
The earth will wear out like a garment,
And its inhabitants will die in the same way.
But Your salvation will last forever,
And Your righteousness will never fail. (Isaiah 51:6)

God was pleased to have all His fullness dwell in Christ and through Him to reconcile all things to Himself, whether things on earth or things in heaven, having made peace through the blood of His cross. (Colossians 1:19–20)

*Pause to reflect upon these biblical affirmations.*

## Thanksgiving

Let those who love the Lord hate evil.
He preserves the souls of His saints
And delivers them from the hand of the wicked.
Light is sown for the righteous
And gladness for the upright in heart. (Psalm 97:10–11)

*Pause to offer your own expressions of thanksgiving.*

## Closing Prayer

The Lord has established His throne in heaven,
And His kingdom rules over all.
Bless the Lord, you His angels,
Mighty in strength who do His bidding,
Obeying the voice of His word.
Bless the Lord, all His hosts,
You His servants who do His will.
Bless the Lord, all His works,
In all places of His dominion.
Bless the Lord, O my soul. (Psalm 103:19–22)

# THE SECOND MONTH
# **DAY 28**

## Adoration

Blessed be the God and Father of our Lord Jesus Christ, who has blessed us with every spiritual blessing in the heavenly realms in Christ. (Ephesians 1:3)

Our Lord Jesus Christ gave Himself for our sins to rescue us from the present evil age, according to the will of our God and Father, to whom be glory for ever and ever. (Galatians 1:3–5)

*Pause to express your thoughts of praise and worship.*

## Confession

Blessed is he whose transgression is forgiven,
Whose sin is covered.
Blessed is the man to whom the Lord does not impute iniquity
And in whose spirit is no deceit.
When I kept silent, my bones wasted away
Through my groaning all day long.
For day and night Your hand was heavy upon me;
My strength was sapped as in the heat of summer.
I acknowledged my sin to You
And did not hide my iniquity.
I said, "I will confess my transgressions to the Lord,"
And You forgave the guilt of my sin. (Psalm 32:1–5)

*Ask the Spirit to search your heart and reveal any areas of unconfessed sin. Acknowledge these to the Lord and thank Him for His forgiveness.*

## Renewal

May I take heed not to practice my righteousness before men to be seen by them. Otherwise, I will have no reward from my Father in heaven. (Matthew 6:1)

May I not fear those who kill the body but cannot kill the soul, but rather, may I fear the One who is able to destroy both soul and body in hell. (Matthew 10:28)

*Pause to add your own prayers for personal renewal.*

## Petition

In You, O Lord, I have taken refuge;
Let me never be ashamed;
Deliver me in Your righteousness.
Since You are my rock and my fortress,
For Your name's sake lead me and guide me.
Into Your hands I commit my spirit;
Redeem me, O Lord, God of truth. (Psalm 31:1, 3, 5)

- **Spiritual Insight**
    - Understanding and insight into the Word
    - Understanding my identity in Christ
        - Who I am
        - Where I came from
        - Where I'm going

- Understanding God's purpose for my life
- My activities for this day
- Special concerns

## Intercession

You have given us a new commandment to love one another even as You have loved us; so we must love one another. By this all men will know that we are Your disciples, if we have love for one another. (John 13:34)

### Believers

- Personal friends
- Those in ministry
- Those who are oppressed and in need
- Special concerns

## Affirmation

Multitudes who sleep in the dust of the earth will awake, some to everlasting life, others to shame and everlasting contempt. Those who are wise will shine like the brightness of the heavens, and those who lead many to righteousness like the stars for ever and ever. (Daniel 12:2–3)

An hour is coming when all who are in the graves will hear the voice of the Son of Man, and will come out—those who have done good to a resurrection of life, and those who have done evil to a resurrection of judgment. (John 5:28–29)

In the resurrection of the dead, the body that is sown is perishable, but it is raised imperishable; it is sown in dishonor, but it is raised in glory; it is sown in weakness, but it is raised in power; it is sown a natural body, but it is raised a spiritual body. If there is a natural body, there is also a spiritual body. (1 Corinthians 15:42–44)

*Pause to reflect upon these biblical affirmations.*

## Thanksgiving

Oh give thanks to the Lord, call upon His name;
Make His deeds known among the nations.
Sing to Him, sing praises to Him;
Tell of all His wonders.
Glory in His holy name;
Let the hearts of those who seek the Lord rejoice.
(Psalm 105:1–3)

*Pause to offer your own expressions of thanksgiving.*

## Closing Prayer

The Lord gives wisdom;
From His mouth come knowledge and understanding.
He stores up sound wisdom for the upright;
He is a shield to those who walk in integrity,
Guarding the paths of justice
And protecting the way of His saints. (Proverbs 2:6–8)

# THE SECOND MONTH
## **DAY 29**

### Adoration

How lovely are Your dwellings,
O Lord of hosts!
My soul longs and even faints for the courts of the Lord;
My heart and my flesh cry out for the living God.
(Psalm 84:1–2)

Your righteousness, O God, reaches to the heavens,
You who have done great things.
O God, who is like You? (Psalm 71:19)

*Pause to express your thoughts of praise and worship.*

### Confession

Does God not see my ways
And count all my steps? (Job 31:4)

*Ask the Spirit to search your heart and reveal any areas of unconfessed sin. Acknowledge these to the Lord and thank Him for His forgiveness.*

## Renewal

The hour has come for me to wake up from sleep, for my salvation is nearer now than when I first believed. The night is nearly over; the day is almost here. Therefore may I cast off the works of darkness and put on the armor of light. (Romans 13:11–12)

Though I walk in the flesh, I do not war according to the flesh. The weapons of my warfare are not fleshly, but divinely powerful to overthrow strongholds, casting down arguments and every pretension that sets itself up against the knowledge of God, and taking every thought captive to the obedience of Christ. (2 Corinthians 10:3–5)

*Pause to add your own prayers for personal renewal.*

## Petition

Just as I received Christ Jesus the Lord, so let me walk in Him, rooted and built up in Him, and established in the faith, as I was taught, and abounding in thanksgiving. (Colossians 2:6–7)

- **Relationships with Others**
    - Greater love and compassion for others
    - Loved ones
    - Those who do not know Christ
    - Those in need
- My activities for this day
- Special concerns

## Intercession

All things are from God, who reconciled us to Himself through Christ and gave us the ministry of reconciliation: namely, that God was reconciling the world to Himself in Christ, not counting their trespasses against them. And He has committed to us the message of reconciliation. Therefore, we are ambassadors for Christ, as though God were appealing through us, as we implore others on Christ's behalf to be reconciled to God. (2 Corinthians 5:18–20)

### Evangelism

- Friends
- Relatives
- Neighbors
- Coworkers
- Special opportunities

## Affirmation

The Lord is the Spirit, and where the Spirit of the Lord is, there is freedom. (2 Corinthians 3:17)

Christ is not weak in dealing with us, but is powerful among us. For though He was crucified in weakness, yet He lives by the power of God. For we are weak in Him, yet by the power of God we will live with Him to serve others. (2 Corinthians 13:3–4)

*Pause to reflect upon these biblical affirmations.*

Daily Prayer Guide

## Thanksgiving

Praise the Lord!
I will thank the Lord with all my heart
In the council of the upright and in the assembly.
Great are the works of the Lord;
They are pondered by all who delight in them.
Splendid and majestic is His work,
And His righteousness endures forever.
He has caused His wonderful acts to be remembered;
The Lord is gracious and compassionate. (Psalm 111:1–4)

*Pause to offer your own expressions of thanksgiving.*

## Closing Prayer

To us a child is born, to us a son is given,
And the government will be on His shoulders.
And he will be called Wonderful Counselor, Mighty God,
Everlasting Father, Prince of Peace.
Of the increase of His government and peace
There will be no end.
He will reign on the throne of David and over His kingdom,
Establishing and upholding it with justice and righteousness
From that time on and forever.
The zeal of the Lord of hosts will accomplish this. (Isaiah 9:6–7)

# THE SECOND MONTH
# **DAY 30**

## Adoration

You are my shield, my very great reward. (Genesis 15:1)

As for God, His way is perfect;
The word of the Lord is proven.
He is a shield to all who take refuge in Him.
For who is God besides the Lord?
And who is the Rock except our God? (Psalm 18:30–31)

*Pause to express your thoughts of praise and worship.*

## Confession

Remember, O Lord, Your compassions and Your mercies,
For they are from of old.
Do not remember the sins of my youth or my transgressions;
According to Your loyal love remember me,
For Your goodness' sake, O Lord. (Psalm 25:6–7)

*Ask the Spirit to search your heart and reveal any areas of unconfessed sin. Acknowledge these to the Lord and thank Him for His forgiveness.*

## Renewal

I do not want even a hint of immorality, or any impurity, or greed in my life, as is proper for a saint. Nor will I give myself to obscenity, foolish talk, or coarse joking, which are not fitting, but rather to giving of thanks. (Ephesians 5:3–4)

Whatever is true, whatever is noble, whatever is right, whatever is pure, whatever is lovely, whatever is of good report—if anything is excellent or praiseworthy—may I think about such things. The things I have learned and received and heard and seen in those who walk with Christ I will practice, and the God of peace will be with me. (Philippians 4:8–9)

*Pause to add your own prayers for personal renewal.*

## Petition

Answer me, O Lord, for Your lovingkindness is good;
In the abundance of Your mercies, turn to me. (Psalm 69:16)

- **Faithfulness as a Steward**
    - Of time
    - Of talents
    - Of treasure
    - Of truth
    - Of relationships
- My activities for this day
- Special concerns

## Intercession

The God of Israel spoke,
The Rock of Israel said to me:
"He who rules over men in righteousness,
Who rules in the fear of God,
Is like the light of morning when the sun rises,
A morning without clouds,
Like the tender grass springing out of the earth
Through the sunshine after rain." (2 Samuel 23:3–4)

## Government

- Spiritual revival
- Local government
- State government
- National government
- Current events and concerns

## Affirmation

Those who belong to Christ Jesus have crucified the flesh with its passions and desires. (Galatians 5:24)

I have put off the old self with its practices and have put on the new self, who is being renewed in full knowledge according to the image of its Creator. (Colossians 3:9–10)

I know that I abide in Christ, and He in me, because He has given me of His Spirit. (1 John 4:13)

*Pause to reflect upon these biblical affirmations.*

## Thanksgiving

I love the Lord, because He has heard
My voice and my supplications.
Because He turned His ear to me,
I will call on Him as long as I live. (Psalm 116:1–2)

I will give thanks to the God of heaven,
For His merciful love endures forever. (Psalm 136:26)

*Pause to offer your own expressions of thanksgiving.*

## Closing Prayer

Behold, the Lord God will come with power,
And His arm will rule for Him.
Behold, His reward is with Him,
And His recompense accompanies Him.
He will feed His flock like a shepherd;
He will gather the lambs in His arms
And carry them close to His heart;
He will gently lead those that have young. (Isaiah 40:10–11)

The Lord's lovingkindness is great toward us,
And the truth of the Lord endures forever.
Praise the Lord! (Psalm 117:2)

# THE SECOND MONTH
## **DAY 31**

### Adoration

Who gave God authority over the earth?
Who put Him in charge of the whole world?
If He set His heart on it and withdrew His spirit and
  His breath,
All flesh would perish together
And man would return to dust. (Job 34:13–15)

Every animal of the forest is Yours,
And the cattle on a thousand hills.
You know every bird in the mountains,
And everything that moves in the field is Yours.
(Psalm 50:10–11)

*Pause to express your thoughts of praise and worship.*

### Confession

All a man's ways are right in his own eyes,
But the Lord weighs the hearts. (Proverbs 21:2)

*Ask the Spirit to search your heart and reveal any areas of unconfessed sin. Acknowledge these to the Lord and thank Him for His forgiveness.*

## Renewal

May I be holy to You, for You the Lord are holy, and You have set me apart to be Your own. (Leviticus 20:26)

May I learn to fear You all the days I live on the earth and teach Your words to my children. (Deuteronomy 4:10)

May I be careful not to forget the Lord my God by failing to observe Your commandments, Your ordinances and Your statutes. (Deuteronomy 8:11)

*Pause to add your own prayers for personal renewal.*

## Petition

I have sought You with my whole heart;
Do not let me stray from Your commands. (Psalm 119:10)

- **Family and Ministry**
  - Family
  - Ministry
    - Sharing Christ with others
    - Helping others grow in Him
  - Career
- My activities for this day
- Special concerns

## Intercession

You have called us to go and make disciples of all nations, baptizing them in the name of the Father and of the Son and of the Holy Spirit, teaching them to observe everything You have commanded us. And surely You are with us always, even to the end of the age. (Matthew 28:19–20)

### Missions

- Local missions
- National missions
- World missions
- The fulfillment of the Great Commission
- Special concerns

## Affirmation

When I seek the Lord my God, I will find Him if I seek Him with all my heart and with all my soul. (Deuteronomy 4:29)

Thus says the Lord who made the earth, the Lord who formed it to establish it—the Lord is His name: "Call to Me, and I will answer you and tell you great and unsearchable things you do not know." (Jeremiah 33:2–3)

The hand of our God is favorable to everyone who looks to Him, but His power and His anger are against all who forsake Him. (Ezra 8:22)

*Pause to reflect upon these biblical affirmations.*

## Thanksgiving

You are my God, and I will give thanks to You;
You are my God, and I will exalt You.
I will give thanks to the Lord, for He is good;
His loyal love endures forever. (Psalm 118:28–29)

*Pause to offer your own expressions of thanksgiving.*

## Closing Prayer

As for me, I will always have hope,
And I will praise You more and more.
My mouth will tell of Your righteousness
And of Your salvation all day long,
Though I know not its measure.
I will come in the strength of the Lord God;
I will proclaim Your righteousness, Yours alone.
Since my youth, O God, You have taught me,
And to this day I declare Your wondrous deeds.
(Psalm 71:14–17)

I will both lie down in peace and sleep,
For You alone, O Lord, make me dwell in safety. (Psalm 4:8)

# The Third Month

# THE THIRD MONTH
## DAY 1

### Adoration

I will bless the Lord at all times;
His praise will always be in my mouth.
My soul will make its boast in the Lord;
The humble will hear and be glad.
O magnify the Lord with me,
And let us exalt His name together. (Psalm 34:1–3)

The Lord is my stronghold,
And my God is a rock of refuge to me. (Psalm 94:22)

*Pause to express your thoughts of praise and worship.*

### Confession

"Come now, let us reason together,"
Says the Lord.
"Though your sins are like scarlet,
They shall be as white as snow;
Though they are red as crimson,
They shall be like wool." (Isaiah 1:18)

*Ask the Spirit to search your heart and reveal any areas of unconfessed sin. Acknowledge these to the Lord and thank Him for His forgiveness.*

## Renewal

May I be strong in the Lord and in His mighty power as I put on the full armor of God, so that I will be able to stand against the schemes of the devil. (Ephesians 6:10–11)

Since I belong to the day, may I be self-controlled, putting on the breastplate of faith and love, and the hope of salvation as a helmet. (1 Thessalonians 5:8)

*Pause to add your own prayers for personal renewal.*

## Petition

O Lord, I cry to You; hasten to me.
Hear my voice when I cry to You.
Let my prayer be set before You like incense,
And the lifting up of my hands like the evening sacrifice. (Psalm 141:1–2)

- **Personal Concerns**
    - Spiritual warfare
        - The world
        - The flesh
        - The devil
    - Growth in character
    - Personal disciplines
    - Physical health and strength
- My activities for this day
- Special concerns

Third Month, Day 1

## Intercession

Restore us again, O God of our salvation,
And put away Your anger toward us.
Will You be angry with us forever?
Will You prolong Your anger to all generations?
Will You not revive us again,
That Your people may rejoice in You?
Show us Your lovingkindness, O Lord,
And grant us Your salvation. (Psalm 85:4–7)

## World Affairs

- The poor and hungry
- The oppressed and persecuted
- Those in authority
- Peace among nations
- Current events and concerns

## Affirmation

The Lord Himself goes before me and will be with me; He will never leave me nor forsake me. I will not be afraid or be dismayed. (Deuteronomy 31:8)

The Lord will guard the feet of His saints,
But the wicked will be silenced in darkness.
It is not by strength that one prevails;
Those who contend with the Lord will be shattered.
He will thunder against them from heaven;
The Lord will judge the ends of the earth.

He will give strength to His king
And exalt the horn of His anointed. (1 Samuel 2:9–10)

*Pause to reflect upon these biblical affirmations.*

## Thanksgiving

In the day that You created man, You made him in Your likeness. You created them male and female and blessed them and called their name Man in the day they were created. (Genesis 5:1–2)

It is God the Lord
Who created the heavens and stretched them out,
Who spread out the earth and all that comes out of it,
Who gives breath to its people,
And spirit to those who walk on it. (Isaiah 42:5)

*Pause to offer your own expressions of thanksgiving.*

## Closing Prayer

I rejoice at Your word
As one who finds great spoil.
I hate and abhor falsehood,
But I love Your law.
Great peace have they who love Your law,
And nothing causes them to stumble.
O Lord, I hope for Your salvation,
And I follow Your commands.

My soul keeps Your testimonies,
For I love them greatly.
I keep Your precepts and Your testimonies,
For all my ways are known to You.
(Psalm 119:162–163, 165–168)

Daily Prayer Guide

# THE THIRD MONTH
# DAY 2

### Adoration

Like the roar of rushing waters and like loud peals of thunder, a great multitude will shout, "Hallelujah! For the Lord God Almighty reigns. Let us rejoice and be glad and give Him glory! For the marriage of the Lamb has come, and His bride has made herself ready." Blessed are those who are invited to the marriage supper of the Lamb. (Revelation 19:6–7, 9)

Lord Jesus, You are the Root and the Offspring of David, the bright Morning Star. (Revelation 22:16)

*Pause to express your thoughts of praise and worship.*

### Confession

Come, let us return to the Lord.
For He has torn us, but He will heal us;
He has injured us but He will bind up our wounds.
After two days He will revive us;
On the third day He will raise us up,
That we may live before Him. (Hosea 6:1–2)

*Ask the Spirit to search your heart and reveal any areas of unconfessed sin. Acknowledge these to the Lord and thank Him for His forgiveness.*

## Renewal

May I rejoice always, pray without ceasing, and give thanks in all circumstances, for this is God's will for me in Christ Jesus. (1 Thessalonians 5:16–18)

I want to know Christ and the power of His resurrection and the fellowship of His sufferings, being conformed to His death, that I may attain to the resurrection from the dead. (Philippians 3:10–11)

*Pause to add your own prayers for personal renewal.*

## Petition

Hear my cry, O God,
And listen to my prayer.
From the ends of the earth I call to You
When my heart grows faint;
Lead me to the rock that is higher than I.
You have been a shelter for me
And a strong tower against the enemy.
I will dwell in Your tent forever
And take refuge in the shelter of Your wings. (Psalm 61:1–4)

- **Growth in Christ**
    - Greater desire to know and please Him
    - Greater love and commitment to Him
    - Grace to practice His presence
    - Grace to glorify Him in my life
- My activities for this day
- Special concerns

## Intercession

There is one body and one Spirit, just as we were called in one hope of our calling; one Lord, one faith, one baptism, one God and Father of all, who is over all and through all and in all. (Ephesians 4:4–6)

### Churches and Ministries

- My local church
- Other churches
- Evangelism and discipleship ministries
- Educational ministries
- Special concerns

## Affirmation

He who is the Glory of Israel does not lie or change His mind, for He is not a man, that He should change His mind. (1 Samuel 15:29)

The counsel of the Lord stands firm forever,
The plans of His heart through all generations. (Psalm 33:11)

The Lord is not slow concerning His promise, as some count slowness, but is patient with us, not wanting anyone to perish, but for all to come to repentance. (2 Peter 3:9)

*Pause to reflect upon these biblical affirmations.*

## Thanksgiving

The Lord your God is a merciful God; He will not forsake you nor destroy you nor forget the covenant with your forefathers, which He swore to them. (Deuteronomy 4:31)

You, O Lord, are a shield around me;
You bestow glory on me and lift up my head. (Psalm 3:3)

*Pause to offer your own expressions of thanksgiving.*

## Closing Prayer

By this the love of God was manifested to us, that God has sent His only begotten Son into the world that we might live through Him. In this is love, not that we loved God, but that He loved us and sent His Son to be the propitiation for our sins. (1 John 4:9–10)

Love is patient, love is kind, it does not envy; love does not boast, it is not arrogant, it does not behave rudely; it does not seek its own, it is not provoked, it keeps no record of wrongs; it does not rejoice in unrighteousness but rejoices with the truth; it bears all things, believes all things, hopes all things, endures all things. Love never fails. (1 Corinthians 13:4–8)

# THE THIRD MONTH
## DAY 3

### Adoration

I will praise You with uprightness of heart
As I learn Your righteous judgments. (Psalm 119:7)

I know that the Lord is great,
And that our Lord is above all gods.
Whatever the Lord pleases He does,
In the heavens and on the earth,
In the seas and all their depths. (Psalm 135:5–6)

*Pause to express your thoughts of praise and worship.*

### Confession

If I say that I have fellowship with God and yet walk in the darkness, I lie and do not practice the truth. But if I walk in the light, as He is in the light, we have fellowship with one another, and the blood of Jesus His Son purifies me from all sin. (1 John 1:6–7)

*Ask the Spirit to search your heart and reveal any areas of unconfessed sin. Acknowledge these to the Lord and thank Him for His forgiveness.*

## Renewal

May I be a doer of the word and not merely a hearer who deceives himself. For if anyone is a hearer of the word and not a doer, he is like a man who looks at his natural face in a mirror, and after looking at himself, goes away, and immediately forgets what kind of person he was. But the one who looks intently into the perfect law of freedom and continues in it and is not a forgetful hearer but a doer of the word, this one will be blessed in what he does. (James 1:22–25)

In obedience to the truth may I purify my soul for a sincere love of the brethren, and love others fervently from the heart. (1 Peter 1:22)

*Pause to add your own prayers for personal renewal.*

## Petition

May I not say when I am tempted, "I am being tempted by God"; for God cannot be tempted by evil, nor does He tempt anyone. But each one is tempted when he is drawn away and enticed by his own lust. Then, after lust has conceived, it gives birth to sin; and sin, when it is full-grown, gives birth to death. (James 1:13–15)

- **Growth in Wisdom**
    - Developing an eternal perspective
    - Renewing my mind with truth
    - Greater skill in each area of life
- My activities for this day
- Special concerns

## Intercession

Far be it from me that I should sin against the Lord by ceasing to pray for others. (1 Samuel 12:23)

### Family

- My immediate family
- My relatives
- Spiritual concerns
- Emotional and physical concerns
- Other concerns

## Affirmation

It is for my good that You returned to the Father, because You have sent the Counselor, the Holy Spirit, to me. (John 16:7)

Jesus told His disciples, "The Spirit will glorify Me by taking from what is Mine and making it known to you. All that belongs to the Father is Mine. Therefore I said that He will take from what is Mine and make it known to you." (John 16:14–15)

*Pause to reflect upon these biblical affirmations.*

## Thanksgiving

I trust in Your loyal love;
My heart rejoices in Your salvation.
I will sing to the Lord,
For He has dealt bountifully with me. (Psalm 13:5–6)

Third Month, Day 3

Blessed be the Lord,
For He has heard the voice of my prayers.
The Lord is my strength and my shield;
My heart trusts in Him, and I am helped.
My heart greatly rejoices,
And I will give thanks to Him in song. (Psalm 28:6–7)

*Pause to offer your own expressions of thanksgiving.*

## Closing Prayer

You are worthy, our Lord and God,
To receive glory and honor and power,
For You created all things,
And by Your will they were created and have their being. (Revelation 4:11)

Every creature in heaven and on earth and under the earth and on the sea and all that is in them, will sing:

> "To Him who sits on the throne and to the Lamb
> Be blessing and honor and glory and power
> For ever and ever!" (Revelation 5:13)

# THE THIRD MONTH
## DAY 4

### Adoration

The Lord stretches out the heavens, lays the foundation of the earth, and forms the spirit of man within him. (Zechariah 12:1)

You are the Lord, the God of the spirits of all flesh. (Numbers 27:16)

Nothing is too difficult for the Lord. (Genesis 18:14)

*Pause to express your thoughts of praise and worship.*

### Confession

Death and Destruction lie open before the Lord;
How much more the hearts of men! (Proverbs 15:11)

*Ask the Spirit to search your heart and reveal any areas of unconfessed sin. Acknowledge these to the Lord and thank Him for His forgiveness.*

### Renewal

May I observe all Your statutes and all Your judgments and follow them; You are the Lord. (Leviticus 19:37)

May I not show partiality in judgment, but hear both small and great alike. May I not be afraid of any man, for judgment belongs to God. (Deuteronomy 1:17)

*Pause to add your own prayers for personal renewal.*

## Petition

No one who waits for You will be ashamed,
But those who are treacherous without cause will be ashamed.
Show me Your ways, O Lord,
Teach me Your paths;
Lead me in Your truth and teach me,
For You are the God of my salvation,
And my hope is in You all day long. (Psalm 25:3–5)

- **Spiritual Insight**
    - Understanding and insight into the Word
    - Understanding my identity in Christ
        - Who I am
        - Where I came from
        - Where I'm going
    - Understanding God's purpose for my life
- My activities for this day
- Special concerns

## Intercession

God's servants have commended themselves in every way: in great endurance, in afflictions, in needs, in distresses, in beatings, in imprisonments, in tumults, in labors, in sleeplessness, in hunger, in purity, in knowledge, in patience, in kindness, in the Holy Spirit, in sincere love, in the word of truth, in the power of God—through the weapons of righteousness in the right hand and in the left, through glory and dishonor, through bad report and good report—as deceivers, and yet true; as unknown, and yet well known; as dying, and yet living; as beaten, and yet not killed; as sorrowful, yet always rejoicing; as poor, yet making many rich; as having nothing, and yet possessing everything. (2 Corinthians 6:4–10)

## Believers

- Personal friends
- Those in ministry
- Those who are oppressed and in need
- Special concerns

## Affirmation

O Lord, what is man that You know him,
Or the son of man that You think of him?
Man is like a breath;
His days are like a passing shadow. (Psalm 144:3–4)

Whoever seeks to keep his life will lose it, and whoever loses his life will preserve it. (Luke 17:33)

Here I do not have an enduring city, but I am seeking the city that is to come. (Hebrews 13:14)

*Pause to reflect upon these biblical affirmations.*

Third Month, Day 4

## Thanksgiving

I will declare Your name to my brothers;
In the midst of the congregation I will praise You.
You who fear the Lord, praise Him!
All you descendants of Jacob, glorify Him!
Stand in awe of Him, all you descendants of Israel!
For He has not despised or disdained the suffering of the afflicted one;
Nor has He hidden His face from him,
But has listened to his cry for help. (Psalm 22:22–24)

*Pause to offer your own expressions of thanksgiving.*

## Closing Prayer

The Lord will be gracious to whom He will be gracious, and He will have compassion on whom He will have compassion. (Exodus 33:19)

You, Lord God, are compassionate and gracious, slow to anger, and abounding in lovingkindness and truth, maintaining love to thousands, and forgiving iniquity, transgression, and sin. (Exodus 34:6–7)

# THE THIRD MONTH
## DAY 5

### Adoration

Where does wisdom come from?
Where does understanding dwell?
It is hidden from the eyes of every living thing
And concealed from the birds of the air.
Destruction and Death say,
"Only a rumor of it has reached our ears."
God understands its way,
And He knows its place.
For He looks to the ends of the earth
And sees everything under the heavens. (Job 28:20–24)

Men fear You,
For You do not regard any who are wise of heart. (Job 37:24)

*Pause to express your thoughts of praise and worship.*

### Confession

O God, You know my foolishness,
And my guilt is not hidden from You.
May those who hope in You not be ashamed because of me,
   O Lord God of hosts;
May those who seek You not be dishonored because of me,
   O God of Israel. (Psalm 69:5–6)

Third Month, Day 5

*Ask the Spirit to search your heart and reveal any areas of unconfessed sin. Acknowledge these to the Lord and thank Him for His forgiveness.*

## Renewal

Solomon said to God, "Give me wisdom and knowledge, that I may lead this people, for who is able to judge this great people of Yours?" God said to Solomon, "Because this was in your heart and you have not asked for riches, wealth, or honor, nor for the life of your enemies, and since you have not asked for a long life but for wisdom and knowledge to judge My people over whom I have made you king, wisdom and knowledge will be given you. And I will also give you riches and wealth and honor, such as no king who was before you ever had and none after you will have." (2 Chronicles 1:10–12)

May I not be worried and troubled about many things; only one thing is needed. Like Mary, may I choose the good part, which will not be taken away from me. (Luke 10:41–42)

*Pause to add your own prayers for personal renewal.*

## Petition

May everything I do be done in love. (1 Corinthians 16:14)

- **Relationships with Others**
    - Greater love and compassion for others
    - Loved ones
    - Those who do not know Christ
    - Those in need
- My activities for this day
- Special concerns

## Intercession

I pray that words may be given to me, that I may open my mouth boldly to make known the mystery of the gospel. (Ephesians 6:19)

### Evangelism

- Friends
- Relatives
- Neighbors
- Coworkers
- Special opportunities

## Affirmation

The mouth of the righteous speaks wisdom,
And his tongue speaks what is just.
The law of his God is in his heart;
His steps do not slide. (Psalm 37:30–31)

Everyone should be quick to hear, slow to speak, and slow to anger, for the anger of man does not produce the righteousness of God. (James 1:19–20)

*Pause to reflect upon these biblical affirmations.*

## Thanksgiving

The heavens declare the glory of God,
And the skies proclaim the work of His hands.
Day after day they pour forth speech;
Night after night they reveal knowledge. (Psalm 19:1–2)

I will exalt You, O Lord, for You lifted me up
And did not let my enemies rejoice over me.
O Lord my God,
I cried to You for help and You healed me. (Psalm 30:1–2)

*Pause to offer your own expressions of thanksgiving.*

## Closing Prayer

As for God, His way is perfect;
The word of the Lord is proven.
He is a shield for all who take refuge in Him.
For who is God besides the Lord?
And who is the Rock except our God? (2 Samuel 22:31–32)

Daily Prayer Guide

# THE THIRD MONTH
# DAY 6

## Adoration

You have chosen me as Your witness and servant so that I may know and believe You and understand that You are the Lord. Before You no god was formed, nor will there be one after You. (Isaiah 43:10)

Thus says the Lord, the King of Israel
And his Redeemer, the Lord of hosts:
I am the first and I am the last;
Apart from Me there is no God. (Isaiah 44:6)

*Pause to express your thoughts of praise and worship.*

## Confession

Can a mortal be more righteous than God?
Can a man be more pure than his Maker? (Job 4:17)

*Ask the Spirit to search your heart and reveal any areas of unconfessed sin. Acknowledge these to the Lord and thank Him for His forgiveness.*

## Renewal

When I have done all the things which are commanded me, let me realize that I am an unworthy servant; I have only done what I ought to have done. (Luke 17:10)

May I do the work of Him who sent me while it is day; night is coming, when no one can work. (John 9:4)

*Pause to add your own prayers for personal renewal.*

## Petition

May I be a person who fears God, loves truth, and hates dishonest gain. (Exodus 18:21)

- **Faithfulness as a Steward**
    - Of time
    - Of talents
    - Of treasure
    - Of truth
    - Of relationships
- My activities for this day
- Special concerns

## Intercession

Righteousness exalts a nation,
But sin is a disgrace to any people. (Proverbs 14:34)

Daily Prayer Guide

## Government

- Spiritual revival
- Local government
- State government
- National government
- Current events and concerns

## Affirmation

You save the humble
But bring low those whose eyes are haughty. (Psalm 18:27)

Pride breeds nothing but strife,
But wisdom is found in those who take advice. (Proverbs 13:10)

When pride comes, then comes dishonor,
But with humility comes wisdom. (Proverbs 11:2)

The proud looks of man will be humbled,
And the loftiness of men brought low;
The Lord alone will be exalted. (Isaiah 2:11)

*Pause to reflect upon these biblical affirmations.*

## Thanksgiving

How great is Your goodness,
Which You have stored up for those who fear You,
Which You have prepared for those who take refuge in You
Before the sons of men! (Psalm 31:19)

Surely God is my helper;
The Lord is the sustainer of my soul. (Psalm 54:4)

*Pause to offer your own expressions of thanksgiving.*

## Closing Prayer

God is my strong fortress,
And He sets the blameless free in His way.
He makes my feet like the feet of a deer;
He enables me to stand on the heights.
He trains my hands for battle,
So that my arms can bend a bow of bronze.
You give me Your shield of salvation;
You stoop down to make me great.
You broaden the path beneath me,
And my feet have not slipped.
(2 Samuel 22:33–37; Psalm 18:33–36)

The Lord lives! Blessed be my Rock!
Exalted be God, the Rock of my salvation!
(2 Samuel 22:47; Psalm 18:46)

Daily Prayer Guide

# THE THIRD MONTH
## DAY 7

### Adoration

We see Jesus, who was made a little lower than the angels, now crowned with glory and honor because He suffered death, that by the grace of God He might taste death for everyone. For it was fitting for Him, for whom are all things and through whom are all things, in bringing many sons to glory, to make the author of their salvation perfect through sufferings. (Hebrews 2:9–10)

You are the King of kings and Lord of lords. (Revelation 19:16)

*Pause to express your thoughts of praise and worship.*

### Confession

I know in my heart that as a man disciplines his son, so the Lord my God disciplines me. (Deuteronomy 8:5)

*Ask the Spirit to search your heart and reveal any areas of unconfessed sin. Acknowledge these to the Lord and thank Him for His forgiveness.*

### Renewal

May I not receive God's grace in vain. For He says, "In the acceptable time I heard you, and in the day of salvation I helped you." Now is the time of God's favor; now is the day of salvation. (2 Corinthians 6:1–2)

May the Lord establish my heart as blameless and holy before our God and Father at the coming of our Lord Jesus with all His saints. (1 Thessalonians 3:13)

*Pause to add your own prayers for personal renewal.*

## Petition

May I obey those who are in authority over me in all things, not with external service as a pleaser of men, but with sincerity of heart, fearing the Lord. Whatever I do, may I work at it with all my heart, as to the Lord and not to men, knowing that I will receive the reward of the inheritance from the Lord. It is the Lord Christ I am serving. (Colossians 3:22–24)

- **Family and Ministry**
    - Family
    - Ministry
        - Sharing Christ with others
        - Helping others grow in Him
    - Career
- My activities for this day
- Special concerns

## Intercession

In the past God overlooked the times of ignorance, but now He commands all people everywhere to repent. For He has set a day when He will judge the world with justice by the Man He has appointed. He has given assurance of this to all men by raising Him from the dead. (Acts 17:30–31)

## Missions

- Local missions
- National missions
- World missions
- The fulfillment of the Great Commission
- Special concerns

## Affirmation

Only in the Lord are righteousness and strength. (Isaiah 45:24)

God, who made the world and everything in it, since He is Lord of heaven and earth, does not dwell in temples built by hands. And He is not served by human hands, as though He needed anything, since He Himself gives all men life and breath and everything else. (Acts 17:24–25)

*Pause to reflect upon these biblical affirmations.*

## Thanksgiving

I will sing of Your strength,
Yes, I will sing of Your mercy in the morning,
For You have been my stronghold,
My refuge in times of trouble.

To You, O my Strength, I will sing praises,
For God is my fortress, my loving God. (Psalm 59:16–17)

*Pause to offer your own expressions of thanksgiving.*

## Closing Prayer

I would have lost heart unless I had believed
That I would see the goodness of the Lord
In the land of the living.
I will hope in the Lord and be of good courage,
And He will strengthen my heart;
Yes, I will hope in the Lord. (Psalm 27:13–14)

My soul waits in hope for the Lord;
He is my help and my shield.
My heart rejoices in Him,
Because I trust in His holy name.
Let Your unfailing love be upon us, O Lord,
Even as we put our hope in You. (Psalm 33:20–22)

Daily Prayer Guide

# THE THIRD MONTH
# DAY 8

## Adoration

The Lord of hosts will be exalted in judgment,
And the holy God will show Himself holy in righteousness.
(Isaiah 5:16)

The Lord longs to be gracious and rises to show compassion.
For the Lord is a God of justice;
Blessed are all those who wait for Him! (Isaiah 30:18)

*Pause to express your thoughts of praise and worship.*

## Confession

There are six things the Lord hates,
Seven that are detestable to Him:
Haughty eyes, a lying tongue,
Hands that shed innocent blood,
A heart that devises wicked plans,
Feet that run swiftly to evil,
A false witness who breathes lies,
And one who causes strife among brothers. (Proverbs 6:16–19)

*Ask the Spirit to search your heart and reveal any areas of unconfessed sin. Acknowledge these to the Lord and thank Him for His forgiveness.*

Third Month, Day 8

## Renewal

I greatly rejoice in my salvation, though now for a little while, if necessary, I have been grieved by various trials, so that the proving of my faith, being much more precious than gold that perishes, even though refined by fire, may be found to result in praise, glory, and honor at the revelation of Jesus Christ. (1 Peter 1:6–7)

Since the day of the Lord will come like a thief, what kind of person should I be in holy conduct and godliness as I look for and hasten the coming of the day of God? But according to His promise, I am looking for new heavens and a new earth, in which righteousness dwells. Therefore, since I am looking for these things, may I be diligent to be found by Him in peace, spotless and blameless. (2 Peter 3:10–14)

*Pause to add your own prayers for personal renewal.*

## Petition

The sons of this world are more shrewd in dealing with their own kind than are the sons of light. May I use worldly wealth to make friends for myself, so that when it is gone, they may welcome me into the eternal dwellings. (Luke 16:8–9)

- **Personal Concerns**
    - Spiritual warfare
        - The world
        - The flesh
        - The devil

- Growth in character
    - Personal disciplines
    - Physical health and strength
- My activities for this day
- Special concerns

## Intercession

The end of all things is near; therefore we should be clear minded and self-controlled for prayer. (1 Peter 4:7)

### World Affairs

- The poor and hungry
- The oppressed and persecuted
- Those in authority
- Peace among nations
- Current events and concerns

## Affirmation

Far be it from You to kill the righteous with the wicked, treating the righteous and the wicked alike. Far be it from You! Will not the Judge of all the earth do right? (Genesis 18:25)

Your eyes are too pure to look at evil;
You cannot look on wickedness. (Habakkuk 1:13)

By the word of God the heavens existed long ago and the earth was formed out of water and by water. By these waters also the world of that time was deluged and destroyed. By the same word the present heavens and earth are reserved for fire, being kept for the day of judgment and destruction of ungodly men. (2 Peter 3:5–7)

*Pause to reflect upon these biblical affirmations.*

## Thanksgiving

I am continually with You;
You hold me by my right hand.
You guide me with Your counsel,
And afterward You will take me to glory. (Psalm 73:23–24)

*Pause to offer your own expressions of thanksgiving.*

## Closing Prayer

I will be still and know that You are God;
You will be exalted among the nations,
You will be exalted in the earth. (Psalm 46:10)

Blessed be the Lord, the God of Israel,
From everlasting to everlasting.
Amen and Amen. (Psalm 41:13)

Daily Prayer Guide

# THE THIRD MONTH
# DAY 9

### Adoration

The Lord my God is a consuming fire, a jealous God. (Deuteronomy 4:24)

The Lord is seated on His throne with all the host of heaven standing by Him on His right and on His left. (1 Kings 22:19)

The heavens and the highest heavens cannot contain the Lord. (2 Chronicles 2:6; 6:18)

*Pause to express your thoughts of praise and worship.*

### Confession

This is what the Lord God, the Holy One of Israel, says:
"In repentance and rest is your salvation;
In quietness and trust is your strength." (Isaiah 30:15)

*Ask the Spirit to search your heart and reveal any areas of unconfessed sin. Acknowledge these to the Lord and thank Him for His forgiveness.*

Third Month, Day 9

## Renewal

Like Asa, may I do what is good and right in the sight of the Lord my God. (2 Chronicles 14:2)

Like Jehoshaphat, let my heart take delight in the ways of the Lord and remove the places of idolatry from my life. (2 Chronicles 17:6)

*Pause to add your own prayers for personal renewal.*

## Petition

May I put away perversity from my mouth
And keep corrupt talk far from my lips. (Proverbs 4:24)

- **Growth in Christ**
  - Greater desire to know and please Him
  - Greater love and commitment to Him
  - Grace to practice His presence
  - Grace to glorify Him in my life
- My activities for this day
- Special concerns

## Intercession

As living stones, we are being built into a spiritual house to be a holy priesthood, offering spiritual sacrifices acceptable to God through Jesus Christ. We are a chosen people, a royal priesthood, a holy nation, a people for God's own possession, that we may declare the praises of Him who called us out of darkness into His marvelous light. (1 Peter 2:5, 9)

## Churches and Ministries

- My local church
- Other churches
- Evangelism and discipleship ministries
- Educational ministries
- Special concerns

## Affirmation

How shall we escape if we ignore God's great salvation? This salvation, which was first announced by the Lord, was confirmed by those who heard Him. God also bore witness to it by signs and wonders and various miracles and gifts of the Holy Spirit distributed according to His will. (Hebrews 2:3–4)

The faith of those chosen of God and the knowledge of the truth, which is according to godliness, is a faith and knowledge resting in the hope of eternal life, which God, who does not lie, promised before the beginning of time. At the appointed time, He manifested His word through the preaching entrusted to the apostles by the command of God our Savior. (Titus 1:1–3)

*Pause to reflect upon these biblical affirmations.*

## Thanksgiving

I will give thanks to the Lord, for He is good;
His lovingkindness endures forever. (Psalm 118:1)

Your word is settled in heaven
Forever, O Lord.
Your faithfulness continues through all generations;
You established the earth, and it stands.
They continue to this day according to Your ordinances,
For all things serve You. (Psalm 119:89–91)

*Pause to offer your own expressions of thanksgiving.*

## Closing Prayer

My soul silently waits for God alone;
My salvation comes from Him.
He alone is my rock and my salvation;
He is my stronghold; I will never be shaken. (Psalm 62:1–2)

Blessed be the Lord, the God of Israel,
From everlasting to everlasting.
Praise the Lord. (Psalm 106:48)

# THE THIRD MONTH
# DAY 10

## Adoration

My soul will rejoice in the Lord
And delight in His salvation. (Psalm 35:9)

O God, You are my God;
Earnestly I seek You;
My soul thirsts for You;
My body longs for You,
In a dry and weary land
Where there is no water. (Psalm 63:1)

*Pause to express your thoughts of praise and worship.*

## Confession

Who is a God like You, who pardons iniquity
And passes over the transgression of the remnant of His
    inheritance?
You do not stay angry forever
But delight to show mercy.
You will have compassion on Your people;
You will tread their iniquities underfoot
And hurl all their sins into the depths of the sea. (Micah 7:18–19)

Third Month, Day 10

*Ask the Spirit to search your heart and reveal any areas of unconfessed sin. Acknowledge these to the Lord and thank Him for His forgiveness.*

## Renewal

May I beware and be on my guard against all covetousness, for my life does not consist in the abundance of my possessions. (Luke 12:15)

May I keep my life free from the love of money and be content with what I have, for You have said, "I will never leave you, nor will I forsake you." (Hebrews 13:5)

*Pause to add your own prayers for personal renewal.*

## Petition

My eyes are upon You, O God the Lord;
In You I take refuge; You will not leave my soul destitute. (Psalm 141:8)

- **Growth in Wisdom**
    - Developing an eternal perspective
    - Renewing my mind with truth
    - Greater skill in each area of life
- My activities for this day
- Special concerns

Handbook to Prayer

## Intercession

May God grant you, according to the riches of His glory, to be strengthened with power through His Spirit in your inner being, so that Christ may dwell in your hearts through faith. And may you, being rooted and grounded in love, be able to comprehend with all the saints what is the width and length and height and depth of the love of Christ, and to know this love that surpasses knowledge, that you may be filled to all the fullness of God. (Ephesians 3:16–19)

### Family

- My immediate family
- My relatives
- Spiritual concerns
- Emotional and physical concerns
- Other concerns

## Affirmation

Faith is the reality of things hoped for and the conviction of things not seen. (Hebrews 11:1)

Without faith it is impossible to please God, for he who comes to Him must believe that He exists, and that He is a rewarder of those who earnestly seek Him. (Hebrews 11:6)

*Pause to reflect upon these biblical affirmations.*

Third Month, Day 10

## Thanksgiving

Even to my old age, You are the same,
And even to my gray hairs You will carry me.
You have made me, and You will bear me;
You will sustain me and You will deliver me. (Isaiah 46:4)

I will watch in hope for the Lord;
I will wait for the God of my salvation;
My God will hear me. (Micah 7:7)

*Pause to offer your own expressions of thanksgiving.*

## Closing Prayer

Ah, Lord God! You have made the heavens and the earth by Your great power and outstretched arm. Nothing is too difficult for You. You are the great and mighty God, whose name is the Lord of hosts. You are great in counsel and mighty in deed, and Your eyes are open to all the ways of the sons of men; You reward everyone according to his ways and according to the fruit of his deeds. (Jeremiah 32:17–19)

I delight to do Your will, O my God,
And Your law is within my heart. (Psalm 40:8)

# THE THIRD MONTH
## DAY 11

### Adoration

Make a joyful shout to God, all the earth!
Sing the glory of His name;
Make His praise glorious.
Say to God, "How awesome are Your works!
Through the greatness of Your power
Your enemies submit themselves to You.
All the earth will worship You
And sing praises to You;
They will sing praise to Your name." (Psalm 66:1–4)

My mouth is filled with Your praise,
And with Your glory all day long. (Psalm 71:8)

*Pause to express your thoughts of praise and worship.*

### Confession

Before his downfall the heart of a man is haughty,
But humility comes before honor. (Proverbs 18:12)

*Ask the Spirit to search your heart and reveal any areas of unconfessed sin. Acknowledge these to the Lord and thank Him for His forgiveness.*

## Renewal

May I not turn my heart away from the Lord, the God of Israel, but keep what the Lord has commanded. (1 Kings 11:9–10)

Like Hezekiah, may I do what is good and right and true before the Lord my God by seeking Him with all my heart. (2 Chronicles 31:20–21)

*Pause to add your own prayers for personal renewal.*

## Petition

Preserve me, O God, for I take refuge in You.
I said to the Lord, "You are my Lord;
I have no goodness apart from You." (Psalm 16:1–2)

- **Spiritual Insight**
    - Understanding and insight into the Word
    - Understanding my identity in Christ
        - Who I am
        - Where I came from
        - Where I'm going
    - Understanding God's purpose for my life
- My activities for this day
- Special concerns

## Intercession

We must all attain to unity of the faith and of the knowledge of the Son of God to a mature man, to the measure of the stature of the fullness of Christ, so that we will no longer be infants, being blown and carried around by every wind of doctrine, by the cunning and craftiness of men in their deceitful scheming; but speaking the truth in love, we must grow up in all things into Him who is the Head, that is, Christ. (Ephesians 4:13–15)

**Believers**

- Personal friends
- Those in ministry
- Those who are oppressed and in need
- Special concerns

## Affirmation

I have come to Mount Zion, to the heavenly Jerusalem, the city of the living God, to myriads of angels, and to the assembly and church of the firstborn, who are enrolled in heaven. I have come to God, the Judge of all men, to the spirits of righteous men made perfect, to Jesus the mediator of a new covenant, and to the sprinkled blood that speaks better things than the blood of Abel. (Hebrews 12:22–24)

He who overcomes will be clothed in white garments, and You will not blot out his name from the book of life, but You will confess his name before Your Father and before His angels. (Revelation 3:5)

*Pause to reflect upon these biblical affirmations.*

## Thanksgiving

God set forth Christ to be a propitiation through faith in His blood. He did this to demonstrate His righteousness, because in His forbearance He passed over the sins committed beforehand; He did it to demonstrate His righteousness at the present time, that He might be just and the justifier of those who have faith in Jesus. Where, then, is boasting? It is excluded. By what law? Of works? No, but by a law of faith. For we maintain that a man is justified by faith apart from works of the law. (Romans 3:25–28)

Having been justified by faith, I have peace with God through the Lord Jesus Christ, through whom I have gained access by faith into this grace in which I stand; and I rejoice in the hope of the glory of God. (Romans 5:1–2)

*Pause to offer your own expressions of thanksgiving.*

## Closing Prayer

Your word is a lamp to my feet
And a light to my path.
I have inclined my heart to perform Your statutes
To the very end. (Psalm 119:105, 112)

## THE THIRD MONTH
## DAY 12

### Adoration

I will exalt the Lord my God and worship Him,
For the Lord God is holy. (Psalm 99:9)

I have tasted and seen that the Lord is good;
Blessed is the man who takes refuge in Him!
O fear the Lord, you His saints,
For those who fear Him lack nothing. (Psalm 34:8–9)

*Pause to express your thoughts of praise and worship.*

### Confession

My little children, I write these things to you that you may not sin. But if anyone sins, we have an Advocate with the Father, Jesus Christ, the Righteous. And He is the propitiation for our sins, and not for ours only but also for the whole world. (1 John 2:1–2)

*Ask the Spirit to search your heart and reveal any areas of unconfessed sin. Acknowledge these to the Lord and thank Him for His forgiveness.*

## Renewal

May I not let my heart be troubled; let me trust in God and trust also in Christ. (John 14:1)

As the Father has loved You, You also have loved me. May I abide in Your love. If I keep Your commandments, I will abide in Your love, just as You kept Your Father's commandments and abide in His love. You have told me this so that Your joy may be in me and that my joy may be full. (John 15:9–11)

May I never boast except in the cross of our Lord Jesus Christ, through which the world has been crucified to me, and I to the world. (Galatians 6:14)

*Pause to add your own prayers for personal renewal.*

## Petition

May I walk in wisdom toward outsiders, making the most of every opportunity. My speech should always be with grace, seasoned with salt, so that I may know how to answer each person. (Colossians 4:5–6)

- **Relationships with Others**
    - Greater love and compassion for others
    - Loved ones
    - Those who do not know Christ
    - Those in need
- My activities for this day
- Special concerns

## Intercession

I pray that God may open to me a door for the word, so that I may speak the mystery of Christ and proclaim it clearly, as I ought to speak. (Colossians 4:3–4)

### Evangelism

- Friends
- Relatives
- Neighbors
- Coworkers
- Special opportunities

## Affirmation

Blessed is the man who makes the Lord his trust,
Who does not look to the proud or those who turn aside to lies.
(Psalm 40:4)

I will call upon You and come and pray to You, and You will listen to me. I will seek You and find You when I search for You with all my heart. (Jeremiah 29:12–13)

*Pause to reflect upon these biblical affirmations.*

## Thanksgiving

If I have been united with Christ in the likeness of His death, I will certainly also be united with Him in the likeness of His resurrection. (Romans 6:5)

Third Month, Day 12

I thank God because of His grace in Christ Jesus. In Him we have been enriched in every way, in all speech and in all knowledge. We do not lack any spiritual gift, as we eagerly wait for the revelation of our Lord Jesus Christ. (1 Corinthians 1:4–5, 7)

*Pause to offer your own expressions of thanksgiving.*

## Closing Prayer

Lord Jesus, You are the stone which was rejected by the builders, but which has become the chief cornerstone. Salvation is found in no one else, for there is no other name under heaven given to men by which we must be saved. (Acts 4:11–12)

I believe that Jesus is the Christ, the Son of God, and by believing, I have life in His name. (John 20:31)

Daily Prayer Guide

# THE THIRD MONTH
# DAY 13

## Adoration

The Lord executes righteousness
And justice for all who are oppressed.
The Lord is compassionate and gracious,
Slow to anger, and abounding in lovingkindness.
(Psalm 103:6, 8)

Righteousness and justice are the foundation of Your throne;
Lovingkindness and truth go before You. (Psalm 89:14)

*Pause to express your thoughts of praise and worship.*

## Confession

What can I say to You? What can I speak? How can I justify myself? You have uncovered the iniquity of Your servant. (Genesis 44:16)

*Ask the Spirit to search your heart and reveal any areas of unconfessed sin. Acknowledge these to the Lord and thank Him for His forgiveness.*

Third Month, Day 13

## Renewal

May I walk properly as in the daytime, not in revellings and drunkenness, not in promiscuity and debauchery, not in strife and jealousy. Rather, may I put on the Lord Jesus Christ and make no provision to gratify the lusts of the flesh. (Romans 13:13–14)

Since I have God's promises, may I cleanse myself from all pollution of body and spirit, perfecting holiness in the fear of God. (2 Corinthians 7:1)

*Pause to add your own prayers for personal renewal.*

## Petition

We are all sons of the light and sons of the day. We do not belong to the night or to the darkness. So then, let us not be like others who are asleep, but let us be alert and self-controlled. (1 Thessalonians 5:5–6)

- **Faithfulness as a Steward**
  - Of time
  - Of talents
  - Of treasure
  - Of truth
  - Of relationships
- My activities for this day
- Special concerns

## Intercession

Trust in the Lord your God and you will be established; believe in His prophets and you will prosper. (2 Chronicles 20:20)

### Government

- Spiritual revival
- Local government
- State government
- National government
- Current events and concerns

## Affirmation

The Son of Man is going to come in the glory of His Father with His angels, and then He will reward each person according to his works. (Matthew 16:27)

If anyone is ashamed of You and Your words in this adulterous and sinful generation, the Son of Man will be ashamed of him when He comes in the glory of His Father with the holy angels. (Mark 8:38; Luke 9:26)

Blessed are the dead who die in the Lord from now on. They will rest from their labor, for their works will follow them. (Revelation 14:13)

*Pause to reflect upon these biblical affirmations.*

## Thanksgiving

I was washed, I was sanctified, I was justified in the name of the Lord Jesus Christ and by the Spirit of our God. (1 Corinthians 6:11)

Thanks be to God, who gives us the victory through our Lord Jesus Christ. Therefore let us be steadfast, immovable, abounding in the work of the Lord, knowing that our labor in the Lord is not in vain. (1 Corinthians 15:57–58)

*Pause to offer your own expressions of thanksgiving.*

## Closing Prayer

God, who said, "Let light shine out of darkness," made His light shine in my heart to give me the light of the knowledge of the glory of God in the face of Christ. But I have this treasure in an earthen vessel to show that this all-surpassing power is from God and not from me. (2 Corinthians 4:6–7)

Your grace is sufficient for me, for Your power is made perfect in weakness. Therefore, I will boast all the more gladly in my weaknesses, that the power of Christ may rest upon me. Therefore, I can be content in weaknesses, in insults, in hardships, in persecutions, in difficulties, for Christ's sake. For when I am weak, then I am strong. (2 Corinthians 12:9–10)

Daily Prayer Guide

# THE THIRD MONTH
# DAY 14

## Adoration

Your lovingkindness, O Lord, reaches to the heavens,
Your faithfulness to the skies.
Your righteousness is like the mountains of God;
Your judgments are like a great deep.
O Lord, You preserve man and beast.
How priceless is Your lovingkindness, O God!
The children of men find refuge in the shadow of Your wings.
For with You is the fountain of life;
In Your light we see light. (Psalm 36:5–7, 9)

I will praise the name of God in song
And magnify Him with thanksgiving. (Psalm 69:30)

*Pause to express your thoughts of praise and worship.*

## Confession

All the paths of the Lord are mercy and truth
For those who keep His covenant and His testimonies.
For Your name's sake, O Lord,
Pardon my iniquity, for it is great. (Psalm 25:10–11)

*Ask the Spirit to search your heart and reveal any areas of unconfessed sin. Acknowledge these to the Lord and thank Him for His forgiveness.*

## Renewal

My struggle is not against flesh and blood, but against the rulers, against the authorities, against the world rulers of this darkness, against the spiritual forces of evil in the heavenly realms. Therefore, I will put on the full armor of God, so that I may be able to resist in the day of evil, and having done all, to stand. (Ephesians 6:12–13)

Since I have been raised with Christ, I should seek the things above, where Christ is seated at the right hand of God. May I set my mind on the things above, not on the things on the earth, for I died, and my life is now hidden with Christ in God. When Christ who is my life appears, then I also will appear with Him in glory. (Colossians 3:1–4)

*Pause to add your own prayers for personal renewal.*

## Petition

In my distress may I seek the favor of the Lord my God, and humble myself greatly before the God of my fathers, for I know that the Lord is God. (2 Chronicles 33:12–13)

- **Family and Ministry**
    - Family
    - Ministry
        - Sharing Christ with others
        - Helping others grow in Him
    - Career
- My activities for this day
- Special concerns

Daily Prayer Guide

## Intercession

Jesus said, "As the Father has sent Me, I also send you." (John 20:21)

### Missions

- Local missions
- National missions
- World missions
- The fulfillment of the Great Commission
- Special concerns

## Affirmation

In his heart a man plans his way,
But the Lord determines his steps. (Proverbs 16:9)

Many are the plans in a man's heart,
But it is the counsel of the Lord that will stand. (Proverbs 19:21)

There is no wisdom or understanding
Or counsel that can succeed against the Lord. (Proverbs 21:30)

The word that goes forth from Your mouth
Will not return to You empty
But will accomplish what You desire
And achieve the purpose for which You sent it. (Isaiah 55:11)

*Pause to reflect upon these biblical affirmations.*

Third Month, Day 14

## Thanksgiving

He who makes me stand firm in Christ and anointed me is God, who also sealed me and gave me the Spirit in my heart as a deposit. (2 Corinthians 1:21–22)

Thanks be to God, who always leads us in triumph in Christ and through us spreads everywhere the fragrance of the knowledge of Him. (2 Corinthians 2:14)

*Pause to offer your own expressions of thanksgiving.*

## Closing Prayer

Through the law I died to the law so that I might live for God. I have been crucified with Christ; and it is no longer I who live, but Christ lives in me; and the life which I now live in the flesh, I live by faith in the Son of God, who loved me and gave Himself for me. (Galatians 2:19–20)

To me, to live is Christ and to die is gain. (Philippians 1:21)

Daily Prayer Guide

# THE THIRD MONTH
# DAY 15

## Adoration

The Lord is upright;
He is my Rock, and there is no unrighteousness in Him.
(Psalm 92:15)

I will seek the Lord and His strength;
I will seek His face continually.
I will remember the wonders He has done,
His miracles, and the judgments of His mouth. (Psalm 105:4–5)

*Pause to express your thoughts of praise and worship.*

## Confession

Pride goes before destruction,
And a haughty spirit before a fall. (Proverbs 16:18)

*Ask the Spirit to search your heart and reveal any areas of unconfessed sin. Acknowledge these to the Lord and thank Him for His forgiveness.*

## Renewal

When Uzziah became strong, his heart became proud and he acted corruptly, and he transgressed against the Lord his God, and entered the temple of the Lord to burn incense on the altar of incense. (2 Chronicles 26:16)

When I am blessed with abundance, may I beware lest my heart becomes proud, and I forget the Lord my God who provided all good things, thinking that it was my power and the strength of my hand that brought this wealth. (Deuteronomy 8:12–14, 17)

*Pause to add your own prayers for personal renewal.*

## Petition

Answer me when I call to You, O my righteous God!
You have relieved me from my distress;
Be merciful to me and hear my prayer. (Psalm 4:1)

- **Personal Concerns**
    - Spiritual warfare
        - The world
        - The flesh
        - The devil
    - Growth in character
    - Personal disciplines
    - Physical health and strength
- My activities for this day
- Special concerns

## Intercession

May I help the weak and remember the words of the Lord Jesus, that He said, "It is more blessed to give than to receive." (Acts 20:35)

### World Affairs

- The poor and hungry
- The oppressed and persecuted
- Those in authority
- Peace among nations
- Current events and concerns

## Affirmation

Your hands made me and fashioned me. (Psalm 119:73)

Before You formed me in the womb, You knew me;
Before I was born, You set me apart. (Jeremiah 1:5)

You know me, O Lord;
You see me and test my thoughts about You. (Jeremiah 12:3)

*Pause to reflect upon these biblical affirmations.*

## Thanksgiving

God made Him who knew no sin to be sin for me, so that in Him I might become the righteousness of God. (2 Corinthians 5:21)

God chose me in Christ before the foundation of the world to be holy and blameless in His sight. In love He predestined me to be adopted as His son through Jesus Christ, according to the good pleasure of His will, to the praise of the glory of His grace, which He bestowed upon me in the One He loves. (Ephesians 1:4–6)

*Pause to offer your own expressions of thanksgiving.*

## Closing Prayer

Christ is the image of the invisible God, the firstborn over all creation. For by Him all things were created that are in heaven and on earth, visible and invisible, whether thrones or dominions or rulers or authorities; all things were created by Him and for Him. And He is before all things, and in Him all things hold together. (Colossians 1:15–17)

To the Lord my God belongs the heavens, even the highest heavens, the earth and everything in it. (Deuteronomy 10:14)

Daily Prayer Guide

# THE THIRD MONTH
# DAY 16

### Adoration

O Lord of hosts, God of Israel, enthroned between the cherubim, You alone are God over all the kingdoms of the earth. You have made heaven and earth. (Isaiah 37:16)

The Mighty One, God, the Lord,
Has spoken and summoned the earth
From the rising of the sun to the place where it sets. (Psalm 50:1)

*Pause to express your thoughts of praise and worship.*

### Confession

There is not a righteous man on earth who continually
   does good
And never sins. (Ecclesiastes 7:20)

*Ask the Spirit to search your heart and reveal any areas of unconfessed sin. Acknowledge these to the Lord and thank Him for His forgiveness.*

### Renewal

Whatever I do, whether in word or in deed, may I do all in the name of the Lord Jesus, giving thanks to God the Father through Him. (Colossians 3:17)

May I abide in Christ, so that when He appears, I will have confidence and not be ashamed before Him at His coming. (1 John 2:28)

*Pause to add your own prayers for personal renewal.*

## Petition

When I am afraid, I will trust in You.
In God, whose word I praise,
In God I have put my trust.
I will not fear;
What can mortal man do to me? (Psalm 56:3–4)

- **Growth in Christ**
  - Greater desire to know and please Him
  - Greater love and commitment to Him
  - Grace to practice His presence
  - Grace to glorify Him in my life
- My activities for this day
- Special concerns

## Intercession

There is neither Jew nor Greek, there is neither slave nor free, there is neither male nor female, for we are all one in Christ Jesus. (Galatians 3:28)

## Churches and Ministries

- My local church
- Other churches
- Evangelism and discipleship ministries
- Educational ministries
- Special concerns

## Affirmation

He who loves his father or mother more than You is not worthy of You; he who loves his son or daughter more than You is not worthy of You. (Matthew 10:37)

He who does not take his cross and follow after You is not worthy of You. He who finds his life will lose it, and he who loses his life for Your sake will find it. (Matthew 10:38–39)

*Pause to reflect upon these biblical affirmations.*

## Thanksgiving

In Christ I have redemption through His blood, the forgiveness of sins, in accordance with the riches of God's grace that He lavished on me with all wisdom and understanding. (Ephesians 1:7–8)

God raised me up with Christ and seated me with Him in the heavenly realms in Christ Jesus, in order that in the coming ages He might show the surpassing riches of His grace in kindness toward me in Christ Jesus. (Ephesians 2:6–7)

Third Month, Day 16

*Pause to offer your own expressions of thanksgiving.*

## Closing Prayer

The secret things belong to the Lord our God, but the things revealed belong to us and to our children forever, that we may observe Your words. (Deuteronomy 29:29)

Be exalted, O Lord, in Your strength;
We will sing and praise Your power. (Psalm 21:13)

# THE THIRD MONTH
## DAY 17

### Adoration

Whoever is wise will consider the lovingkindness of the Lord. (Psalm 107:43)

The sum of Your words is truth,
And all of Your righteous judgments are eternal. (Psalm 119:160)

You are the God of Abraham, the God of Isaac, and the God of Jacob. (Exodus 3:6)

*Pause to express your thoughts of praise and worship.*

### Confession

I have blotted out your transgressions like a thick cloud,
And your sins like the morning mist.
Return to Me, for I have redeemed you. (Isaiah 44:22)

*Ask the Spirit to search your heart and reveal any areas of unconfessed sin. Acknowledge these to the Lord and thank Him for His forgiveness.*

Third Month, Day 17

## Renewal

Let me stop trusting in man, whose breath is in his nostrils. For in what should he be esteemed? (Isaiah 2:22)

May I trust in You enough to honor You as holy in the sight of others. (Numbers 20:12)

*Pause to add your own prayers for personal renewal.*

## Petition

Keep falsehood and lies far from me;
Give me neither poverty nor riches;
Give me only my daily bread,
Lest I be full and deny You and say, "Who is the Lord?"
Or lest I become poor and steal,
And profane the name of my God. (Proverbs 30:8–9)

- **Growth in Wisdom**
    - Developing an eternal perspective
    - Renewing my mind with truth
    - Greater skill in each area of life
- My activities for this day
- Special concerns

## Intercession

May your love abound more and more in full knowledge and depth of insight, so that you may be able to approve the things that are excellent, in order to be sincere and blameless until the day of Christ—having been filled with the fruit of righteousness that comes through Jesus Christ, to the glory and praise of God. (Philippians 1:9–11)

**Family**

- My immediate family
- My relatives
- Spiritual concerns
- Emotional and physical concerns
- Other concerns

## Affirmation

Jesus preached the gospel of the kingdom of God, and said, "The time is fulfilled, and the kingdom of God is at hand. Repent and believe the good news." (Mark 1:14–15)

You have called me to go and proclaim the kingdom of God. (Luke 9:60)

As I follow You, You will make me a fisher of men. (Matthew 4:19; Mark 1:17)

*Pause to reflect upon these biblical affirmations.*

## Thanksgiving

I will not forget the God of my salvation;
I will remember the Rock of my refuge. (Isaiah 17:10)

O Lord, You are my God;
I will exalt You and praise Your name,
For You have done wonderful things,
Things planned long ago in perfect faithfulness. (Isaiah 25:1)

*Pause to offer your own expressions of thanksgiving.*

## Closing Prayer

Great is our Lord and mighty in power;
His understanding is infinite. (Psalm 147:5)

The fear of the Lord is the beginning of wisdom;
All who practice His commandments have a good understanding.
His praise endures forever. (Psalm 111:10)

## THE THIRD MONTH
# DAY 18

### Adoration

O Sovereign Lord, You are God! Your words are true, and You have promised good things to Your servant. (2 Samuel 7:28)

I will sing of Your lovingkindness and justice;
To You, O Lord, I will sing praises. (Psalm 101:1)

*Pause to express your thoughts of praise and worship.*

### Confession

This is the one You esteem:
He who is humble and contrite of spirit,
And who trembles at Your word. (Isaiah 66:2b)

*Ask the Spirit to search your heart and reveal any areas of unconfessed sin. Acknowledge these to the Lord and thank Him for His forgiveness.*

### Renewal

May I love the Lord my God and serve Him with all my heart and with all my soul. (Deuteronomy 11:13)

May I set my heart to honor Your name. (Malachi 2:2)

May I worship the Lord my God, and serve Him only. (Matthew 4:10)

*Pause to add your own prayers for personal renewal.*

## Petition

May I take courage and not be afraid, for the Lord Jesus is with me. (Mark 6:50)

- **Spiritual Insight**
    - Understanding and insight into the Word
    - Understanding my identity in Christ
        - Who I am
        - Where I came from
        - Where I'm going
    - Understanding God's purpose for my life
- My activities for this day
- Special concerns

## Intercession

The one who loves his brother abides in the light, and there is no cause for stumbling in him. But the one who hates his brother is in the darkness and walks in the darkness and does not know where he is going, because the darkness has blinded his eyes. (1 John 2:10–11)

## Believers

- Personal friends
- Those in ministry
- Those who are oppressed and in need
- Special concerns

## Affirmation

A disciple is not above his teacher, nor a servant above his master. It is enough for the disciple to be like his teacher, and the servant like his master. (Matthew 10:24–25)

The greatest among us should be like the youngest, and the one who rules like the one who serves. For who is greater, the one who is at the table or the one who serves? Is it not the one who is at the table? But Jesus came among us as the One who serves. (Luke 22:26–27)

If anyone wants to be first, he must be the last of all and the servant of all. (Mark 9:35)

*Pause to reflect upon these biblical affirmations.*

## Thanksgiving

You raised up Pharaoh for this purpose, that You might show him Your power and that Your name might be proclaimed through all the earth. (Exodus 9:16)

Third Month, Day 18

Others may intend evil, but You can use it for good to accomplish Your loving purposes. (Genesis 50:20)

*Pause to offer your own expressions of thanksgiving.*

## Closing Prayer

There is none like You, O Lord;
You are great, and Your name is mighty in power.
Who should not revere You, O King of the nations?
It is Your rightful due.
For among all the wise men of the nations
And in all their kingdoms,
There is no one like You. (Jeremiah 10:6–7)

Father in heaven,
Hallowed be Your name.
Your kingdom come;
Your will be done
On earth as it is in heaven. (Matthew 6:9–10)

Daily Prayer Guide

# THE THIRD MONTH
# DAY 19

## Adoration

The Lord of hosts is wonderful in counsel and great in wisdom. (Isaiah 28:29)

You are the Lord,
And there is no savior besides You.
From ancient days You are He,
And no one can deliver out of Your hand;
You act, and who can reverse it? (Isaiah 43:11, 13)

*Pause to express your thoughts of praise and worship.*

## Confession

Lord Jesus, You were despised and rejected by men,
A man of sorrows, and acquainted with grief.
And like one from whom men hide their faces,
You were despised, and we did not esteem You.
Surely You have borne our infirmities
And carried our sorrows;
Yet we considered You stricken,
Smitten by God, and afflicted.
But You were pierced for our transgressions,
You were crushed for our iniquities;
The punishment that brought us peace was upon You,
And by Your wounds we are healed.

Third Month, Day 19

All of us like sheep have gone astray,
Each of us has turned to his own way,
And the Lord has laid on You the iniquity of us all.
(Isaiah 53:3–6)

*Ask the Spirit to search your heart and reveal any areas of unconfessed sin. Acknowledge these to the Lord and thank Him for His forgiveness.*

## Renewal

May I not become weary in doing good, for at the proper time I will reap a harvest if I do not give up. (Galatians 6:9)

May I not grieve the Holy Spirit of God by whom I was sealed for the day of redemption. (Ephesians 4:30)

May I work out my salvation with fear and trembling, for it is God who works in me to will and to act according to His good purpose. (Philippians 2:12–13)

*Pause to add your own prayers for personal renewal.*

## Petition

May I obey those who are in authority over me with fear and trembling and with sincerity of heart, as to Christ; not with external service as a pleaser of men, but as a slave of Christ, doing the will of God from my heart. With good will may I serve as to the Lord and not to men, knowing that I will receive back from the Lord whatever good I do. (Ephesians 6:5–8)

- **Relationships with Others**
    - Greater love and compassion for others
    - Loved ones
    - Those who do not know Christ
    - Those in need
- My activities for this day
- Special concerns

## Intercession

May the Lord make me increase and abound in my love for believers and for unbelievers. (1 Thessalonians 3:12)

## Evangelism

- Friends
- Relatives
- Neighbors
- Coworkers
- Special opportunities

## Affirmation

Jesus is Your beloved Son in whom You are well pleased. (Matthew 3:17; Mark 1:11; Luke 3:22)

Jesus is the Christ, the Son of the living God. (Matthew 16:16)

Jesus is the Christ, the Son of God, who came into the world. (John 11:27)

Jesus is Your Son, whom You have chosen. (Luke 9:35)

The Father loves the Son and has given all things into His hand. (John 3:35)

*Pause to reflect upon these biblical affirmations.*

## Thanksgiving

I will give thanks to the Lord, for He is good;
His love endures forever. (1 Chronicles 16:34)

In my distress I called to the Lord
And cried to my God for help.
He heard my voice from His temple,
And my cry came before Him, into His ears.
He brought me out into a broad place;
He rescued me because He delighted in me. (Psalm 18:6, 19)

*Pause to offer your own expressions of thanksgiving.*

## Closing Prayer

"I know the plans I have for you," declares the Lord, "plans to prosper you and not to harm you, plans to give you a future and a hope." (Jeremiah 29:11)

Peace You leave with me; Your peace You give to me. Not as the world gives, do You give to me. I will not let my heart be troubled nor let it be fearful. (John 14:27)

Daily Prayer Guide

# THE THIRD MONTH
# DAY 20

## Adoration

Thus says the Lord, your Redeemer,
Who formed you in the womb:
I am the Lord, who makes all things,
Who alone stretches out the heavens,
Who spread out the earth by Myself. (Isaiah 44:24)

Blessing and glory and wisdom
And thanksgiving and honor and power and strength
Be to our God for ever and ever. Amen. (Revelation 7:12)

*Pause to express your thoughts of praise and worship.*

## Confession

All a man's ways are pure in his own eyes,
But the Lord weighs the motives. (Proverbs 16:2)

*Ask the Spirit to search your heart and reveal any areas of unconfessed sin. Acknowledge these to the Lord and thank Him for His forgiveness.*

## Renewal

May I revere this glorious and awesome name—the Lord my God. (Deuteronomy 28:58)

Third Month, Day 20

May I serve the Lord with fear and rejoice with trembling. (Psalm 2:11)

May I give You my heart
And let my eyes delight in Your ways. (Proverbs 23:26)

*Pause to add your own prayers for personal renewal.*

## Petition

May I learn to be content in whatever circumstances I am. Whether I am abased or in abundance, whether I am filled or hungry, let me learn the secret of being content in any and every situation. I can do all things through Him who strengthens me. (Philippians 4:11–13)

- **Faithfulness as a Steward**
  - Of time
  - Of talents
  - Of treasure
  - Of truth
  - Of relationships
- My activities for this day
- Special concerns

## Intercession

We have acted very corruptly toward You and have not obeyed the commandments, statutes, and ordinances which You commanded Your servant Moses. (Nehemiah 1:7)

## Government

- Spiritual revival
- Local government
- State government
- National government
- Current events and concerns

## Affirmation

Christ was in the world, and the world was made through Him, and the world did not know Him. He came to His own, but His own did not receive Him. (John 1:10–11)

No one has ever seen God, but the only begotten God, who is in the bosom of the Father, has made Him known. (John 1:18)

*Pause to reflect upon these biblical affirmations.*

## Thanksgiving

God's power toward us who believe is according to the working of His mighty strength, which He exerted in Christ when He raised Him from the dead and seated Him at His right hand in the heavenly realms, far above all rule and authority, power and dominion, and every title that can be given, not only in the present age but also in the one to come. (Ephesians 1:19–21)

God, who is rich in mercy, because of His great love with which He loved me, made me alive with Christ, even when I was dead in transgressions; it is by grace I have been saved. (Ephesians 2:4–5)

Third Month, Day 20

*Pause to offer your own expressions of thanksgiving.*

## Closing Prayer

Now to Him who is able to establish us by the gospel and the proclamation of Jesus Christ, according to the revelation of the mystery which was kept secret for long ages past, but now is manifested, and through the Scriptures of the prophets by the command of the eternal God, has been made known to all nations for obedience to the faith—to the only wise God, through Jesus Christ, be the glory forever. Amen. (Romans 16:25–27)

# THE THIRD MONTH
## DAY 21

### Adoration

I will express the memory of Your abundant goodness
And joyfully sing of Your righteousness.
The Lord is gracious and compassionate,
Slow to anger, and great in lovingkindness.
The Lord is good to all,
And His tender mercies are over all His works. (Psalm 145:7–9)

My Redeemer, the Lord of hosts is Your name;
You are the Holy One of Israel. (Isaiah 47:4)

*Pause to express your thoughts of praise and worship.*

### Confession

Out of the depths I have called to You, O Lord.
O Lord, hear my voice,
And let Your ears be attentive
To the voice of my supplications.
If You, Lord, should mark iniquities,
O Lord, who could stand?
But there is forgiveness with You,
That You may be feared. (Psalm 130:1–4)

*Ask the Spirit to search your heart and reveal any areas of unconfessed sin. Acknowledge these to the Lord and thank Him for His forgiveness.*

## Renewal

If I died with Christ, I believe that I will also live with Him, knowing that Christ, having been raised from the dead, cannot die again; death no longer has dominion over Him. For the death that He died, He died to sin once for all; but the life that He lives, He lives to God. In the same way, may I consider myself to be dead to sin, but alive to God in Christ Jesus. (Romans 6:8–11)

Having begun in the Spirit, may I not seek to be perfected by the flesh. (Galatians 3:3)

*Pause to add your own prayers for personal renewal.*

## Petition

May I not hate my brother in my heart, but reprove my neighbor frankly and not incur sin because of him. May I not take vengeance or bear a grudge against others, but love my neighbor as myself. (Leviticus 19:17–18)

- **Family and Ministry**
  - Family
  - Ministry

- - Sharing Christ with others
  - Helping others grow in Him
  - Career
- My activities for this day
- Special concerns

## Intercession

Finally, brethren, pray for us that the word of the Lord may spread rapidly and be glorified, just as it is with you, and that we may be delivered from perverse and evil men, for not all have faith. (2 Thessalonians 3:1–2)

### Missions

- Local missions
- National missions
- World missions
- The fulfillment of the Great Commission
- Special concerns

## Affirmation

If the many died by the trespass of the one man, how much more did the grace of God and the gift that came by the grace of the one Man, Jesus Christ, abound to the many. And the gift of God is not like the result of the one man's sin, for the judgment followed one sin and brought condemnation, but the gift followed many trespasses and brought justification. (Romans 5:15–16)

The law was added that the transgression might increase. But where sin increased, grace abounded all the more, so that just as sin reigned in death, so also grace might reign through righteousness to bring eternal life through Jesus Christ our Lord. (Romans 5:20–21)

*Pause to reflect upon these biblical affirmations.*

## Thanksgiving

Once I was alienated from God and was an enemy in my mind because of my evil works. But now He has reconciled me by His fleshly body through death to present me holy and blameless in His sight and free from reproach. (Colossians 1:21–22)

My citizenship is in heaven, from which I also eagerly await a Savior, the Lord Jesus Christ, who will transform my lowly body and conform it to His glorious body, according to the exertion of His ability to subject all things to Himself. (Philippians 3:20–21)

*Pause to offer your own expressions of thanksgiving.*

## Closing Prayer

Blessed be the God and Father of our Lord Jesus Christ, the Father of mercies and the God of all comfort. (2 Corinthians 1:3)

The God of hope will fill me with all joy and peace as I trust in Him, so that I may overflow with hope by the power of the Holy Spirit. (Romans 15:13)

Daily Prayer Guide

# THE THIRD MONTH
# DAY 22

## Adoration

You are the Lord; You do not change. (Malachi 3:6)

God is light; in Him there is no darkness at all. (1 John 1:5)

Fear God and give Him glory, because the hour of His judgment has come. Worship Him who made the heavens and the earth, the sea and the springs of water. (Revelation 14:7)

*Pause to express your thoughts of praise and worship.*

## Confession

My ears had heard of You
But now my eyes have seen You.
Therefore I despise myself
And repent in dust and ashes. (Job 42:5–6)

*Ask the Spirit to search your heart and reveal any areas of unconfessed sin. Acknowledge these to the Lord and thank Him for His forgiveness.*

## Renewal

May I not let any corrupt word come out of my mouth, but only what is helpful for building others up according to their needs, that it may impart grace to those who hear. (Ephesians 4:29)

I have been born again, not of perishable seed, but of imperishable, through the living and abiding word of God. Therefore, may I put away all malice and all guile and hypocrisy and envy and all slander. (1 Peter 1:23; 2:1)

Since I have been approved by God to be entrusted with the gospel, let me speak not as pleasing men but God, who tests my heart. May I not seek glory from men. (1 Thessalonians 2:4, 6)

*Pause to add your own prayers for personal renewal.*

## Petition

May I not follow the crowd in doing wrong. (Exodus 23:2)

May I not accept a bribe, for a bribe blinds those who see and perverts the words of the righteous. (Exodus 23:8)

- **Personal Concerns**
    - Spiritual warfare
        - The world
        - The flesh
        - The devil
    - Growth in character
    - Personal disciplines
    - Physical health and strength
- My activities for this day
- Special concerns

## Intercession

Salvation belongs to the Lord.
May Your blessing be on Your people. (Psalm 3:8)

### World Affairs

- The poor and hungry
- The oppressed and persecuted
- Those in authority
- Peace among nations
- Current events and concerns

## Affirmation

God set me apart from my mother's womb and called me through His grace. (Galatians 1:15)

I have believed in the Lord Jesus, so that I will be saved—me and my household. (Acts 16:31)

He who is joined to the Lord is one with Him in spirit. (1 Corinthians 6:17)

None of us lives to himself alone and none of us dies to himself alone. If we live, we live to the Lord; and if we die, we die to the Lord. So, whether we live or die, we belong to the Lord. (Romans 14:7–8)

*Pause to reflect upon these biblical affirmations.*

Third Month, Day 22

## Thanksgiving

When I was dead in my trespasses and in the uncircumcision of my flesh, God made me alive with Christ. He forgave me all my trespasses, having canceled the written code, with its regulations, that was against me and was contrary to me; He took it away, nailing it to the cross. And having disarmed the powers and authorities, He made a public spectacle of them, triumphing over them by the cross. (Colossians 2:13–15)

God did not appoint me to suffer wrath but to obtain salvation through my Lord Jesus Christ. He died for me, so that, whether I am awake or asleep, I may live together with Him. (1 Thessalonians 5:9–10)

*Pause to offer your own expressions of thanksgiving.*

## Closing Prayer

The grace of the Lord Jesus Christ and the love of God and the fellowship of the Holy Spirit are with us. (2 Corinthians 13:14)

Blessed be the Lord forever!
Amen and Amen. (Psalm 89:52)

Daily Prayer Guide

# THE THIRD MONTH
## DAY 23

### Adoration

Will God indeed dwell on earth? Heaven and the highest heaven cannot contain You. (1 Kings 8:27)

God's voice thunders in marvelous ways;
He does great things which we cannot comprehend. (Job 37:5)

*Pause to express your thoughts of praise and worship.*

### Confession

O Lord, do not rebuke me in Your anger
Or chasten me in Your wrath.
Be merciful to me, Lord, for I am weak;
O Lord, heal me, for my bones are in distress.
My soul also is greatly troubled;
But You, O Lord, how long? (Psalm 6:1–3)

*Ask the Spirit to search your heart and reveal any areas of unconfessed sin. Acknowledge these to the Lord and thank Him for His forgiveness.*

### Renewal

May I be self-controlled and alert; my adversary the devil prowls around like a roaring lion looking for someone to devour.

But may I resist him, standing firm in the faith, knowing that my brothers throughout the world are undergoing the same kind of sufferings. (1 Peter 5:8–9)

I will stand firm, having girded my waist with truth, having put on the breastplate of righteousness, and having shod my feet with the readiness of the gospel of peace; above all, taking up the shield of faith with which I will be able to quench all the fiery darts of the evil one. I will take the helmet of salvation and the sword of the Spirit, which is the word of God. With all prayer and petition, I will pray always in the Spirit, and to this end I will be watchful with all perseverance and petition for all the saints. (Ephesians 6:14–18)

*Pause to add your own prayers for personal renewal.*

## Petition

Oh, that You would bless me and enlarge my territory! Let Your hand be with me and keep me from evil, so it may not grieve me. (1 Chronicles 4:10)

- **Growth in Christ**
    - Greater desire to know and please Him
    - Greater love and commitment to Him
    - Grace to practice His presence
    - Grace to glorify Him in my life
- My activities for this day
- Special concerns

## Intercession

Grace has been given to each one of us according to the measure of the gift of Christ. And He gave some to be apostles, some to be prophets, some to be evangelists, and some to be pastors and teachers, for the equipping of the saints for the work of ministry, for the building up of the body of Christ. (Ephesians 4:7, 11–12)

### Churches and Ministries

- My local church
- Other churches
- Evangelism and discipleship ministries
- Educational ministries
- Special concerns

## Affirmation

As Moses lifted up the serpent in the desert, so the Son of Man had to be lifted up, that everyone who believes in Him may have eternal life. (John 3:14–15)

He who believes in God's Son is not condemned, but he who does not believe is condemned already, because he has not believed in the name of the only begotten Son of God. (John 3:18)

*Pause to reflect upon these biblical affirmations.*

## Thanksgiving

We should not be ignorant about those who fall asleep or grieve like the rest of men, who have no hope. For if we believe that Jesus died and rose again, even so God will bring with Him those who have fallen asleep in Jesus. According to the Lord's own word, we who are alive and remain until the coming of the Lord will not precede those who have fallen asleep. For the Lord Himself will come down from heaven, with a loud command, with the voice of the archangel, and with the trumpet of God, and the dead in Christ will rise first. Then we who are alive and remain will be caught up together with them in the clouds to meet the Lord in the air. And so we will be with the Lord forever. (1 Thessalonians 4:13–17)

*Pause to offer your own expressions of thanksgiving.*

## Closing Prayer

You are my hiding place;
You will preserve me from trouble
And surround me with songs of deliverance. (Psalm 32:7)

You will instruct me and teach me in the way I should go;
You will counsel me and watch over me. (Psalm 32:8)

Daily Prayer Guide

# THE THIRD MONTH
# DAY 24

### Adoration

Praise the Lord!
Praise the Lord, O my soul!
I will praise the Lord while I live;
I will sing praises to my God while I have my being.
(Psalm 146:1–2)

My mouth will speak the praise of the Lord,
And all flesh will bless His holy name for ever and ever.
(Psalm 145:21)

*Pause to express your thoughts of praise and worship.*

### Confession

O my God, I am too ashamed and disgraced to lift up my face to you, my God, because my sins have risen higher than my head and my guilt has reached to the heavens. (Ezra 9:6)

*Ask the Spirit to search your heart and reveal any areas of unconfessed sin. Acknowledge these to the Lord and thank Him for His forgiveness.*

Third Month, Day 24

## Renewal

My attitude should be the same as that of Christ Jesus, who, being in the form of God, did not consider equality with God something to be grasped, but emptied Himself, taking the form of a servant, being made in the likeness of men. And being found in appearance as a man, He humbled Himself and became obedient to death, even death on a cross. (Philippians 2:5–8)

May I not seek my own interests, but those of Christ Jesus. (Philippians 2:21)

*Pause to add your own prayers for personal renewal.*

## Petition

May I be strong and not lose courage, for my work will be rewarded. (2 Chronicles 15:7)

- **Growth in Wisdom**
  - Developing an eternal perspective
  - Renewing my mind with truth
  - Greater skill in each area of life
- My activities for this day
- Special concerns

## Intercession

We must encourage one another daily, as long as it is still called "Today," lest any of us be hardened by the deceitfulness of sin. (Hebrews 3:13)

## Family

- My immediate family
- My relatives
- Spiritual concerns
- Emotional and physical concerns
- Other concerns

## Affirmation

Christ is the end of the law for righteousness to everyone who believes. (Romans 10:4)

Faith comes from hearing, and hearing by the word of Christ. (Romans 10:17)

My faith does not rest on the wisdom of men, but on the power of God. (1 Corinthians 2:5)

*Pause to reflect upon these biblical affirmations.*

## Thanksgiving

It is a trustworthy saying, that deserves full acceptance, that Christ Jesus came into the world to save sinners. I obtained mercy as the worst of sinners, so that Christ Jesus might display His unlimited patience as an example for those who would believe on Him for eternal life. (1 Timothy 1:15–16)

God has saved me and called me with a holy calling, not according to my works but according to His own purpose and grace. (2 Timothy 1:9a)

*Pause to offer your own expressions of thanksgiving.*

## Closing Prayer

There is now no condemnation for those who are in Christ Jesus, because the law of the Spirit of life in Christ Jesus has set me free from the law of sin and death. (Romans 8:1–2)

In Christ I have obtained an inheritance, having been predestined according to the plan of Him who works all things according to the counsel of His will, that we who have trusted in Christ should be to the praise of His glory. (Ephesians 1:11–12)

Daily Prayer Guide

# THE THIRD MONTH
# DAY 25

### Adoration

To God belong wisdom and power;
Counsel and understanding are His. (Job 12:13)

You are holy;
You are enthroned on the praise of Israel. (Psalm 22:3)

*Pause to express your thoughts of praise and worship.*

### Confession

What is man that You should magnify him,
That you should set Your heart on him,
That You examine him every morning
And test him every moment? (Job 7:17–18)

*Ask the Spirit to search your heart and reveal any areas of unconfessed sin. Acknowledge these to the Lord and thank Him for His forgiveness.*

### Renewal

May I flee youthful lusts and pursue righteousness, faith, love, and peace, with those who call on the Lord out of a pure heart. (2 Timothy 2:22)

Third Month, Day 25

May I avoid foolish and ignorant disputes, knowing that they produce quarrels. The Lord's servant must not quarrel, but be gentle toward all, able to teach, and patient. (2 Timothy 2:23–24)

*Pause to add your own prayers for personal renewal.*

## Petition

This is the will of God, my sanctification, that I abstain from immorality and learn to possess my own vessel in sanctification and honor. For God did not call me to be impure, but to live a holy life. (1 Thessalonians 4:3–4, 7)

- **Spiritual Insight**
  - Understanding and insight into the Word
  - Understanding my identity in Christ
    - Who I am
    - Where I came from
    - Where I'm going
  - Understanding God's purpose for my life
- My activities for this day
- Special concerns

## Intercession

May I owe nothing to anyone except to love them, for he who loves his neighbor has fulfilled the law. For the commandments, "You shall not commit adultery," "You shall not murder," "You shall not steal," "You shall not covet," and if there is any other commandment, it is summed up in this saying: "You shall love your neighbor as yourself." Love does no harm to a neighbor; therefore love is the fulfillment of the law. (Romans 13:8–10)

## Believers

- Personal friends
- Those in ministry
- Those who are oppressed and in need
- Special concerns

## Affirmation

In Christ are hidden all the treasures of wisdom and knowledge. (Colossians 2:3)

In Christ all the fullness of the Godhead lives in bodily form. (Colossians 2:9)

I have set my hope on the living God, who is the Savior of all men, especially of those who believe. (1 Timothy 4:10)

*Pause to reflect upon these biblical affirmations.*

## Thanksgiving

God's grace was given to us in Christ Jesus before the beginning of time and has now been revealed through the appearing of our Savior, Christ Jesus, who abolished death and brought life and immortality to light through the gospel. (2 Timothy 1:9b–10)

The grace of my Lord was poured out on me abundantly, along with the faith and love that are in Christ Jesus. (1 Timothy 1:14)

*Pause to offer your own expressions of thanksgiving.*

## Closing Prayer

I have seen You in the sanctuary
And beheld Your power and Your glory.
Because Your lovingkindness is better than life,
My lips will praise You.
So I will bless You as long as I live;
I will lift up my hands in Your name.
My soul will be satisfied as with the richest of foods,
And my mouth will praise You with joyful lips. (Psalm 63:2–5)

God is able to do immeasurably more than all that we ask or think, according to His power that is at work within us. To Him be glory in the church and in Christ Jesus throughout all generations, for ever and ever. (Ephesians 3:20–21)

Daily Prayer Guide

# THE THIRD MONTH
# DAY 26

### Adoration

You, O Lord, are a compassionate and gracious God,
Slow to anger, and abounding in lovingkindness and truth.
(Psalm 86:15)

My flesh trembles for fear of You;
I stand in awe of Your judgments. (Psalm 119:120)

*Pause to express your thoughts of praise and worship.*

### Confession

Good and upright is the Lord;
Therefore He instructs sinners in His ways.
The Lord guides the humble in what is right
And teaches the humble His way. (Psalm 25:8–9)

*Ask the Spirit to search your heart and reveal any areas of unconfessed sin. Acknowledge these to the Lord and thank Him for His forgiveness.*

### Renewal

My son, keep my words
And store up my commands within you.

Keep my commands and live,
And my law as the apple of your eye.
Bind them on your fingers;
Write them on the tablet of your heart.
Say to wisdom, "You are my sister,"
And call understanding your kinsman. (Proverbs 7:1–4)

May I carefully observe all the commandment to love the Lord my God, to walk in all His ways and to hold fast to Him. (Deuteronomy 11:22)

*Pause to add your own prayers for personal renewal.*

## Petition

May I be an example for other believers in speech, in behavior, in love, in faith, and in purity. (1 Timothy 4:12)

- **Relationships with Others**
  - Greater love and compassion for others
  - Loved ones
  - Those who do not know Christ
  - Those in need
- My activities for this day
- Special concerns

## Intercession

May I have mercy on those who are doubting. (Jude 22)

Daily Prayer Guide

## Evangelism

- Friends
- Relatives
- Neighbors
- Coworkers
- Special opportunities

## Affirmation

During the days of His flesh, Jesus offered up prayers and petitions with loud cries and tears to the One who could save Him from death, and He was heard because of His devoutness. Although He was a Son, He learned obedience by the things which He suffered; and being perfected, He became the source of eternal salvation for all who obey Him, being designated by God as a high priest according to the order of Melchizedek. (Hebrews 5:7–10)

When Christ came as high priest of the good things that have come, He went through the greater and more perfect tabernacle that is not made with hands, that is to say, not a part of this creation. Not through the blood of goats and calves but through His own blood, He entered the Most Holy Place once for all, having obtained eternal redemption. (Hebrews 9:11–12)

*Pause to reflect upon these biblical affirmations.*

Third Month, Day 26

## Thanksgiving

We are looking for the blessed hope and the glorious appearing of our great God and Savior, Christ Jesus, who gave Himself for us to redeem us from all iniquity and to purify for Himself a people for His own possession, zealous for good works. (Titus 2:13–14)

The Lord will deliver me from every evil work and will bring me safely to His heavenly kingdom. To Him be glory forever and ever. (2 Timothy 4:18)

*Pause to offer your own expressions of thanksgiving.*

## Closing Prayer

God comforts us in all our afflictions, so that we can comfort those in any affliction with the comfort we ourselves have received from God. (2 Corinthians 1:4)

Satisfy us in the morning with Your loyal love,
That we may sing for joy and be glad all our days. (Psalm 90:14)

Daily Prayer Guide

# THE THIRD MONTH
# DAY 27

### Adoration

The Lord is righteous in all His ways
And gracious in all His works. (Psalm 145:17)

You declare the end from the beginning,
And from ancient times things that have not yet been done,
Saying, "My purpose will stand,
And I will do all My pleasure." (Isaiah 46:10)

*Pause to express your thoughts of praise and worship.*

### Confession

I have sinned greatly in what I have done. But now, O Lord, take away the iniquity of Your servant, for I have acted very foolishly. (2 Samuel 24:10)

*Ask the Spirit to search your heart and reveal any areas of unconfessed sin. Acknowledge these to the Lord and thank Him for His forgiveness.*

### Renewal

May I return to my God,
Maintain mercy and justice,
And wait on my God continually. (Hosea 12:6)

Third Month, Day 27

May I not live on bread alone, but on every word that comes from the mouth of God. (Matthew 4:4)

*Pause to add your own prayers for personal renewal.*

## Petition

May I be above reproach, blameless as a steward of God, not self-willed, not quick-tempered, not given to wine, not violent, not fond of dishonest gain, but hospitable, a lover of what is good, sensible, just, holy, and self-controlled. (Titus 1:6–8)

- **Faithfulness as a Steward**
    - Of time
    - Of talents
    - Of treasure
    - Of truth
    - Of relationships
- My activities for this day
- Special concerns

## Intercession

When the children of Judah were victorious, it was because they relied on the Lord, the God of their fathers. (2 Chronicles 13:18)

### Government

- Spiritual revival
- Local government

- State government
- National government
- Current events and concerns

## Affirmation

What we must do to work the works of God is to believe in Him whom He has sent. (John 6:28–29)

This is God's commandment: that we believe in the name of His Son, Jesus Christ, and love one another as He commanded us. (1 John 3:23)

The Father has sent the Son to be the Savior of the world. Whoever confesses that Jesus is the Son of God, God abides in him and he in God. (1 John 4:14–15)

*Pause to reflect upon these biblical affirmations.*

## Thanksgiving

When the kindness and love of God my Savior appeared, He saved me, not by works of righteousness which I have done, but according to His mercy. He saved me through the washing of regeneration and renewal by the Holy Spirit whom He poured out on me abundantly through Jesus Christ my Savior, so that having been justified by His grace, I might become an heir according to the hope of eternal life. (Titus 3:4–7)

My hope in God is an anchor of my soul, both sure and steadfast, and it enters the inner sanctuary behind the veil, where Jesus the forerunner has entered on my behalf, having become a high priest forever, according to the order of Melchizedek. (Hebrews 6:19–20)

*Pause to offer your own expressions of thanksgiving.*

## Closing Prayer

The Father has qualified me to share in the inheritance of the saints in the light. For He has rescued me from the dominion of darkness and brought me into the kingdom of His beloved Son, in whom I have redemption, the forgiveness of sins. (Colossians 1:12–14)

I make it my ambition to please the Lord, whether I am at home in the body or away from it. For we must all appear before the judgment seat of Christ, that each one may receive what is due for the things done while in the body, whether good or bad. (2 Corinthians 5:9–10)

# THE THIRD MONTH
## DAY 28

### Adoration

And the four living creatures, each having six wings, were full of eyes around and within; and they do not rest day or night, saying,

"Holy, holy, holy is the Lord God Almighty,
Who was, and is, and is to come." (Revelation 4:8)

Then a voice came from the throne, saying: "Praise our God, all you his servants, you who fear Him, both small and great!" (Revelation 19:5)

*Pause to express your thoughts of praise and worship.*

### Confession

Truly I have sinned against the Lord, the God of Israel. (Joshua 7:20)

*Ask the Spirit to search your heart and reveal any areas of unconfessed sin. Acknowledge these to the Lord and thank Him for His forgiveness.*

Third Month, Day 28

## Renewal

May I love my enemies and pray for those who persecute me. (Matthew 5:44)

Whatever I want others to do to me, may I also do to them, for this is the Law and the Prophets. (Matthew 7:12)

*Pause to add your own prayers for personal renewal.*

## Petition

Since I have a great high priest who has passed through the heavens, Jesus the Son of God, I will hold firmly to the faith I confess. For I do not have a high priest who is unable to sympathize with my weaknesses, but one who has been tempted in every way, just as I am, yet without sin. Therefore, I will approach the throne of grace with confidence, so that I may receive mercy and find grace to help in time of need. (Hebrews 4:14–16)

- **Family and Ministry**
    - Family
    - Ministry
        - Sharing Christ with others
        - Helping others grow in Him
    - Career
- My activities for this day
- Special concerns

## Intercession

May I not forget to do good and to share with others, for with such sacrifices God is well pleased. (Hebrews 13:16)

### Missions

- Local missions
- National missions
- World missions
- The fulfillment of the Great Commission
- Special concerns

## Affirmation

Jesus said, "My Father loves Me because I lay down My life that I may take it up again. No one takes it from Me, but I lay it down of My own accord. I have authority to lay it down and authority to take it up again. This command I received from My Father." (John 10:17–18)

Unless a grain of wheat falls to the ground and dies, it remains alone. But if it dies, it bears much fruit. The one who loves his life will lose it, and the one who hates his life in this world will keep it for eternal life. (John 12:24–25)

*Pause to reflect upon these biblical affirmations.*

Third Month, Day 28

## Thanksgiving

I have been chosen according to the foreknowledge of God the Father, in sanctification of the Spirit, for obedience to Jesus Christ and sprinkling of His blood; grace and peace are mine in abundance. (1 Peter 1:2)

Through Jesus, I will continually offer to God a sacrifice of praise, that is, the fruit of lips that give thanks to His name. (Hebrews 13:15)

*Pause to offer your own expressions of thanksgiving.*

## Closing Prayer

May our Lord Jesus Christ Himself and God our Father, who has loved us and has given us eternal consolation and good hope by grace, comfort our hearts and strengthen us in every good work and word. (2 Thessalonians 2:16–17)

God is the blessed and only Sovereign, the King of kings and Lord of lords, who alone has immortality and dwells in unapproachable light, whom no one has seen or can see. To Him be honor and eternal dominion. (1 Timothy 6:15b–16)

Daily Prayer Guide

# THE THIRD MONTH
# DAY 29

## Adoration

The Lord reigns; He is clothed with majesty;
The Lord is robed in majesty and is armed with strength.
Indeed, the world is firmly established; it cannot be moved.
Your throne is established from of old;
You are from everlasting.
Your testimonies stand firm;
Holiness adorns Your house,
O Lord, forever. (Psalm 93:1–2, 5)

God sits enthroned above the circle of the earth,
And its inhabitants are like grasshoppers.
He stretches out the heavens like a curtain
And spreads them out like a tent to dwell in.
He reduces rulers to nothing
And makes the judges of this world meaningless.
(Isaiah 40:22–23)

*Pause to express your thoughts of praise and worship.*

## Confession

Forgive me when I desert the Rock who begot me,
And forget the God who gave me birth. (Deuteronomy 32:18)

Third Month, Day 29

*Ask the Spirit to search your heart and reveal any areas of unconfessed sin. Acknowledge these to the Lord and thank Him for His forgiveness.*

## Renewal

By Your grace, I want to hear the words, "Well done, good and faithful servant; you have been faithful with a few things; I will put you in charge of many things. Enter into the joy of your Lord." (Matthew 25:21)

May I not love praise from men more than praise from God. (John 12:43)

I am the Lord's servant; let Your will be done in me according to Your word. (Luke 1:38)

*Pause to add your own prayers for personal renewal.*

## Petition

May I not throw away my confidence; it will be richly rewarded. Let me persevere so that when I have done the will of God, I will receive what He has promised. (Hebrews 10:35–36)

- **Personal Concerns**
    - Spiritual warfare
        - The world
        - The flesh
        - The devil

- Growth in character
- Personal disciplines
- Physical health and strength
- My activities for this day
- Special concerns

## Intercession

Many are saying, "Who will show us any good?"
O Lord, lift up the light of Your countenance upon us.
(Psalm 4:6)

### World Affairs

- The poor and hungry
- The oppressed and persecuted
- Those in authority
- Peace among nations
- Current events and concerns

## Affirmation

God raised Jesus from the dead, freeing Him from the agony of death, because it was impossible for Him to be held by it. (Acts 2:24)

Just as the Father raises the dead and gives them life, even so the Son gives life to whom He wishes. (John 5:21)

God gives life to the dead and calls into being things that do not exist. (Romans 4:17)

He who believes in the Son of God has everlasting life. (John 6:47)

God both raised the Lord and will also raise me up through His power. (1 Corinthians 6:14)

*Pause to reflect upon these biblical affirmations.*

## Thanksgiving

Though I have not seen Jesus, I love Him; and though I do not see Him now but believe in Him, I rejoice with joy inexpressible and full of glory, for I am receiving the end of my faith, the salvation of my soul. (1 Peter 1:8–9)

Since I am receiving a kingdom that cannot be shaken, may I be thankful and so worship God acceptably with reverence and awe, for my God is a consuming fire. (Hebrews 12:28–29)

*Pause to offer your own expressions of thanksgiving.*

## Closing Prayer

I will ascribe to the Lord glory and strength.
I will ascribe to the Lord the glory due His name
And worship the Lord in the beauty of holiness. (Psalm 29:1–2)

To the King eternal, immortal, invisible, the only God, be honor and glory forever and ever. (1 Timothy 1:17)

Daily Prayer Guide

# THE THIRD MONTH
# DAY 30

### Adoration

There is but one God, the Father, from whom all things came and for whom I live; and there is but one Lord, Jesus Christ, through whom all things came and through whom I live. (1 Corinthians 8:6)

The Son is the radiance of God's glory and the exact representation of His being, upholding all things by His powerful word. After He cleansed our sins, He sat down at the right hand of the Majesty on high, having become as much superior to angels as the name He has inherited is more excellent than theirs. (Hebrews 1:3–4)

*Pause to express your thoughts of praise and worship.*

### Confession

The Lord does not see as man sees. Man looks at the outward appearance, but the Lord looks at the heart. (1 Samuel 16:7)

*Ask the Spirit to search your heart and reveal any areas of unconfessed sin. Acknowledge these to the Lord and thank Him for His forgiveness.*

## Renewal

May I be a person of faith, who does not doubt the promises of God, and not a double-minded man, who is unstable in all his ways. (James 1:6, 8)

May I walk worthy of God who calls me into His kingdom and glory. (1 Thessalonians 2:12)

If I live according to the flesh, I will die; but if by the Spirit I put to death the deeds of the body, I will live. For those who are led by the Spirit of God are sons of God. (Romans 8:13–14)

*Pause to add your own prayers for personal renewal.*

## Petition

Since I have a great cloud of witnesses surrounding me, may I lay aside every impediment and the sin that so easily entangles, and run with endurance the race that is set before me, fixing my eyes on Jesus, the author and perfecter of my faith, who for the joy set before Him endured the cross, despising the shame, and sat down at the right hand of the throne of God. May I consider Him who endured such hostility from sinners, so that I will not grow weary and lose heart. (Hebrews 12:1–3)

- **Growth in Christ**
    - Greater desire to know and please Him
    - Greater love and commitment to Him
    - Grace to practice His presence
    - Grace to glorify Him in my life

Daily Prayer Guide

- My activities for this day
- Special concerns

## Intercession

Just as the body is one, but has many members, and all the members of the body, being many, are one body; so also is Christ. (1 Corinthians 12:12)

### Churches and Ministries

- My local church
- Other churches
- Evangelism and discipleship ministries
- Educational ministries
- Special concerns

## Affirmation

The Lord is my portion and my inheritance. (Numbers 18:20)

As for me and my household, we will serve the Lord. (Joshua 24:15)

You will honor those who honor You, but those who despise You will be disdained. (1 Samuel 2:30)

*Pause to reflect upon these biblical affirmations.*

## Thanksgiving

I was not redeemed with perishable things such as silver or gold from the aimless way of life handed down to me from my forefathers, but with the precious blood of Christ, as of a lamb without blemish or defect. (1 Peter 1:18–19)

How great is the love the Father has lavished on me, that I should be called a child of God—and I am! Therefore the world does not know me, because it did not know Him. (1 John 3:1)

*Pause to offer your own expressions of thanksgiving.*

## Closing Prayer

I am not ashamed, because I know whom I have believed and am convinced that He is able to guard what I have entrusted to Him until that day. (2 Timothy 1:12)

May the God of peace, who through the blood of the eternal covenant brought back from the dead our Lord Jesus, that great Shepherd of the sheep, equip us in every good thing to do His will, working in us what is pleasing in His sight, through Jesus Christ, to whom be glory forever and ever. (Hebrews 13:20–21)

Daily Prayer Guide

# THE THIRD MONTH
# DAY 31

### Adoration

You are He; You are the first,
And You are also the last. (Isaiah 48:12)

In the beginning was the Word, and the Word was with God, and the Word was God. He was in the beginning with God. (John 1:1–2)

The Lord Jesus, who is holy and true, holds the key of David. What He opens no one can shut, and what He shuts no one can open. (Revelation 3:7)

*Pause to express your thoughts of praise and worship.*

### Confession

Oh, my Lord, please do not hold against me the sin in which I have acted foolishly. (Numbers 12:11)

*Ask the Spirit to search your heart and reveal any areas of unconfessed sin. Acknowledge these to the Lord and thank Him for His forgiveness.*

Third Month, Day 31

## Renewal

May I guard my heart with all diligence,
For out of it flow the issues of life. (Proverbs 4:23)

May I not worry about tomorrow, for tomorrow will worry about itself. Each day has enough trouble of its own. (Matthew 6:34)

May I be ready, for the Son of Man will come at an hour when I do not expect Him. (Matthew 24:44; Luke 12:40)

*Pause to add your own prayers for personal renewal.*

## Petition

May I not live the rest of my time in the flesh for the lusts of men, but for the will of God. For I have spent enough time in the past in doing the will of those without God, when I walked in licentiousness, lusts, drunkenness, carousals, drinking parties, and detestable idolatries. (1 Peter 4:2–3)

- **Growth in Wisdom**
    - Developing an eternal perspective
    - Renewing my mind with truth
    - Greater skill in each area of life
- My activities for this day
- Special concerns

## Intercession

My soul, wait silently for God alone,
For my hope comes from Him.
He alone is my rock and my salvation;
He is my fortress, I will not be shaken.
In God is my salvation and my glory;
My rock of strength, my refuge is in God.
Trust in Him at all times, O people;
Pour out your heart before Him;
God is our refuge. (Psalm 62:5–8)

### Family

- My immediate family
- My relatives
- Spiritual concerns
- Emotional and physical concerns
- Other concerns

## Affirmation

I have not yet come to the resting place and the inheritance the Lord my God is giving me. (Deuteronomy 12:9)

The steps of a man are ordered by the Lord,
And He will delight in his way;
Though he stumbles, he will not be cast down,
For the Lord upholds him with His hand. (Psalm 37:23–24)

I have made the Lord, my refuge,
Even the Most High, my habitation. (Psalm 91:9)

*Pause to reflect upon these biblical affirmations.*

## Thanksgiving

You have given me life and shown me favor,
And Your care has preserved my spirit. (Job 10:12)

My shield is God Most High,
Who saves the upright in heart. (Psalm 7:10)

I will be glad and rejoice in Your love,
For You saw my affliction
And have known the anguish of my soul. (Psalm 31:7)

*Pause to offer your own expressions of thanksgiving.*

## Closing Prayer

Blessed be the God and Father of our Lord Jesus Christ, who according to His great mercy has given us new birth into a living hope through the resurrection of Jesus Christ from the dead, and into an inheritance that is incorruptible and undefiled and unfading, reserved in heaven for us. (1 Peter 1:3–4)

The God of all grace, who called me to His eternal glory in Christ, after I have suffered a little while, will Himself perfect, confirm, strengthen, and establish me. To Him be the glory and dominion for ever and ever. Amen. (1 Peter 5:10–11)

# PART THREE

# ONE-WEEK PRAYER GUIDE

One-Week Prayer Guide

# Sunday

### Adoration

Not to us, O Lord, not to us,
But to Your name give glory,
Because of Your lovingkindness and truth. (Psalm 115:1)

It is good to give thanks to the Lord
And to sing praises to Your name, O Most High,
To declare Your lovingkindness in the morning
And Your faithfulness at night. (Psalm 92:1–2)

Great and marvelous are Your works,
Lord God Almighty!
Righteous and true are Your ways,
King of the nations!
Who will not fear You, O Lord,
And glorify Your name?
For You alone are holy.
All nations will come and worship before You,
For Your righteous acts have been revealed. (Revelation 15:3–4)

O sing to the Lord a new song;
Sing to the Lord, all the earth.
Sing to the Lord, bless His name;
Proclaim the good news of His salvation day after day.
Declare His glory among the nations,

His marvelous works among all people.
Great is the Lord and most worthy of praise;
He is to be feared above all gods.
For all the gods of the nations are idols,
But the Lord made the heavens.
Splendor and majesty are before Him;
Strength and beauty are in His sanctuary. (Psalm 96:1–6)

*Pause to express your thoughts of praise and worship.*

## Confession

This is the one You esteem:
He who is humble and contrite of spirit,
And who trembles at Your word. (Isaiah 66:2b)

Has the Lord as much delight in burnt offerings and sacrifices
As in obeying the voice of the Lord?
To obey is better than sacrifice,
And to heed is better than the fat of rams. (1 Samuel 15:22)

The sacrifices of God are a broken spirit;
A broken and contrite heart,
O God, You will not despise. (Psalm 51:17)

If I confess my sins, He is faithful and just and will forgive me my sins and purify me from all unrighteousness. (1 John 1:9)

The Lord does not see as man sees. Man looks at the outward appearance, but the Lord looks at the heart. (1 Samuel 16:7)

One-Week Prayer Guide

*Ask the Spirit to search your heart and reveal any areas of unconfessed sin. Acknowledge these to the Lord and thank Him for His forgiveness.*

*Thank You that You have said:*

Come now, let us reason together.
Though your sins are like scarlet,
They shall be as white as snow;
Though they are red as crimson,
They shall be like wool. (Isaiah 1:18)

## Renewal

*Lord, renew me by Your Spirit as I offer these prayers to You:*

By Your grace, I want to hear the words, "Well done, good and faithful servant; you have been faithful with a few things; I will put you in charge of many things. Enter into the joy of your Lord." (Matthew 25:21)

May I be careful to lead a blameless life.
May I walk in the integrity of my heart in the midst of
   my house.
May I set no wicked thing before my eyes.
I hate the work of those who fall away;
May it not cling to me. (Psalm 101:2–3)

With regard to my former way of life, may I put off my old self, which is being corrupted by its deceitful desires, and be renewed in the spirit of my mind; and may I put on the new self, which was created according to God in righteousness and true holiness. (Ephesians 4:22–24)

May I consecrate myself and be holy, because You are the Lord my God. May I keep Your statutes and practice them, for You are the Lord who sanctifies me. (Leviticus 20:7–8)

*Pause to add your own prayers for personal renewal.*

## Petition

*Father, using Your Word as a guide, I offer You my prayers concerning **dedication to You**.*

Since I have been raised with Christ, I should seek the things above, where Christ is seated at the right hand of God. May I set my mind on the things above, not on the things on the earth, for I died, and my life is now hidden with Christ in God. When Christ who is my life appears, then I also will appear with Him in glory. (Colossians 3:1–4)

In view of God's mercy, may I present my body as a living sacrifice, holy and pleasing to God, which is my reasonable service. May I not be conformed to the pattern of this world but be transformed by the renewing of my mind, that I may prove that the will of God is good and acceptable and perfect. (Romans 12:1–2)

May I cast down arguments and every pretension that sets itself up against the knowledge of You, and take every thought captive to the obedience of Christ. (2 Corinthians 10:5)

May I take my cross and lose my life for Your sake: He who does not take his cross and follow after You is not worthy of You. He who finds his life will lose it, and he who loses his life for Your sake will find it. (Matthew 10:38–39)

May I trust in the Lord and do good;
May I dwell in the land and feed on Your faithfulness.
When I delight myself in the Lord,
You will give me the desires of my heart.
I will commit my way to the Lord
And trust in You, and You will bring it to pass.
You will bring forth my righteousness like the light,
And my justice like the noonday. (Psalm 37:3–6)

Come, my children, listen to me;
I will teach you the fear of the Lord.
Who is the man who desires life
And loves many days that he may see good?
Keep your tongue from evil
And your lips from speaking guile.
Depart from evil and do good;
Seek peace and pursue it.
The eyes of the Lord are on the righteous,
And His ears are attentive to their cry. (Psalm 34:11–15)

May I learn the fear of the Lord.
Show me Your ways, O Lord,
Teach me Your paths;
Lead me in Your truth and teach me,
For You are the God of my salvation,
And my hope is in You all day long.

Sunday

Remember, O Lord, Your compassions and Your mercies,
For they are from of old. (Psalm 25:4–6)

O Lord my God, may I fear You, walk in all Your ways, love You, and serve You with all my heart and with all my soul. (Deuteronomy 10:12)

Father in heaven,
Hallowed be Your name.
Your kingdom come;
Your will be done
On earth as it is in heaven.
Give me today my daily bread,
And forgive me my debts as I also have forgiven my debtors.
And lead me not into temptation,
But deliver me from the evil one.
For Yours is the kingdom and the power and the glory forever.
(Matthew 6:9–13)

*Pause here to express any additional personal requests, especially concerning **growth in Christ**:*

- Greater desire to know and please Him
- Greater love and commitment to Him
- Grace to practice His presence
- Grace to glorify Him in my life

*I pray also for:*

- My activities for this day
- Special concerns

## Intercession

*Lord, I now prepare my heart for intercessory prayer for **churches and ministries**.*

May our Lord Jesus Christ Himself and God our Father, who has loved us and has given us eternal consolation and good hope by grace, comfort our hearts and strengthen us in every good work and word. (2 Thessalonians 2:16–17)

We should bear one another's burdens and so fulfill the law of Christ. (Galatians 6:2)

Confess your sins to one other and pray for one other so that you may be healed. The prayer of a righteous man accomplishes much. (James 5:16)

*In the spirit of these passages, I pray for:*

- My local church
- Other churches
- Evangelism and discipleship ministries
- Educational ministries
- Special concerns

## Affirmation

*Feed my mind and heart, O Lord, as I affirm these truths from Your Word concerning **salvation**:*

You are the resurrection and the life. He who believes in You will live, even though he dies, and whoever lives and believes in You will never die. (John 11:25–26)

I am convinced that neither death nor life, nor angels nor principalities, nor things present nor things to come, nor powers, nor height nor depth, nor anything else in all creation, will be able to separate me from the love of God that is in Christ Jesus my Lord. (Romans 8:38–39)

By grace I have been saved through faith, and this not of myself; it is the gift of God, not of works, so that no one can boast. For I am God's workmanship, created in Christ Jesus for good works, which God prepared beforehand for me to do. (Ephesians 2:8–10)

Your sheep hear Your voice, and You know them, and they follow You. You give them eternal life, and they shall never perish; no one can snatch them out of Your hand. The Father, who has given them to You, is greater than all; no one can snatch them out of the Father's hand. You and the Father are one. (John 10:27–30)

The Father has qualified me to share in the inheritance of the saints in the light. For He has rescued me from the dominion of darkness and brought me into the kingdom of His beloved Son, in whom I have redemption, the forgiveness of sins. (Colossians 1:12–14)

*Pause to reflect upon these biblical affirmations.*

## Thanksgiving

*For who You are and for what You have done, accept my thanks, O Lord.*

I will greatly rejoice in the Lord;
My soul will be joyful in my God.
For He has clothed me with garments of salvation
And arrayed me in a robe of righteousness,
As a bridegroom decks himself with ornaments,
And as a bride adorns herself with her jewels. (Isaiah 61:10)

My soul silently waits for God alone;
My salvation comes from Him.
He alone is my rock and my salvation;
He is my stronghold; I will never be shaken. (Psalm 62:1–2)

I will both lie down in peace and sleep,
For You alone, O Lord, make me dwell in safety. (Psalm 4:8)

The Lord is my rock and my fortress and my deliverer;
My God is my rock; I will take refuge in Him,
My shield and the horn of my salvation,
My stronghold and my refuge—
My Savior; You save me from violence. (2 Samuel 22:2–3)

*Pause to offer your own expressions of thanksgiving.*

## Closing Prayer

Satisfy us in the morning with Your loyal love,
That we may sing for joy and be glad all our days. (Psalm 90:14)

The God of all grace, who called me to His eternal glory in Christ, after I have suffered a little while, will Himself perfect, confirm, strengthen, and establish me. To him be the glory and dominion for ever and ever. Amen. (1 Peter 5:10–11)

To You who are able to keep me from falling and to present me before Your glorious presence faultless and with great joy—to the only God my Savior, through Jesus Christ my Lord, be glory, majesty, dominion, and authority, before all ages and now and forever. Amen. (Jude 24–25)

One-Week Prayer Guide

# Monday

**Adoration**

I will exalt You, my God and King;
I will bless Your name for ever and ever.
Every day I will bless You,
And I will praise Your name for ever and ever.
Great is the Lord and most worthy of praise;
His greatness is unsearchable.
One generation shall praise Your works to another,
And shall declare Your mighty acts.
I will meditate on the glorious splendor of Your majesty
And on Your wonderful works.
Men shall speak of the might of Your awesome works,
And I will proclaim Your great deeds.
I will express the memory of Your abundant goodness
And joyfully sing of Your righteousness.
The Lord is gracious and compassionate,
Slow to anger, and great in lovingkindness.
The Lord is good to all,
And His tender mercies are over all His works. (Psalm 145:1–9)

O Lord, our Lord,
How majestic is Your name in all the earth!
You have set Your glory above the heavens! (Psalm 8:1)

Lord Jesus, You are the Root and the Offspring of David, the bright Morning Star. (Revelation 22:16)

Monday

Blessed be the Lord God, the God of Israel,
Who alone does wonderful things.
And blessed be His glorious name forever;
May the whole earth be filled with His glory.
Amen and Amen. (Psalm 72:18–19)

*Pause to express your thoughts of praise and worship.*

## Confession

You were pierced for our transgressions,
You were crushed for our iniquities;
The punishment that brought us peace was upon You,
And by Your wounds we are healed.
All of us like sheep have gone astray,
Each of us has turned to his own way,
And the Lord has laid on You the iniquity of us all.
(Isaiah 53:5–6)

"Even now," declares the Lord,
"Return to Me with all your heart,
With fasting and weeping and mourning.
So rend your heart and not your garments."
Return to the Lord your God,
For He is gracious and compassionate,
Slow to anger and abounding in lovingkindness,
And He relents from sending calamity. (Joel 2:12–13)

The Lord is close to the brokenhearted
And saves those who are crushed in spirit. (Psalm 34:18)

Lord, I have heard of Your fame, and I stand in awe of
Your deeds.
O Lord, revive Your work in the midst of the years,
In our time make them known;
In wrath remember mercy. (Habakkuk 3:2)

*Ask the Spirit to search your heart and reveal any areas of unconfessed sin. Acknowledge these to the Lord and thank Him for His forgiveness.*

*Thank You, Lord, that You have said:*

For a brief moment I forsook you,
But with great compassion I will gather you.
In a flood of anger I hid My face from you for a moment,
But I will have compassion on you with everlasting kindness.
(Isaiah 54:7–8)

## Renewal

*Lord, renew me by Your Spirit as I offer these prayers to You:*

May I keep the commandments of the Lord my God, to walk in His ways and to fear Him. May I follow the Lord my God and fear Him; may I keep Your commandments, hear Your voice, serve You, and hold fast to You. (Deuteronomy 8:6; 13:4)

May I know God and serve Him with a whole heart and with a willing mind; for the Lord searches all hearts and understands every motive behind the thoughts. (1 Chronicles 28:9)

May I love the Lord my God and serve Him with all my heart and with all my soul. (Deuteronomy 11:13)

May I love my enemies, do good to those who hate me, bless those who curse me, and pray for those who mistreat me. Just as I want others to do to me, may I do to them in the same way. (Luke 6:27–28, 31)

*Pause to add your own prayers for personal renewal.*

## Petition

*Father, using Your Word as a guide, I offer You my prayers concerning **the things of the world**.*

*May these beatitudes be a reality in my life:*

Blessed are the poor in spirit, for theirs is the kingdom
   of heaven.
Blessed are those who mourn, for they will be comforted.
Blessed are the meek, for they will inherit the earth.
Blessed are those who hunger and thirst for righteousness, for
   they shall be satisfied.
Blessed are the merciful, for they shall obtain mercy.
Blessed are the pure in heart, for they shall see God.
Blessed are the peacemakers, for they shall be called sons of God.
Blessed are those who are persecuted for the sake of
   righteousness, for theirs is the kingdom of heaven.
   (Matthew 5:3–10)

May I seek first Your kingdom and Your righteousness, and all these things will be added to me. (Matthew 6:33)

When I have found one pearl of great value, may I go away and sell all that I have and buy it. (Matthew 13:46)

Incline my heart to Your testimonies
And not to selfish gain.
Turn my eyes away from worthless things,
And revive me in Your way. (Psalm 119:36–37)

May I keep my life free from the love of money and be content with what I have, for You have said, "I will never leave you, nor will I forsake you." (Hebrews 13:5)

May I not be like those among the thorns on whom seed was sown, who hear the word, but the worries of this world, the deceitfulness of riches and pleasures, and the desires for other things come in and choke the word, making it immature and unfruitful. Instead, may I be like the good soil on whom seed was sown, who with a noble and good heart hear the word, understand and accept it, and with perseverance, bear fruit, yielding thirty, sixty, or a hundred times what was sown. (Matthew 13:22–23; Mark 4:18–20; Luke 8:14–15)

As a servant of Christ and a steward of His possessions, it is required that I be found faithful. (1 Corinthians 4:1–2)

No one can serve two masters; for either he will hate the one and love the other, or he will be devoted to the one and despise the other. I cannot serve God and wealth. (Matthew 6:24; Luke 16:13)

By Your grace, I want to hear the words, "Well done, good and faithful servant; you have been faithful with a few things; I will put you in charge of many things. Enter into the joy of your Lord." (Matthew 25:21)

May I never boast except in the cross of our Lord Jesus Christ, through which the world has been crucified to me, and I to the world. (Galatians 6:14)

Lord, make me to know my end
And what is the measure of my days;
Let me know how fleeting is my life. (Psalm 39:4)

Teach me to number my days,
That I may gain a heart of wisdom. (Psalm 90:12)

May the favor of the Lord our God rest upon us,
And establish the work of our hands for us—
Yes, confirm the work of our hands. (Psalm 90:17)

*Pause here to express any additional requests, especially concerning* ***growth in wisdom***:

- Developing an eternal perspective
- Renewing my mind with truth
- Greater skill in each area of life

*I pray also for:*

- My activities for this day
- Special concerns

## Intercession

*Lord, I now prepare my heart for intercessory prayer for **my family**.*

May the Lord make me increase and abound in my love for believers and for unbelievers. May He establish my heart as blameless and holy before our God and Father at the coming of our Lord Jesus with all His saints. (1 Thessalonians 3:12–13)

May Your commandments be upon my heart, so that I may teach them diligently to my children and talk about them when I sit in my house and when I walk along the way and when I lie down and when I rise up. (Deuteronomy 6:6–7)

*In the spirit of these passages, I pray for:*

- My immediate family
- My relatives
- Spiritual concerns
- Emotional and physical concerns
- Other concerns

Monday

## Affirmation

*Feed my mind and heart, O Lord, as I affirm these truths from Your Word concerning the **benefits of salvation**:*

Having been justified by faith, I have peace with God through the Lord Jesus Christ, through whom I have gained access by faith into this grace in which I stand; and I rejoice in the hope of the glory of God. (Romans 5:1–2)

Lord, You have said, "Come to Me, all you who labor and are heavy laden, and I will give you rest. Take My yoke upon you and learn from Me, for I am gentle and humble in heart, and you will find rest for your souls. For My yoke is easy, and My burden is light." (Matthew 11:28–30)

You are the light of the world. He who follows You will not walk in the darkness but will have the light of life. (John 8:12)

You are the bread of life. He who comes to You will never hunger, and he who believes in You will never thirst. (John 6:35)

Everyone who drinks ordinary water will be thirsty again, but whoever drinks the water You give will never thirst. Indeed, the water You give becomes in us a spring of water welling up to eternal life. (John 4:13–14)

*Pause to reflect upon these biblical affirmations.*

## Thanksgiving

*For who You are and for what You have done, accept my thanks, O Lord.*

Bless the Lord, O my soul,
And all that is within me, bless His holy name.
Bless the Lord, O my soul,
And forget not all His benefits;
Who forgives all your iniquities
And heals all your diseases;
Who redeems your life from the pit
And crowns you with love and compassion;
Who satisfies your desires with good things,
So that your youth is renewed like the eagle's. (Psalm 103:1–5)

I will give thanks to the Lord, for He is good;
His love endures forever. (1 Chronicles 16:34)

For who is God besides the Lord?
And who is the Rock except our God?
God is my strong fortress,
And He sets the blameless free in His way.
He makes my feet like the feet of a deer;
He enables me to stand on the heights. (2 Samuel 22:32–34)

I will give thanks to the Lord, for He is good;
His lovingkindness endures forever.
I will give thanks to the Lord for His unfailing love
And His wonderful acts to the children of men. (Psalm 107:1, 8)

*Pause to offer your own expressions of thanksgiving.*

## Closing Prayer

This is the day the Lord has made;
I will rejoice and be glad in it. (Psalm 118:24)

The grace of the Lord Jesus Christ and the love of God and the fellowship of the Holy Spirit are with us. (2 Corinthians 13:14)

Now to Him who is able to establish us by the gospel and the proclamation of Jesus Christ, according to the revelation of the mystery which was kept secret for long ages past, but now is manifested, and through the Scriptures of the prophets by the command of the eternal God, has been made known to all nations for obedience to the faith—to the only wise God, through Jesus Christ, be the glory forever. Amen. (Romans 16:25–27)

# Tuesday

**Adoration**

I will bless the Lord at all times;
His praise will always be in my mouth.
My soul will make its boast in the Lord;
The humble will hear and be glad.
O magnify the Lord with me,
And let us exalt His name together. (Psalm 34:1–3)

Rejoice in the Lord, O you righteous;
Praise is becoming to the upright. (Psalm 33:1)

As for me, I will always have hope,
And I will praise You more and more.
My mouth will tell of Your righteousness
And of Your salvation all day long,
Though I know not its measure.
I will come in the strength of the Lord God;
I will proclaim Your righteousness, Yours alone.
Since my youth, O God, You have taught me,
And to this day I declare Your wondrous deeds.
(Psalm 71:14–17)

Shout joyfully to the Lord, all the earth.
Worship the Lord with gladness;
Come before Him with joyful singing.
The Lord, He is God.

Tuesday

It is He who made us, and not we ourselves;
We are His people and the sheep of His pasture.
I will enter Your gates with thanksgiving
And Your courts with praise;
I will give thanks to You and bless Your name.
For the Lord is good
And Your lovingkindness endures forever;
Your faithfulness continues through all generations.
(Psalm 100:1–5)

*Pause to express your thoughts of praise and worship.*

## Confession

Have mercy on me, O God,
According to Your loyal love;
According to the greatness of Your compassion
Blot out my transgressions.
Wash me completely from my iniquity
And cleanse me from my sin.
For I know my transgressions,
And my sin is ever before me.
Against You, You only, have I sinned
And done what is evil in Your sight,
So that You are justified when You speak
And blameless when You judge. (Psalm 51:1–4)

Who can discern his errors?
Cleanse me from hidden faults.
Keep Your servant also from presumptuous sins;
Let them not rule over me.

Then will I be blameless,
And innocent of great transgression. (Psalm 19:12–13)

*Ask the Spirit to search your heart and reveal any areas of unconfessed sin. Acknowledge these to the Lord and thank Him for His forgiveness.*

Purge me with hyssop, and I will be clean;
Wash me, and I will be whiter than snow.
Cause me to hear joy and gladness,
That the bones You have crushed may rejoice.
Hide Your face from my sins
And blot out all my iniquities.
Create in me a clean heart, O God,
And renew a steadfast spirit within me.
Do not cast me from Your presence
Or take Your Holy Spirit from me.
Restore to me the joy of Your salvation
And uphold me with a willing spirit.
Then I will teach transgressors Your ways,
And sinners will be converted to You. (Psalm 51:7–13)

## Renewal

*Lord, renew me by Your Spirit as I offer these prayers to You:*

May I return to my God,
Maintain mercy and justice,
And wait on my God continually. (Hosea 12:6)

May I rejoice in my tribulations, knowing that tribulation produces perseverance; and perseverance, character; and character, hope. And hope does not disappoint, because the love of God has been poured out into my heart through the Holy Spirit who was given to me. (Romans 5:3–5)

May I rejoice in hope, persevere in affliction, and continue steadfastly in prayer. (Romans 12:12)

May I not become weary in doing good, for at the proper time I will reap a harvest if I do not give up. (Galatians 6:9)

*Pause to add your own prayers for personal renewal.*

## Petition

*Father, using Your Word as a guide, I offer You my prayers concerning **growth in holiness**.*

If I abide in You, and Your words abide in me, I can ask whatever I wish, and it will be done for me. By this is Your Father glorified, that I bear much fruit, showing myself to be Your disciple. As the Father has loved You, You also have loved me. May I abide in Your love. If I keep Your commandments, I will abide in Your love, just as You kept Your Father's commandments and abide in His love. You have told me this so that Your joy may be in me and that my joy may be full. (John 15:7–11)

Search me, O God, and know my heart;
Try me and know my anxious thoughts,
And see if there is any wicked way in me,
And lead me in the way everlasting. (Psalm 139:23–24)

O Lord, set a guard over my mouth;
Keep watch over the door of my lips.
Do not let my heart turn aside to any evil thing. (Psalm 141:3–4a)

Direct my footsteps according to Your word,
And let no iniquity have dominion over me. (Psalm 119:133)

May I be diligent to add to my faith, virtue; and to virtue, knowledge; and to knowledge, self-control; and to self-control, perseverance; and to perseverance, godliness; and to godliness, brotherly kindness; and to brotherly kindness, love. For if these qualities are mine in increasing measure, they will keep me from being barren and unfruitful in the full knowledge of our Lord Jesus Christ. (2 Peter 1:5–8)

I will not let sin reign in my mortal body that I should obey its lusts. Nor will I present the members of my body to sin, as instruments of wickedness, but I will present myself to God as one who is alive from the dead and my members as instruments of righteousness to God. (Romans 6:12–13)

As an alien and a stranger in the world, may I abstain from fleshly lusts, which war against my soul. (1 Peter 2:11)

The works of the flesh are evident, which are: immorality, impurity, sensuality, idolatry, sorcery, hatred, discord, jealousy, fits of rage, selfish ambition, dissensions, factions, envyings, drunkenness, revelries, and the like. Those who practice such things will not inherit the kingdom of God. But the fruit of the Spirit is love, joy, peace, patience, kindness, goodness, faithfulness, gentleness, self-control; against such things there is no law. (Galatians 5:19–23)

May I put away all filthiness and the overflow of wickedness, and in meekness accept the word planted in me, which is able to save my soul. May I be a doer of the word and not merely a hearer who deceives himself. (James 1:21–22)

As I walk in the Spirit, I will not fulfill the desires of the flesh. For the flesh desires what is contrary to the Spirit, and the Spirit what is contrary to the flesh; for they oppose each other, so that I may not do the things that I wish. But if I am led by the Spirit, I am not under the law. (Galatians 5:16–18)

*Pause here to express any additional personal requests, especially concerning **spiritual insight**:*

- Understanding and insight into the Word
- Understanding my identity in Christ
    - Who I am
    - Where I came from
    - Where I am going
- Understanding God's purpose for my life

One-Week Prayer Guide

*I pray also for:*

- My activities for this day
- Special concerns

## Intercession

*Lord, I now prepare my heart for intercessory prayer for **believers**.*

May your love abound more and more in full knowledge and depth of insight, so that you may be able to approve the things that are excellent, in order to be sincere and blameless until the day of Christ—having been filled with the fruit of righteousness that comes through Jesus Christ, to the glory and praise of God. (Philippians 1:9–11)

Beloved, I pray that you may prosper in all things and be in good health, even as your soul prospers. (3 John 2)

*In the spirit of these passages, I pray for:*

- Personal friends
- Those in ministry
- Those who are oppressed and in need
- Special concerns

## Affirmation

*Feed my mind and heart, O Lord, as I affirm these truths from Your Word concerning my **identity in Christ**:*

If anyone is in Christ, he is a new creation; the old things passed away; behold, they have become new. (2 Corinthians 5:17)

I have been crucified with Christ; and it is no longer I who live, but Christ lives in me; and the life which I now live in the flesh, I live by faith in the Son of God, who loved me and gave Himself for me. (Galatians 2:20)

If I died with Christ, I believe that I will also live with Him, knowing that Christ, having been raised from the dead, cannot die again; death no longer has dominion over Him. For the death that He died, He died to sin once for all; but the life that He lives, He lives to God. In the same way, may I consider myself to be dead to sin, but alive to God in Christ Jesus. (Romans 6:8–11)

I did not receive a spirit of slavery again to fear, but I received the Spirit of adoption by whom I cry, "Abba, Father." The Spirit Himself testifies with my spirit that I am a child of God. (Romans 8:15–16)

My body is a temple of the Holy Spirit, who is in me, whom I have from God, and I am not my own. For I was bought at a price; therefore may I glorify God in my body. (1 Corinthians 6:19–20)

*Pause to reflect upon these biblical affirmations.*

## Thanksgiving

*For who You are and for what You have done, accept my thanks, O Lord.*

He who dwells in the shelter of the Most High
Will rest in the shadow of the Almighty.
I will say of the Lord, "He is my refuge and my fortress,
My God, in whom I trust." (Psalm 91:1–2)

The Lord is my light and my salvation;
Whom shall I fear?
The Lord is the strength of my life;
Of whom shall I be afraid? (Psalm 27:1)

*Lord, thank You that You have made these promises:*

For those who revere Your name, the Sun of righteousness will rise with healing in His wings. And they will go out and leap like calves released from the stall. (Malachi 4:2)

Because I love You, You will deliver me;
You will protect me, for I acknowledge Your name.
I will call upon You, and You will answer me;
You will be with me in trouble,
You will deliver me and honor me.
With long life You will satisfy me
And show me Your salvation. (Psalm 91:14–16)

*Pause to offer your own expressions of thanksgiving.*

## Closing Prayer

Surely goodness and mercy will follow me all the days of
   my life,
And I will dwell in the house of the Lord forever. (Psalm 23:6)

Every creature in heaven and on earth and under the earth
   and on the sea and all that is in them, will sing:
"To Him who sits on the throne and to the Lamb
Be blessing and honor and glory and power
For ever and ever!" (Revelation 5:13)

May the God of peace, who through the blood of the eternal covenant brought back from the dead our Lord Jesus, that great Shepherd of the sheep, equip us in every good thing to do His will, working in us what is pleasing in His sight, through Jesus Christ, to whom be glory forever and ever. (Hebrews 13:20–21)

# Wednesday

## Adoration

I have tasted and seen that the Lord is good;
Blessed is the man who takes refuge in Him!
O fear the Lord, you His saints,
For those who fear Him lack nothing. (Psalm 34:8–9)

I thank You because I am fearfully and wonderfully made;
Your works are wonderful,
And my soul knows it full well. (Psalm 139:14)

All Your works will praise you, O Lord,
And Your saints will bless You.
They will speak of the glory of Your kingdom
And talk of Your power,
So that all men may know of Your mighty acts
And the glorious majesty of Your kingdom.
Your kingdom is an everlasting kingdom,
And Your dominion endures through all generations.
(Psalm 145:10–13)

Blessed are You, O Lord, God of Israel, our father, forever and ever. Yours, O Lord, is the greatness and the power and the glory and the victory and the majesty, for everything in heaven and earth is Yours. Yours, O Lord, is the kingdom, and You are exalted as head over all. Both riches and honor come from You, and You are the ruler of all things. In Your hand is power and might to exalt and to give strength to all. Therefore, my God, I give You thanks and praise Your glorious name. (1 Chronicles 29:10–13)

*Pause to express your thoughts of praise and worship.*

## Confession

God is wise in heart and mighty in strength.
Who has resisted Him without harm? (Job 9:4)

Blessed is he whose transgression is forgiven,
Whose sin is covered.
Blessed is the man to whom the Lord does not impute iniquity
And in whose spirit is no deceit.
When I kept silent, my bones wasted away
Through my groaning all day long.
For day and night Your hand was heavy upon me;
My strength was sapped as in the heat of summer.
I acknowledged my sin to You
And did not hide my iniquity.
I said, "I will confess my transgressions to the Lord,"
And You forgave the guilt of my sin. (Psalm 32:1–5)

Come, let us return to the Lord.
For He has torn us, but He will heal us;
He has injured us but He will bind up our wounds.
After two days He will revive us;
On the third day He will raise us up,
That we may live before Him. (Hosea 6:1–2)

*Ask the Spirit to search your heart and reveal any areas of unconfessed sin. Acknowledge these to the Lord and thank Him for His forgiveness.*

I, even I, am He who blots out your transgressions for My
   own sake,
And I will not remember your sins. (Isaiah 43:25)

This what the Lord God, the Holy One of Israel, says:
"In repentance and rest is your salvation;
In quietness and trust is your strength." (Isaiah 30:15)

## Renewal

*Lord, renew me by Your Spirit as I offer these prayers to You:*

May I not profane Your holy name, but acknowledge You as holy before others. You are the Lord, who sanctifies me. (Leviticus 22:32)

May I be a person of faith, who does not doubt the promises of God, and not a double-minded man, who is unstable in all his ways. (James 1:6, 8)

May I abound in love and faith toward the Lord Jesus and to all the saints. (Philemon 5)

May I be strong in the grace that is in Christ Jesus.
(2 Timothy 2:1)

*Pause to add your own prayers for personal renewal.*

## Petition

*Father, using Your Word as a guide, I offer You my prayers concerning **my love for others**.*

Concerning love, You have said: "You shall love the Lord your God with all your heart and with all your soul and with all your mind." This is the first and great commandment. And the second is like it: "You shall love your neighbor as yourself." All the Law and the Prophets hang on these two commandments. (Matthew 22:37–40)

Whatever I want others to do to me, may I also do to them, for this is the Law and the Prophets. (Matthew 7:12)

Love is patient, love is kind, it does not envy; love does not boast, it is not arrogant, it does not behave rudely; it does not seek its own, it is not provoked, it keeps no record of wrongs; it does not rejoice in unrighteousness but rejoices with the truth; it bears all things, believes all things, hopes all things, endures all things. Love never fails. (1 Corinthians 13:4–8)

May I love my enemies and pray for those who persecute me. (Matthew 5:44)

May I be an imitator of God as a beloved child, and walk in love, just as Christ loved me and gave Himself up for me as a fragrant offering and sacrifice to God. (Ephesians 5:1–2)

May I sanctify Christ as Lord in my heart, always being ready to make a defense to everyone who asks me to give the reason for the hope that is in me, but with gentleness and respect. (1 Peter 3:15)

I should walk in wisdom toward outsiders, making the most of every opportunity. My speech should always be with grace, seasoned with salt, so that I may know how to answer each person. (Colossians 4:5–6)

Is this not the fast You have chosen:
To loose the bonds of wickedness,
To undo the cords of the yoke,
And to let the oppressed go free
And break every yoke?
Is it not to share our food with the hungry
And to provide the poor wanderer with shelter;
When we see the naked, to clothe him,
And not to turn away from our own flesh?
Then our light will break forth like the dawn,
And our healing will quickly appear,
And our righteousness will go before us;
The glory of the Lord will be our rear guard.
Then we will call, and the Lord will answer;
We will cry, and He will say, "Here I am." (Isaiah 58:6–9)

May I not let any corrupt word come out of my mouth, but only what is helpful for building others up according to their needs, that it may impart grace to those who hear. May I not grieve the Holy Spirit of God by whom I was sealed for the day of redemption. May I put away all bitterness and anger and wrath and shouting and slander, along with all malice. And may I be kind and compassionate to others, forgiving them just as God in Christ also forgave me. (Ephesians 4:29–32)

May I do nothing out of selfish ambition or vain conceit, but in humility may I esteem others as more important than myself. Let me look not only to my own interests, but also to the interests of others. (Philippians 2:3–4)

May I be of one mind with others and be sympathetic: loving them as brothers and sisters, being compassionate and humble. May I not return evil for evil or insult for insult, but blessing instead, because to this I was called, that I may inherit a blessing. (1 Peter 3:8–9)

*Pause here to express any additional personal requests, especially concerning **relationships with others**:*

- Greater love and compassion for others
- Loved ones
- Those who do not know Christ
- Those in need

*I pray also for:*

- My activities for this day
- Special concerns

## Intercession

*Lord, I now prepare my heart for intercessory prayer for **evangelism**.*

May I devote myself to prayer, being watchful in it with thanksgiving. I pray that God may open to me a door for the word, so that I may speak the mystery of Christ and proclaim it clearly, as I ought to speak. (Colossians 4:2–4)

I pray that words may be given to me, that I may open my mouth boldly to make known the mystery of the gospel. (Ephesians 6:19)

*In the spirit of these passages, I pray for those who do not know Christ:*

- Friends
- Relatives
- Neighbors
- Coworkers
- Special opportunities

## Affirmation

*Feed my mind and heart, O Lord, as I affirm these truths from Your Word concerning my **life in Christ**:*

You have shown me what is good;
And what does the Lord require of me
But to act justly and to love mercy
And to walk humbly with my God? (Micah 6:8)

Though I walk in the flesh, I do not war according to the flesh. The weapons of my warfare are not fleshly, but divinely powerful to overthrow strongholds, casting down arguments and every pretension that sets itself up against the knowledge of God, and taking every thought captive to the obedience of Christ. (2 Corinthians 10:3–5)

May I not love the world or the things in the world. If anyone loves the world, the love of the Father is not in him. For all that is in the world—the lust of the flesh, the lust of the eyes, and the pride of life—is not of the Father but of the world. And the world and its lusts are passing away, but the one who does the will of God abides forever. (1 John 2:15–17)

I will not lay up for myself treasures on earth, where moth and rust destroy and where thieves break in and steal. But I will lay up for myself treasures in heaven, where moth and rust do not destroy and where thieves do not break in and steal. For where my treasure is, there my heart will be also. (Matthew 6:19–21; Luke 12:34)

I make it my ambition to please the Lord, whether I am at home in the body or away from it. For we must all appear before the judgment seat of Christ, that each one may receive what is due for the things done while in the body, whether good or bad. (2 Corinthians 5:9–10)

*Pause to reflect upon these biblical affirmations.*

One-Week Prayer Guide

## Thanksgiving

*For who You are and for what You have done, accept my thanks, O Lord.*

Blessed be the God and Father of our Lord Jesus Christ, who according to His great mercy has given us new birth into a living hope through the resurrection of Jesus Christ from the dead, and into an inheritance that is incorruptible and undefiled and unfading, reserved in heaven for us who through faith are guarded by the power of God for salvation that is ready to be revealed in the last time. (1 Peter 1:3–5)

Whom have I in heaven but You?
And there is nothing on earth I desire besides You.
My flesh and my heart may fail,
But God is the strength of my heart and my portion forever. (Psalm 73:25–26)

Why are you downcast, O my soul?
Why are you disturbed within me?
Hope in God, for I will yet praise Him,
The help of my countenance and my God. (Psalm 42:11)

I call this to mind,
And therefore I have hope:
The Lord's mercies never cease,
For His compassions never fail.
They are new every morning;
Great is Your faithfulness. (Lamentations 3:21–23)

*Pause to offer your own expressions of thanksgiving.*

## Closing Prayer

Let the words of my mouth and the meditation of my heart
Be pleasing in Your sight,
O Lord, my Rock and my Redeemer. (Psalm 19:14)

God is able to do immeasurably more than all that we ask or think, according to His power that is at work within us. To Him be glory in the church and in Christ Jesus throughout all generations, for ever and ever. (Ephesians 3:20–21)

# Thursday

## Adoration

Praise the Lord!
For it is good to sing praises to our God,
Because praise is pleasant and beautiful. (Psalm 147:1)

Blessed be the name of God for ever and ever,
For wisdom and power belong to Him.
He changes the times and the seasons;
He raises up kings and deposes them.
He gives wisdom to the wise
And knowledge to those who have understanding.
He reveals deep and hidden things;
He knows what is in the darkness,
And light dwells with Him. (Daniel 2:20–22)

O God, You are my God;
Earnestly I seek You;
My soul thirsts for You;
My body longs for You,
In a dry and weary land
Where there is no water.
I have seen You in the sanctuary
And beheld Your power and Your glory.
Because Your lovingkindness is better than life,
My lips will praise You.

So I will bless You as long as I live;
I will lift up my hands in Your name.
My soul will be satisfied as with the richest of foods,
And my mouth will praise You with joyful lips.
When I remember You on my bed,
I meditate on You through the watches of the night.
Because You have been my help,
I will rejoice in the shadow of Your wings.
My soul clings to You;
Your right hand upholds me. (Psalm 63:1–8)

The Lord lives! Blessed be my Rock!
Exalted be God, the Rock of my salvation!
(2 Samuel 22:47; Psalm 18:46)

*Pause to express your thoughts of praise and worship.*

## Confession

O Lord, do not rebuke me in Your anger
Or chasten me in Your wrath.
Be merciful to me, Lord, for I am weak;
O Lord, heal me, for my bones are in distress.
My soul also is greatly troubled;
But You, O Lord, how long? (Psalm 6:1–3)

Woe to me, for I am undone!
Because I am a man of unclean lips,
And I live among a people of unclean lips;
For my eyes have seen the King,
The Lord of hosts. (Isaiah 6:5)

There is not a righteous man on earth who continually
  does good
And never sins. (Ecclesiastes 7:20)

Truly I have sinned against the Lord, the God of Israel. (Joshua 7:20)

If I claim to be without sin, I deceive myself, and the truth is not in me. If I confess my sins, He is faithful and just and will forgive me my sins and purify me from all unrighteousness. If I claim I have not sinned, I make Him a liar and His word is not in me. (1 John 1:8–10)

*Ask the Spirit to search your heart and reveal any areas of unconfessed sin. Acknowledge these to the Lord and thank Him for His forgiveness.*

I will sing praises to the Lord
And give thanks at the remembrance of His holy name.
For His anger lasts only a moment,
But His favor is for a lifetime;
Weeping may endure for a night,
But joy comes in the morning. (Psalm 30:4–5)

## Renewal

*Lord, renew me by Your Spirit as I offer these prayers to You:*

May I love the Lord my God, obey His voice, and hold fast to Him. For the Lord is my life and the length of my days. (Deuteronomy 30:20)

# Thursday

May I be holy to You, for You the Lord are holy, and You have set me apart to be Your own. (Leviticus 20:26)

I have been born again, not of perishable seed, but of imperishable, through the living and abiding word of God. Therefore, may I put away all malice and all guile and hypocrisy and envy and all slander. (1 Peter 1:23; 2:1)

Since I call on the Father who judges each man's work impartially, may I conduct myself in fear during the time of my sojourn on earth. (1 Peter 1:17)

*Pause to add your own prayers for personal renewal.*

## Petition

*Father, using Your Word as a guide, I offer You my prayers concerning these **practical exhortations**.*

May the God of my Lord Jesus Christ, the Father of glory, give me a spirit of wisdom and of revelation in the full knowledge of Him, and may the eyes of my heart be enlightened, in order that I may know what is the hope of His calling, what are the riches of His glorious inheritance in the saints, and what is the incomparable greatness of His power toward us who believe. God's power is according to the working of His mighty strength, which He exerted in Christ when He raised Him from the dead and seated Him at His right hand in the heavenly realms, far above all rule and authority, power and dominion, and every title that can be given, not only in the present age but also in the one to come. (Ephesians 1:17–21)

May I rejoice always, pray without ceasing, and give thanks in all circumstances, for this is God's will for me in Christ Jesus. May I examine all things, hold fast to the good, and abstain from every form of evil. (1 Thessalonians 5:16–18, 21–22)

I will consider it all joy whenever I fall into various trials, knowing that the testing of my faith produces endurance. And I will let endurance finish its work, so that I may be mature and complete, lacking in nothing. If I lack wisdom, may I ask of God, who gives generously to all without reproach, and it will be given to me. (James 1:2–5)

May I be steadfast, immovable, abounding in the work of the Lord, knowing that my labor in the Lord is not in vain. (1 Corinthians 15:58)

May I be strong in the Lord and in His mighty power as I put on the full armor of God, so that I will be able to stand against the schemes of the devil. (Ephesians 6:10–11)

May I prepare my mind for action and be self-controlled, setting my hope fully on the grace to be brought to me at the revelation of Jesus Christ. As an obedient child, may I not conform myself to the former lusts I had when I lived in ignorance, but as He who called me is holy, so may I be holy in all my conduct, because it is written: "You shall be holy, for I am holy." (1 Peter 1:13–16)

May I be anxious for nothing, but in everything by prayer and petition with thanksgiving, let my requests be known to God.

Thursday

And the peace of God, which transcends all understanding, will guard my heart and my mind in Christ Jesus. (Philippians 4:6–7)

Whatever is true, whatever is noble, whatever is right, whatever is pure, whatever is lovely, whatever is of good report—if anything is excellent or praiseworthy—may I think about such things. (Philippians 4:8)

*Pause here to express any additional personal requests, especially concerning **faithfulness as a steward**:*

- Of time
- Of talents
- Of treasure
- Of truth
- Of relationships

*I pray also for:*

- My activities for this day
- Special concerns

## Intercession

*Lord, I now prepare my heart for intercessory prayer for **government**.*

We should offer petitions, prayers, intercessions, and thanksgivings on behalf of all men, for kings and all those who are in authority, that we may live peaceful and quiet lives in all godliness and reverence. This is good and acceptable in the sight of God our Savior, who desires all men to be saved and to come to the knowledge of the truth. (1 Timothy 2:1–4)

*In the spirit of this passage, I pray for:*

- Spiritual revival
- Local government
- State government
- National government
- Current events and concerns

## Affirmation

*Feed my mind and heart, O Lord, as I affirm these truths from Your Word concerning **the Scriptures**:*

All Scripture is God-breathed and is useful for teaching, for reproof, for correction, for training in righteousness, that the man of God may be thoroughly equipped for every good work. (2 Timothy 3:16–17)

The word of God is living and active and sharper than any double-edged sword, piercing even to the dividing of soul and spirit and of joints and marrow, and it judges the thoughts and attitudes of the heart. And there is no creature hidden from His sight, but everything is uncovered and laid bare before the eyes of Him to whom we must give account. (Hebrews 4:12–13)

Your word is a lamp to my feet
And a light to my path. (Psalm 119:105)

Thursday

Like Ezra, I want to set my heart to study the word of the Lord, and to do it, and to teach it to others. (Ezra 7:10)

I delight to do Your will, O my God,
And Your law is within my heart. (Psalm 40:8)

*Pause to reflect upon these biblical affirmations.*

## Thanksgiving

*For who You are and for what You have done, accept my thanks, O Lord.*

The Lord is great and greatly to be praised;
He is to be feared above all gods.
For all the gods of the nations are idols,
But the Lord made the heavens.
Splendor and majesty are before Him;
Strength and joy are in His place.
I will ascribe to the Lord glory and strength.
I will ascribe to the Lord the glory due His name
And worship the Lord in the beauty of holiness.
(1 Chronicles 16:25–29)

Through Jesus, I will continually offer to God a sacrifice of praise, that is, the fruit of lips that give thanks to His name. (Hebrews 13:15)

God is my refuge and strength,
An ever-present help in trouble. (Psalm 46:1)

My heart rejoices in the Lord;
My horn is exalted in the Lord.
My mouth boasts over my enemies,
For I delight in Your salvation.
There is no one holy like the Lord;
There is no one besides You;
Nor is there any Rock like our God. (1 Samuel 2:1–2)

*Pause to offer your own expressions of thanksgiving.*

## Closing Prayer

The Lord will keep me from all evil;
He will preserve my soul.
The Lord will watch over my coming and going
From this time forth and forever. (Psalm 121:7–8)

The Lord bless you and keep you;
The Lord make His face shine upon you
And be gracious to you;
The Lord turn His face toward you
And give you peace. (Numbers 6:24–26)

The God of hope will fill me with all joy and peace as I trust in Him, so that I may overflow with hope by the power of the Holy Spirit. (Romans 15:13)

# Friday

## Adoration

How great You are, O Sovereign Lord! There is no one like You, and there is no God besides You, according to all that I have heard with my ears. (2 Samuel 7:22; 1 Chronicles 17:20)

O Lord, the God of our fathers, are You not the God who is in heaven? Are You not the ruler over all the kingdoms of the nations? Power and might are in Your hand, and no one is able to withstand You. (2 Chronicles 20:6)

For with You is the fountain of life;
In Your light we see light. (Psalm 36:9)

O come, let us sing to the Lord;
Let us shout joyfully to the Rock of our salvation.
Let us come before His presence with thanksgiving;
Let us shout for joy to Him with psalms.
The Lord is the great God,
The great King above all gods.
O come, let us worship and bow down,
Let us kneel before the Lord our Maker.
He is our God and we are the people of His pasture
And the sheep under His care. (Psalm 95:1–3, 6–7)

I will sing to the Lord as long as I live;
I will sing praise to my God while I have my being.
May my meditation be pleasing to Him;
I will be glad in the Lord. (Psalm 104:33–34)

*Pause to express your thoughts of praise and worship.*

## Confession

Out of the depths I have called to You, O Lord.
O Lord, hear my voice,
And let Your ears be attentive
To the voice of my supplications.
If You, Lord, should mark iniquities,
O Lord, who could stand?
But there is forgiveness with You,
That You may be feared. (Psalm 130:1–4)

You have been just in all that has happened to me; You have acted faithfully, while I did wrong. (Nehemiah 9:33)

I return to the Lord my God,
For I have stumbled because of my iniquity.
I take words with me and return to the Lord,
Saying, "Take away all iniquity and receive me graciously,
That I may offer the fruit of my lips." (Hosea 14:1–2)

*Ask the Spirit to search your heart and reveal any areas of unconfessed sin. Acknowledge these to the Lord and thank Him for His forgiveness.*

The Lord is compassionate and gracious,
Slow to anger, and abounding in lovingkindness.
God will not always strive with us,
Nor will He harbor His anger forever;
He does not treat us as our sins deserve
Or repay us according to our iniquities.
For as high as the heavens are above the earth,
So great is His love for those who fear Him;
As far as the east is from the west,
So far has He removed our transgressions from us.
As a father has compassion on His children,
So the Lord has compassion on those who fear Him.
You know how I am formed;
You remember that I am dust. (Psalm 103:8–14)

## Renewal

*Lord, renew me by Your Spirit as I offer these prayers to You:*

Who is the faithful and wise servant, whom the master has put in charge of his household to give them their food at the proper time? Blessed is that servant whom his master finds so doing when he comes. (Matthew 24:45–46)

May I watch and pray so that I will not fall into temptation; the spirit is willing, but the flesh is weak. (Matthew 26:41)

May I abide in Christ, so that when He appears, I will have confidence and not be ashamed before Him at His coming. (1 John 2:28)

May I be ready, for the Son of Man will come at an hour when I do not expect Him. (Matthew 24:44; Luke 12:40)

*Pause to add your own prayers for personal renewal.*

## Petition

*Father, using Your Word as a guide, I offer You my prayers concerning my **need for wisdom**.*

May God grant me, according to the riches of His glory, to be strengthened with power through His Spirit in my inner being, so that Christ may dwell in my heart through faith. And may I, being rooted and grounded in love, be able to comprehend with all the saints what is the width and length and height and depth of the love of Christ, and to know this love that surpasses knowledge, that I may be filled to all the fullness of God. (Ephesians 3:16–19)

If I have found grace in Your sight, teach me Your ways, so I may know You and continue to find favor with You. (Exodus 33:13)

Whatever I do, may I do all to the glory of God.
(1 Corinthians 10:31)

May I not let Your word depart from my mouth, but meditate on it day and night, so that I may be careful to do according to all that is written in it; for then I will make my way prosperous, and I will act wisely. (Joshua 1:8)

May I meditate on Your precepts
And consider Your ways.
May I delight in Your statutes,
And not forget Your word.
Deal bountifully with Your servant,
That I may live and keep Your word.
Open my eyes that I may see
Wonderful things from Your law. (Psalm 119:15–18)

Let me be quick to hear, slow to speak, and slow to anger, for the anger of man does not produce the righteousness of God. (James 1:19–20)

May I guard my heart with all diligence,
For out of it flow the issues of life.
May I put away perversity from my mouth
And keep corrupt talk far from my lips.
May I let my eyes look straight ahead,
And fix my gaze straight before me.
May I ponder the path of my feet
So that all my ways will be established.
May I not turn to the right or to the left
But keep my foot from evil. (Proverbs 4:23–27)

Let my light shine before men, that they may see my good deeds and praise my Father in heaven. (Matthew 5:13–16)

May I do all things without complaining or arguing, so that I may become blameless and pure, a child of God without fault in the midst of a crooked and perverse generation, among whom I shine as a light in the world, holding fast the word of life. (Philippians 2:14–16)

May I clothe myself with humility toward others, for God opposes the proud but gives grace to the humble. May I humble myself under the mighty hand of God, that He may exalt me in due time, casting all my anxiety upon Him, because He cares for me. (1 Peter 5:5–7)

*Pause here to express any additional personal requests, especially concerning **family and ministry**:*

- Family
- Ministry
    - Sharing Christ with others
    - Helping others grow in Him
- Career

*I pray also for:*

- My activities for this day
- Special concerns

## Intercession

*Lord, I now prepare my heart for intercessory prayer for **missions**.*

Finally, brethren, pray for us that the word of the Lord may spread rapidly and be glorified, just as it is with you, and that we may be delivered from perverse and evil men, for not all have faith. (2 Thessalonians 3:1–2)

The harvest is plentiful, but the workers are few. Therefore, I will pray that the Lord of the harvest will send out workers into His harvest. (Matthew 9:37–38; Luke 10:2)

*In the spirit of these passages, I pray for:*

- Local missions
- National missions
- World missions
- The fulfillment of the Great Commission
- Special concerns

## Affirmation

*Feed my mind and heart, O Lord, as I affirm these truths from Your Word concerning **my hope as a follower of Christ**:*

I do not lose heart; even though my outward man is perishing, yet my inner man is being renewed day by day. For this light affliction which is momentary is working for me a far more exceeding and eternal weight of glory, while I do not look at the things which are seen but at the things which are unseen. For the things which are seen are temporary, but the things which are unseen are eternal. (2 Corinthians 4:16–18)

Peace You leave with me; Your peace You give to me. Not as the world gives, do You give to me. I will not let my heart be troubled nor let it be fearful. (John 14:27)

Those who wait for the Lord
Will renew their strength;
They will mount up with wings like eagles;
They will run and not grow weary;
They will walk and not be faint. (Isaiah 40:31)

I am always of good courage and know that as long as I am at home in the body, I am away from the Lord. For I live by faith, not by sight. I am of good courage and would prefer to be absent from the body and to be at home with the Lord. (2 Corinthians 5:6–8)

Since I am a child of God, I am an heir of God and a joint heir with Christ, if indeed I share in His sufferings in order that I may also share in His glory. For I consider that the sufferings of this present time are not worth comparing with the glory that will be revealed to me. (Romans 8:17–18)

*Pause to reflect upon these biblical affirmations.*

## Thanksgiving

*For who You are and for what You have done, accept my thanks, O Lord.*

I will praise You, O Lord, with all my heart;
I will tell of all Your wonders.
I will be glad and rejoice in You;
I will sing praise to Your name, O Most High. (Psalm 9:1–2)

Friday

We give thanks to You, Lord God Almighty, the One who is and who was, because You have taken Your great power and have begun to reign. (Revelation 11:17)

I will sing of Your strength,
Yes, I will sing of Your mercy in the morning,
For You have been my stronghold,
My refuge in times of trouble.
To You, O my Strength, I will sing praises,
For God is my fortress, my loving God. (Psalm 59:16–17)

*Pause to offer your own expressions of thanksgiving.*

## Closing Prayer

Teach me to number my days,
That I may gain a heart of wisdom. (Psalm 90:12)

Better is one day in Your courts than a thousand elsewhere;
I would rather be a doorkeeper in the house of my God
Than dwell in the tents of the wicked.
For the Lord God is a sun and shield;
The Lord will give grace and glory;
No good thing does He withhold
From those who walk in integrity.
O Lord of hosts,
Blessed is the man who trusts in You! (Psalm 84:10–12)

To the King eternal, immortal, invisible, the only God, be honor and glory forever and ever. (1 Timothy 1:17)

# Saturday

**Adoration**

Bless the Lord, O my soul.
O Lord, my God, You are very great;
You are clothed with splendor and majesty.
The Lord covers Himself in light as with a garment;
He stretches out the heavens like a tent curtain. (Psalm 104:1–2)

Make a joyful shout to God, all the earth!
Sing the glory of His name;
Make His praise glorious.
Say to God, "How awesome are Your works!
Through the greatness of Your power
Your enemies submit themselves to You.
All the earth will worship You
And sing praises to You;
They will sing praise to Your name." (Psalm 66:1–4)

The Lord is righteous in all His ways
And gracious in all His works.
The Lord is near to all who call upon Him,
To all who call upon Him in truth.
He fulfills the desire of those who fear Him;
He hears their cry and saves them.

Saturday

The Lord preserves all who love Him,
But all the wicked He will destroy.
My mouth will speak the praise of the Lord,
And all flesh will bless His holy name for ever and ever.
(Psalm 145:17–21)

*Pause to express your thoughts of praise and worship.*

## Confession

Remember, O Lord, Your compassions and Your mercies,
For they are from of old.
Do not remember the sins of my youth or my transgressions;
According to Your loyal love remember me,
For Your goodness' sake, O Lord.
Good and upright is the Lord;
Therefore He instructs sinners in His ways.
The Lord guides the humble in what is right
And teaches the humble His way.
All the paths of the Lord are mercy and truth
For those who keep His covenant and His testimonies.
For Your name's sake, O Lord,
Pardon my iniquity, for it is great. (Psalm 25:6–11)

O God, You know my foolishness,
And my guilt is not hidden from You.
May those who hope in You not be ashamed because of me,
O Lord God of hosts;
May those who seek You not be dishonored because of me,
O God of Israel. (Psalm 69:5–6)

O Lord, be gracious to me;
Heal my soul, for I have sinned against You. (Psalm 41:4)

Heal me, O Lord, and I will be healed;
Save me, and I will be saved,
For You are my praise. (Jeremiah 17:14)

*Ask the Spirit to search your heart and reveal any areas of unconfessed sin. Acknowledge these to the Lord and thank Him for His forgiveness.*

I will cleanse them from all their iniquity they have committed against Me, and I will pardon all their iniquities which they have committed against Me, and by which they have transgressed against Me. (Jeremiah 33:8)

Search me, O God, and know my heart;
Try me and know my anxious thoughts,
And see if there is any wicked way in me,
And lead me in the way everlasting. (Psalm 139:23–24)

## Renewal

*Lord, renew me by Your Spirit as I offer these prayers to You:*

I am the Lord's servant; let Your will be done in me according to Your word. (Luke 1:38)

Since the day of the Lord will come like a thief, what kind of person should I be in holy conduct and godliness as I look for and hasten the coming of the day of God? But according to

His promise, I am looking for new heavens and a new earth, in which righteousness dwells. Therefore, since I am looking for these things, may I be diligent to be found by Him in peace, spotless and blameless. (2 Peter 3:10–14)

May I not love with words or tongue, but in deed and in truth. By this I will know that I am of the truth and will assure my heart before Him; for if my heart condemns me, God is greater than my heart, and knows all things. If my heart does not condemn me, I have confidence before God and receive from Him whatever I ask, because I keep His commandments and do the things that are pleasing in His sight. (1 John 3:18–22)

Examine me, O Lord, and try me;
Purify my mind and my heart;
For Your lovingkindness is ever before me,
And I have walked in Your truth. (Psalm 26:2–3)

*Pause to add your own prayers for personal renewal.*

## Petition

*Father, using Your Word as a guide, I offer You my prayers concerning **my spiritual walk**.*

Since I live in the Spirit, may I also walk in the Spirit. (Galatians 5:25)

May God fill me with the knowledge of His will through all spiritual wisdom and understanding, so that I may walk worthy of the Lord and please Him in every way, bearing fruit in every good work, and growing in the knowledge of God; strengthened with all power according to His glorious might, so that I may have great endurance and patience; joyfully giving thanks to the Father who has qualified me to share in the inheritance of the saints in the light. (Colossians 1:9–12)

The Lord my God, the Lord is one. May I love the Lord my God with all my heart and with all my soul and with all my strength. (Deuteronomy 6:4–5)

May I have no other gods before You.
May I not make for myself an idol in any form.
May I not take the name of the Lord my God in vain, for the
   Lord will not hold anyone guiltless who misuses His name.
May I honor my father and my mother.
May I not murder.
May I not commit adultery.
May I not steal.
May I not bear false witness against my neighbor.
May I not covet my neighbor's house, my neighbor's wife,
   his manservant or maidservant, his ox or donkey, or
   anything that belongs to my neighbor. (Exodus 20:3–17;
   Deuteronomy 5:7–21)

My struggle is not against flesh and blood, but against the rulers, against the authorities, against the world rulers of this darkness, against the spiritual forces of evil in the heavenly realms. Therefore, I will put on the full armor of God, so that I may be able to resist in the day of evil, and having done all, to stand. I will stand firm, having girded my waist with truth, having put on the breastplate of righteousness, and having shod my feet with the readiness of the gospel of peace; above all, taking up the shield of faith with which I will be able to quench all the fiery darts of the evil one. I will take the helmet of salvation and the sword of the Spirit, which is the word of God. With all prayer and petition, I will pray always in the Spirit, and to this end I will be watchful with all perseverance and petition for all the saints. (Ephesians 6:12–18)

May my love abound more and more in full knowledge and depth of insight, so that I may be able to approve the things that are excellent, in order to be sincere and blameless until the day of Christ—having been filled with the fruit of righteousness that comes through Jesus Christ, to the glory and praise of God. (Philippians 1:9–11)

As one who has been chosen of God, holy and beloved, may I put on a heart of compassion, kindness, humility, gentleness, and patience, bearing with others and forgiving others even as the Lord forgave me; and above all these things, may I put on love, which is the bond of perfection. Let the peace of Christ rule in my heart, to which I was called as a member of one body, and let me be thankful. Let the word of Christ dwell in me richly as I teach and admonish others with all wisdom, singing psalms, hymns, and spiritual songs with gratitude in my heart to God. And whatever I do, whether in word or in deed, may I do all in the name of the Lord Jesus, giving thanks to God the Father through Him. (Colossians 3:12–17)

Since I have a great cloud of witnesses surrounding me, may I lay aside every impediment and the sin that so easily entangles, and run with endurance the race that is set before me, fixing my eyes on Jesus, the author and perfecter of my faith, who for the joy set before Him endured the cross, despising the shame, and sat down at the right hand of the throne of God. May I consider Him who endured such hostility from sinners, so that I will not grow weary and lose heart. (Hebrews 12:1–3)

May I consider all things loss compared to the surpassing greatness of knowing Christ Jesus my Lord, for whose sake I have suffered the loss of all things and consider them rubbish, that I may gain Christ and be found in Him, not having a righteousness of my own that comes from the law, but that which is through faith in Christ—the righteousness that comes from God on the basis of faith. I want to know Christ and the power of His resurrection and the fellowship of His sufferings, being conformed to His death. (Philippians 3:8–10)

I have not been made perfect, but I press on to lay hold of that for which Christ Jesus also laid hold of me. I do not consider myself yet to have attained it, but one thing I do: forgetting what is behind and stretching forward to what is ahead, I press on toward the goal to win the prize of the upward call of God in Christ Jesus. (Philippians 3:12–14)

May the proving of my faith, being much more precious than gold that perishes, even though refined by fire, be found to result in praise, glory, and honor at the revelation of Jesus Christ. (1 Peter 1:7)

*Pause here to express any additional requests, especially these **personal concerns**:*

- Spiritual warfare
    - The world
    - The flesh
    - The devil
- Growth in character
- Personal disciplines
- Physical health and strength

*I pray also for:*

- My activities for this day
- Special concerns

## Intercession

*Lord, I now prepare my heart for intercessory prayer for **world affairs**.*

Father in heaven,
Hallowed be Your name.
Your kingdom come;
Your will be done
On earth as it is in heaven. (Matthew 6:9–10)

The end of all things is near; therefore we should be clear minded and self-controlled for prayer. (1 Peter 4:7)

*In the spirit of these passages, I pray for:*

- The poor and hungry
- The oppressed and persecuted
- Those in authority
- Peace among nations
- Current events and concerns

## Affirmation

*Feed my mind and heart, O Lord, as I affirm these timeless truths from **Your Word**:*

"Not by might nor by power, but by My Spirit," says the Lord of hosts. (Zechariah 4:6)

The fear of the Lord is the beginning of wisdom,
And the knowledge of the Holy One is understanding.
(Proverbs 9:10)

Your grace is sufficient for me, for Your power is made perfect in weakness. Therefore, I will boast all the more gladly in my weaknesses, that the power of Christ may rest upon me. Therefore, I can be content in weaknesses, in insults, in hardships, in persecutions, in difficulties, for Christ's sake. For when I am weak, then I am strong. (2 Corinthians 12:9–10)

No temptation has overtaken me except what is common to man. And God is faithful, who will not let me be tempted beyond what I am able, but with the temptation will also provide a way out, so that I may be able to endure it. (1 Corinthians 10:13)

Saturday

Without faith it is impossible to please God, for he who comes to Him must believe that He exists, and that He is a rewarder of those who earnestly seek Him. (Hebrews 11:6)

If I cry for discernment
And lift up my voice for understanding,
If I seek her as silver
And search for her as for hidden treasures,
Then I will understand the fear of the Lord
And find the knowledge of God.
For the Lord gives wisdom;
From His mouth come knowledge and understanding.
He stores up sound wisdom for the upright;
He is a shield to those who walk in integrity,
Guarding the paths of justice
And protecting the way of His saints. (Proverbs 2:3–8)

*Pause to reflect upon these biblical affirmations.*

## Thanksgiving

*For who You are and for what You have done, accept my thanks, O Lord.*

I will sing of the mercies of the Lord forever;
With my mouth I will make Your faithfulness known through all generations.
I will declare that Your lovingkindness will be built up forever,
That You will establish Your faithfulness in the heavens.
(Psalm 89:1–2)

Lovingkindness and truth have met together;
Righteousness and peace have kissed each other.
Truth shall spring forth from the earth,
And righteousness looks down from heaven. (Psalm 85:10–11)

I will watch in hope for the Lord;
I will wait for the God of my salvation;
My God will hear me. (Micah 7:7)

Blessed be the Lord,
For He has heard the voice of my prayers.
The Lord is my strength and my shield;
My heart trusts in Him, and I am helped.
My heart greatly rejoices,
And I will give thanks to Him in song. (Psalm 28:6–7)

*Pause to offer your own expressions of thanksgiving.*

## Closing Prayer

May we rejoice, become complete, be of good comfort, be of one mind, and live in peace; and the God of love and peace will be with us. May the grace of the Lord Jesus Christ and the love of God and the fellowship of the Holy Spirit be with us. (2 Corinthians 13:11, 14)

Blessing and glory and wisdom
And thanksgiving and honor and power and strength
Be to our God for ever and ever. Amen. (Revelation 7:12)

May our Lord Jesus Christ Himself and God our Father, who has loved us and has given us eternal consolation and good hope by grace, comfort our hearts and strengthen us in every good work and word. (2 Thessalonians 2:16–17)

# PART FOUR

# PERSONAL PRAYER PAGES

Personal Prayer Pages

Personal Prayer Pages

Personal Prayer Pages

Personal Prayer Pages

Personal Prayer Pages

Personal Prayer Pages

Personal Prayer Pages

# ABOUT THE AUTHOR

Kenneth Boa is engaged in a ministry of relational evangelism and discipleship, teaching, writing, and speaking. He holds a BS from Case Institute of Technology, a ThM from Dallas Theological Seminary, a PhD from New York University, and a DPhil from the University of Oxford in England.

Dr. Boa is the president and founder of Trinity House Publishers, Reflections Ministries, and Omnibus Media Ministries. Trinity House is dedicated to publishing materials that help people manifest eternal values in a temporal arena. Reflections seeks to encourage, teach, and equip people to know Christ, follow Him, become progressively conformed to His image, and reproduce His life in others. The mission of Omnibus Media is to generate transformative media to encourage global audiences to think, live, and act as they really are in Christ.

Dr. Boa's more than seventy books and publications include *Shaped by Suffering*, *Life in the Presence of God*, *Rewriting Your Broken Story*, *Conformed to His Image*, *Faith Has Its Reasons*, *20 Compelling Evidences that God Exists*, and *Augustine to Freud*. He is a consulting editor of the *Zondervan NASB Study Bible* and has been a contributing editor for multiple other Bibles. He writes a free monthly teaching letter called *Reflections*; you can sign up to receive it and other resources at kenboa.org.

# OTHER TRINITY HOUSE PUBLICATIONS

*Handbook to Prayer* is the first in a series of handbooks designed to enhance the devotional life and renew the minds of people who want to grow in faith, hope, and love. Other titles in this series include:

- *Handbook to Renewal*
- *Handbook to Scripture*
- *Handbook to Leadership*
- *Handbook to Wisdom*
- *Simple Prayers*
- *Handbook to Spiritual Growth*
- *Handbook to God's Promises*
- *Scripture Prayer Guide*

Also from Trinity House:

- *A Guide to Practicing God's Presence*
- *A Journal of Sacred Readings*

Purchase, or register to purchase and distribute, other Trinity House Publishers products at trinityhousepublishers.org.